W9-ASL-780

ANTHROPOLOGY

BOARD OF ACADEMIC EDITORIAL ADVISERS

Professor Joseph Bram, *Anthropology*

Professor Harry A. Charipper, *Biology and Zoology*

Professor Isidor Chein, *Psychology*

Professor Hollis R. Cooley, *Mathematics*

Associate Professor William J. Crotty, *Botany*

Professor Jotham Johnson, *Archaeology*

Professor Serge A. Korff, *Astronomy and Physics*

Professor James E. Miller, *Meteorology*

Professor George M. Murphy, *Chemistry and Science*

Professor Gerhard Neumann, *Oceanography*

Professor Joseph Pick, M.D., *Anatomy and Physiology*

Dean John R. Ragazzini, *Engineering*

Professor Leslie E. Spock, *Geology*

THE NEW YORK UNIVERSITY LIBRARY OF SCIENCE

ANTHROPOLOGY

EDITED BY

Samuel Rapport AND *Helen Wright*

ACADEMIC EDITORIAL ADVISER

JOSEPH BRAM

*Professor of Sociology and Anthropology,
Washington Square College,
New York University*

NEW YORK • NEW YORK UNIVERSITY PRESS
LONDON • UNIVERSITY OF LONDON PRESS LIMITED
1967

031217

© 1967 by New York University
Library of Congress Catalog Card Number: 66-12601
Manufactured in the United States of America
Designed by Andor Braun

ACKNOWLEDGMENTS

"Subject, Method and Scope" from *Argonauts of the Western Pacific* by Bronislaw Malinowski. Reprinted by permission of E. P. Dutton & Co., Inc. and of Routledge & Kegan Paul, Ltd.

"The Perfect Circle" from *Raw Material* by Oliver La Farge. Copyright © 1945 by Oliver La Farge. Reprinted by permission of Houghton Mifflin Co.

"The Strategy of Physical Anthropology" from *Anthropology Today* by S. L. Washburn. Copyright © 1962 by the University of Chicago Press and reprinted with their permission.

"Today's Crisis in Anthropology" by C. Lévi-Strauss, reprinted from *UNESCO Courier,* a United Nations publication.

"The Search for Man's Ancestors" from *Adam's Ancestors* by L. S. B. Leakey. Reprinted by permission of Harper & Row, Publishers, Inc., and of Methuen & Co., Ltd.

"The Discovery of Zinjanthropus" by L. S. B. Leakey. Copyright © 1960 by National Geographic Society. Reprinted with revisions by permission of the National Geographic Society and the author.

"The Peking Man" from *Children of the Yellow Earth* by Gunnar J. Andersson. Reprinted by permission of Routledge & Kegan Paul, Ltd.

"The Great Piltdown Hoax" by William L. Straus. Copyright © 1954 by the American Association for the Advancement of Science. Originally published in *Science,* February 1954. Reprinted by permission of *Science* and of the author.

"Races of Mankind" from *Man in the Primitive World* by E. Adamson Hoebel. Copyright © 1958 by McGraw-Hill Book Company and used with their permission.

"Language" by Harry Hoijer from *Man, Culture, and Society,* edited by Harry L. Shapiro. Copyright © 1956 by Oxford University Press, Inc. and reprinted with their permission.

"The Family" by C. Lévi-Strauss from *Man, Culture, and Society,* edited by Harry L. Shapiro. Copyright © 1956 by Oxford University Press, Inc. and reprinted with their permission.

"Law and the Social Order" from *Man in the Primitive World* by E. Adamson Hoebel. Copyright © 1958 by McGraw-Hill Book Company and used with their permission.

"Religion" by Ruth Benedict from *General Anthropology*, edited by Franz Boas. Copyright © 1930 by D. C. Heath & Co. and reprinted with their permission.

"The Lapps" from *Primitive Man and His Ways* by Kaj Birket-Smith, translated by Roy Duffell. Reprinted by permission of The World Publishing Co. and of Odhams Press Ltd.

"The Lesson of the Pygmies" by Colin M. Turnbull. Reprinted with permission. Copyright © 1963 by Scientific American, Inc. All rights reserved.

"Pitcairn" by Harry L. Shapiro from the UNESCO pamphlet, *Race Mixture*.

"The Navajos" from *On the Gleaming Way* by John Collier. Copyright © 1949 by John Collier. Reprinted by permission of Sage Books (Alan Swallow, publisher).

"The Old Order Amish of Pennsylvania" from *The Ways of Men* by John Gillin. Copyright © 1948 by D. Appleton-Century Company, Inc.

CONTENTS

IV. Some Primitive Cultures

FOREWORD

THE UTILITARIAN BENT in contemporary American civilization is so all-pervasive that we naturally approach any new field of knowledge with such questions as "what is it good for?" or "what problems can it help to solve?" . . . Although, where anthropology is concerned, valid positive answers can be given to these questions, many an anthropologist would be tempted to play them down and instead assert defiantly the worthwhileness of his pursuit, with no strings attached, of *pure* knowledge.

Men have always tended not only to live but at the same time to observe themselves living. For better or for worse human beings must be described as introspective, self-reflective and self-conscious creatures. Anthropology is engaged in satisfying just such urges! What sets it apart from idle curiosity is the fact that, similar to other scientific disciplines, it strives to perform its task in a systematic and self-critical manner.

Our insatiable inquisitiveness regarding ourselves and our fellow-men nevertheless remains the principal driving force behind most anthropological research, along with the sense of wonder with which we respond to the archaic, the primitive and the exotic. When an individual anthropologist has succeeded in breaking through the barrier of diffidence, shyness, and an unknown tongue into the inner world of a foreign culture, he does not really feel the need to justify his accomplishment in terms of practical results.

One of the oldest and most successful branches of anthropology, known as prehistoric archaeology, derives its thrills from the deeds and thoughts of men who left the historical stage thousands of years ago. The lifeways of these distant ancestors of ours have to be reconstructed on the basis of voiceless and fragmentary evidence salvaged from the destructive action of time. The protagonists of prehistoric archaeology are dead, but the tools, the weapons and the dwellings which they made and used have been forced to yield plausible and dramatic stories of their existence. Why strain oneself in the effort to prove the *usefulness* of this pursuit? Oakeshott, the British historian, speaking for his own field, has expressed this attitude neatly thus: "The attempt to imagine and elucidate a past, lost and different world from that in which the historian lives, is, taken by itself, completely satisfying."

The branch of anthropology which deals with the languages of nonliterate societies has also been often involved in seemingly impractical ventures. Individual anthropologist-linguists have been known to spend several years in the effort to unravel and record the speech of a vanishing ethnic group of one or two dozen members. Their interest is in reconstructing a hitherto unknown language—a unique system of sounds, forms, syntactic patterns, and meanings. They are not disturbed by the fact that the knowledge of such a tongue is no contribution to the expansion of foreign trade or of tourism.

A discerning reader might see at this point that all these non-utilitarian studies, whether in cultural anthropology, prehistoric archaeology or anthropological linguistics, have one thing in common, namely their sympathetic reverence for all the creative efforts of men, whoever and wherever they are. As one follows the writings of field-anthropologists one cannot help feeling that, all the seeming oddities of their beliefs and conduct notwithstanding, the Masai of East Africa, the Chukchee of Northern Siberia, and the Arunta of Central Australia are as "normal" and "legitimate" as the bank clerks of London and the fishermen of Norway. In fact, as one unravels the thoughts and the emotions of these tribal aborigines the sense of common humanity may make one say ". . . there but for the grace of God go I."

Strangeness is really, like beauty, in the eyes of the beholder. Our own way of life, which we take for granted, may easily appear intriguing and upsetting to many unprepared foreign visitors to our shores. A Hindu friend once told me that when, upon his arrival in this country, he, for the first time, entered a cafeteria in Seattle, and had one look at the counter with its display of roasts and fowl, he fainted. He added with a smile that of course he knew that Americans ate meat, but somehow had never realized that this was done "so brazenly."

The reader who keeps hoping for a practical justification of anthropology may perk up at this point and ask whether this scholarly discipline could be useful by facilitating understanding among men of different cultures. It is undeniable that anthropology often has performed this function. Missionary societies, the Peace Corps, the State Department, and other such organizations have found it useful to give their field-personnel an awareness of cultural diversity in general, and knowledge of specific cultures in the areas of their activities in particular. It would be unwise, however, to assume that communication and understanding between societies with cultures of their own will necessarily lead to reciprocal acceptance and amity. The French saying that "comprendre c'est pardonner" is not often borne out by the events of history.

The understanding of human cultures may serve, however, more far-reaching purposes than the ideals of international tolerance and harmony. In human affairs whatever action or inaction one decides upon, the decision is always predicated upon some implicit image of human nature. This elusive entity, i.e., human nature, has been pondered by generations of philosophers, psychologists, and biologists. The discipline of anthropology, however, has its own peculiar contribution to make to this common search for "basic" man. This contribution grows out of the comparative point of view which is the very heart of anthropology.

When, for instance, we read a nineteenth-century French novel which deals with a case of unrequited love, we cannot automatically assume that similar interpersonal difficulties will be found in all human societies and in all historical periods. Our data restrict us in this case to nineteenth-century France. In fact, we learn from comparative materials that the torments of unrequited love are not universal phenomena and thus cannot be regarded as part and parcel of human nature. We know furthermore that even the same ethnic group undergoes considerable changes in its behavior and emotional life through the successive centuries of its history. Thus the people of Elizabethan England, those of the Victorian era, and the English of today differ substantially among themselves.

What we call human nature is never found *in vacuo*. It is always anchored in a particular time period and a specific culture. Santayana once said that no human being speaks just . . . language, he always speaks *a* language. Using this remark as a model we can draw a distinction between what is *generic* in man (for instance, the universal human ability to produce and perceive distinct sounds for the purposes of communicating meanings which a particular group has agreed to attach to them) and what is *specific* (that is any particular language such as Homeric Greek, Mandarin Chinese, Navajo, or Maori).

Following this paradigm we can say that all human groups have methods of child-care, which differ, however, from one group to another. Magic and religion are found in all human societies, yet every one of them has its own magical and religious systems.

This preoccupation with the *generic* and the *specific* in the cultures of mankind not only leads the anthropologist to the formulation of a common denominator (consisting of generic traits), but occasionally makes him discover some human potentialities which only very few cultures have cultivated.

Anthropological comparativism becomes a useful corrective to the viewpoints of philosophers and psychologists, which often stem from their authors' culture-bound or parochial knowledge of the human world. Sumner was strongly critical of the belief that any thinker could escape being the creature of this culture. He said that

> . . . it is vain to imagine that any man can lift himself out of these characteristic features in the mores of the group to which he belongs, especially when he is dealing with the nearest and most familiar phenomena of everyday life. It is vain to imagine that a "scientific man" can divest himself of prejudice or previous opinion, and put

himself in an attitude of neutral independence towards the
mores. . . . The most learned scholar reveals all the philis-
tinism and prejudice of the man-on-the-curbstone when
mores are in discussion . . .

We know that an English professor involved in a class-
room discussion of Tom Jones or Becky Sharp is easily made
unhappy by a somewhat argumentative student who has
been contaminated with the comparative point of view of cultural anthropology. Similarly orthodox Marxians or Freudians
have been made uncomfortable by references to cross-cul-
tural data which fail to bear out their respective creeds.

Cultural anthropology (along with prehistory and linguistics) must also be recognized as a valuable substitute for direct experimentation on humans. For obvious moral and legal
reasons, for instance, no social scientist could permit himself
to contrive polyandrous marriages (i.e., marriages of several
men to one woman) for purposes of observation. To an anthropologist this is not an issue, since he is aware of a number of societies where this particular form of marriage is
practiced and is regarded as proper. One thus substitutes a
field-trip for an illicit experiment and observes human beings
under, to us, unusual circumstances. We can treat all the cultures of mankind as so many laboratories where specific historical developments have produced forms of behavior and
personality types not found elsewhere.

An occasional skeptic attempts to upset the anthropologist
with a vision of the future as marked by cultural uniformity.
Reference is made to the forces of modern technology and to
their leveling impact on the life of mankind. To this alleged
"threat" there are two answers. First, there is every reason to
believe that while the more obvious overt cultural contrasts
may recede into the past, the subtler invisible aesthetic,
moral, and intellectual idiosyncrasies will persevere and even
proliferate among the societies of the world. If cultural uniformity, however, is really to invade our planet, it will then
become dramatically important to keep before men's eyes an
understanding of the man-made nature of such a uniform
worldwide culture. In such a situation cultural anthropology
alone would be there to prevent men from identifying their

uniform lifeways with the innate, instinctive, and inevitable human nature.

It is most important to remember that the many cultures of mankind are of man's own making. Their very diversity testifies to their birth in the creative and inventive minds of men. With one global culture left in the world (if it ever came to pass), it would be difficult to persuade men that cultural uniformity was the result of their own choice and that what was done could be undone if it failed to make them satisfied with their lot.

Anthropology can thus be seen as dealing not only with numerous particular cultures but with culture as a phenomenon *sui generis*—a realm of existence with its own laws of invention, imitation, diffusion, change, evolution, decay, psychological patterning, and other properties.

Behind it all, setting the cultural realm in motion and pulling its strings, is the chief protagonist of anthropology—*Homo sapiens*—with his myths and memories of the past, his plans for the future, and his unceasing creative and destructive impulses and an over-all Promethean restlessness.

Joseph Bram

INTRODUCTION

IN HIS ILLUMINATING small book *Aspects of Culture,* Harry Shapiro contrasts the knowledge of mankind possessed by Herodotus, "one of the most widely traveled and erudite men of his time," with that of the well-educated person of today. In both space and time, the information available to this ancient historian was extremely limited. He knew only the world bordering the Mediterranean. The civilizations of China and India, for example, might have been nonexistent. Historically, his knowledge was even more restricted. Homer, who lived only four or five hundred years before him, was a shadowy figure. Today, we have examined the culture of the remote tribes of New Guinea and the upper Amazon. We have information about the precursors of *Homo sapiens* who lived millions of years ago. What we have learned has been acquired in large part through the branch of knowledge known as anthropology.

By definition, anthropology is the science of man. The word itself stems from "anthropo," a Greek root referring to man the human being, and "-ology," also from the Greek, a noun termination referring variously to a speaking, an account, a study, a science. A related group of words combining the root "anthropo" with various suffixes, such as anthropometry, anthropoid, and anthropozoic, refer to specific aspects of the study of man, his ancestors, and the various breeds with which he has a close biological connection. The definition, however, requires limitation. Under it, the study of medicine might be considered a branch of anthropology. It is not so considered. In a sense, all human knowledge and endeavor are related to the study of man. To arrive at a more exact definition of the science, it is necessary to examine the parts of which it is composed and the activities in which anthropologists engage. To throw light on their aims and methods is part of the purpose of this book.

Anthropology is usually considered to have two major divisions—physical and cultural. As its name indicates, physical anthropology is concerned with the general physical characteristics of the human family. One of its subsections deals with the roots from which *Homo sapiens* has sprung—the branch of the biological tree known as hominids, of which the human race is a single part. Prehistoric anthropology consists largely of the search for and study of fossil remains. So far, fragments of several hundred fossil men and numerous nonhuman primates have been collected. The relationship among them is in many cases doubtful and the theories regarding them controversial. Nevertheless, the evidence is now sufficient to give us in broad outline the story of man's prehistoric past. The discovery of new evidence and the rigorous scientific thinking whereby anthropologists are attempting to close the gaps in our knowledge are among the most fascinating aspects of anthropological research.

The other division of physical anthropology deals with man as he exists today. Here of course much of the evidence must be obtained in field-trips to remote sections of the globe. The anthropologist makes comparative analysis of the various races—their anatomy and physiology, their psychology as well—attempting to differentiate among them and to arrive at theories which will explain the differentiations. The science of anthropometry, the measurement of physical characteristics, has developed detailed techniques for such analyses. Frequently, the anthropologist's research has been used by propagandists to further the belief that certain races are inherently superior, and hence that others are inferior. Bitter controversy has resulted. Among reputable anthropologists there has been controversy of another sort. It is felt that too much emphasis has been placed on the mere collection of statistical data. The physical anthropologist of today must take cognizance of new discoveries in biology, particularly in human genetics, to learn the causes of man's evolutionary development and racial differentiation.

The study of the patterns of human behavior in social organizations is known as cultural anthropology. All societies have patterns which differ in varying degrees and which in sum make up their individual cultures. The function of the anthropologist consists of the study of each element—sexual customs, family life, legal codes, language, and the like—and the attempt to understand how all these elements become integrated parts of a total cultural framework.

One branch of anthropology, prehistoric archaeology or simply prehistory, the recovery and study of the material cultures of ancient man, is claimed simultaneously by anthropology and archaeology. The literature in this field is extremely rich and varied, and for editorial reasons it has been decided to include selections on prehistory in a separate volume entitled *Archaeology*, which is part of the New York University Library of Science.

In recent years, anthropological knowledge has increased with accelerated speed. This is due in large part to advances in other sciences which have placed powerful tools at anthropology's disposal. New techniques in genetics have aided the physical anthropologist in his study of race. The prehistoric anthropologist leans heavily on Carbon 14 dating, developed by Willard F. Libby in 1946 and the years following, and on other developments in physics and chemistry. We shall see, for example, how with their aid the Piltdown hoax was exposed. The anthropologist has refined his techniques for the study of man's forebears, of linguistics, and of cultural evolution. Two world wars have brought him in touch with hitherto almost inaccessible cultures. They have, however, made immediate study imperative before such cultures go the way of the dinosaur. In another development, anthropology has impinged increasingly on the realm of sociology. In past generations, the study of Western cultures was considered outside the anthropologist's domain. More recently such an eminent anthropologist as Clyde Kluckhohn included a chapter entitled "An Anthropologist looks at the United States" in his book *A Mirror for Man*. Popular works like Galbraith's *The Folklore of Capitalism* have used descriptive techniques not unlike those of anthropologists studying the head hunters of New Guinea. This development has an interesting corollary. Anthropology serves as a guide for the Westerner attempting to understand the alien cultures of the Far North, of Africa, or of the islands of the Pacific. Lévi-Strauss, the French anthropologist, suggests in his article "Today's Crisis in Anthropology" that this process may some day be reversed. Not only must we learn to study our own culture from an anthropological point of view; might we not also invite "African or Melanesian anthropologists to come and study us in the same way that up to now only we have studied them?"

It is difficult to overemphasize the importance of such mutual study. In the words of E. Adamson Hoebel, it helps us "break through the mental crust formed by our own cake of custom." By observing the development of other cultures, we learn to understand our own. As we weigh other standards and values, we are likely to reappraise and criticize those which we have previously accepted without question. Through such criticism lies a possible solution of the modern dilemma. We have developed our capacity for destruction to a degree which is almost absolute. Our military strategists talk not of "kill" but of "overkill." Our civilization is desperately in need of a strategy of peace which is equally efficient. It could be a function of anthropology to supply us with some data on which to develop it. In *The Ways of Man* John Gillin observes that "it is desirable that we may inquire into the conditions of man and the conditions under which he operates, so that we may place in his hands the scientific tools whereby he may abolish or avert certain of the disagreeable events of his own making." Professor Gillin's reference to "disagreeable events" is an understatement. They involve nothing less than the survival of the human race. The possibility that anthropology can contribute in however small a measure to a solution of this problem would of itself be sufficient justification for its existence.

ANTHROPOLOGY is one of the books in the series entitled THE NEW YORK UNIVERSITY LIBRARY OF SCIENCE. Other volumes, dealing with individual sciences, have been published; still others are in preparation. Because of limitation of space, certain articles have been presented in abbreviated form; and as the primary audience is intended to be the lay reader, most footnotes and other scholarly apparatus have been omitted. The series as a whole will encompass much of the universe of modern man, for that universe has been shaped in greatest measure by science, the branch of human activity which is derived from the Latin *scire*—to know.

I. The Evolution of Man

I. The Evolution of Man

More than any other branch of anthropology, the search
for man's ancestors has captured the imagination of the general
public. It has been a dramatic story. Discoveries have been
made in the farthest corners of the earth. At times they have
been the result of pure accident; at others, as in the case
described in the article below, chance, to borrow Pasteur's
phrase, has favored the prepared mind. The subject has been
intimately connected with some of mankind's most deeply
held convictions. A century ago, the idea that man has
evolved from some lower form was anathema to many. It
seemed to strike at the very foundations of the Christian
religion. Much of the controversy surrounding Darwin's theory
of evolution resulted from this single aspect of his hypothesis.
The conflict raged with great bitterness. In 1860, in a
debate with T. H. Huxley, Bishop Samuel Wilberforce asked
whether it was on his mother's side or his father's that Huxley
claimed descent from the monkeys. Huxley made a crushing
rejoinder, in which he challenged both the knowledge and
the good faith of his opponent. It was one of the early
battles in a war which gradually was won for science.
However, even today a rearguard action is being waged
by the fundamentalists.

While there remains no doubt among educated people
that man has evolved from earlier forms, the question of
exactly how this evolution took place is still uncertain. Nor is
this fact surprising. Russian scientists are said to harbor the
hope that one day they will find the undecomposed body
of one of man's forebears preserved in the Siberian ice, as
they have already discovered prehistoric animals. So far,
however, the evidence consists of bits and pieces, with long
gaps in the chronology. Moreover, false clues have hampered
research. As recently as 1953, when the following article was
written, the puzzle of Piltdown man remained unsolved. How

3

it was proved to be an ingenious hoax is described in an article
by William L. Straus, Jr., which appears later in this book.

L. S. B. Leakey is one of the leaders in the search for
primitive man. He was born in Kenya in 1903, the son of a
missionary, and has been at home with African tribal customs
since his youth. He was educated at Cambridge and in 1924
returned to Africa, where he began his career of searching for
fossil remains of early man. In 1945 he was appointed Curator
of the Cryndon Museum at Nairobi and is now Honorary
Director of the Museum Centre for Prehistory and Pale-
ontology. He has made an intensive study of the Olduvai gorge,
where some of his greatest finds were made. He is noted
for his studies of the Stone Age in East Africa, of Miocene
apes, and of Kikuyu culture and languages. He has recently
announced the discovery of skeletal fragments of a new
species which he has entitled "homo habilis," which lived
some 1,820,000 years ago and which may be more closely
related to modern man than any other fossils hitherto
unearthed.

THE SEARCH FOR MAN'S ANCESTORS

L. S. B. LEAKEY

IT IS not so very long ago—a matter of about a hundred
years only—that most people still accepted the opinion of
Bishop Usher that man was created in 4004 B.C., and that
Adam was the first representative of humanity on earth.

Today the position has changed to such an extent that the
discovery of any new piece of evidence relating to human
evolution is considered important news by the press and is
also often discussed at length in the wireless programs of
most countries.

Most educated people believe in evolution in the animal
and plant kingdoms, and consequently are more than usually
interested in any light that can be thrown on the stages of
evolution of man himself.

The first discovery to be made of an authenticated fossil human skull was that of the Gibraltar skull, found in 1848, but its significance was not realized until some twenty years later, by which time its pride of place had been taken by the discovery of the famous Neanderthal skull in 1856, which has given its name to a whole race of extinct humanity which, until relatively recently, was regarded as being in the direct line of ancestry leading to man as we know him today.

Since these early discoveries, finds of fossil human and sub-human remains have been made in ever-increasing numbers, and whereas most of the early discoveries were to a great extent accidental, and incidental to a search for other things, today the search for the ancestors and cousins of *Homo sapiens* is being conducted increasingly by trained scientists in a determined effort to clear up the story of man's early history.

The study of prehistory is a complicated subject and is not only confined to the search for and interpretation of fossil human remains. This aspect of the subject is in fact only one very small part, although it is the central figure of the picture, so to speak, but the background is made up of studies of the climate, geography, cultures, and associated fauna and flora of the periods in the past history of the earth when man was gradually and slowly evolving into the creature we call *Homo sapiens* today. Let us briefly consider some of the ways in which the evidence is found.

It has to be admitted that even today, when the search for Stone Age cultures and fossil humans is more scientifically organized than ever before, luck still plays a very major part in most discoveries of importance.

After all, the surface of the earth is immense, and a very large part of the earth's crust is covered up by vegetation and by surface deposits of humus and hillwash and other superficial deposits, so that, to a considerable extent, the search for evidence of man's past in geological deposits is governed by chance. Rivers and other forces of nature cut through geological deposits containing the evidence which we seek, and it is a matter of luck whether this erosion takes place at a time when some trained scientist is on the spot to recognize the hidden treasures so exposed.

Similarly, commercial undertakings carried out for the exploitation of river gravels and brick earths, or alluvial deposits containing gold or diamonds or tin are often the means by which deposits containing missing parts of the giant jigsaw puzzle are revealed. Here again it is a matter of pure luck whether a person qualified to recognize the stone tools and fossils is present before they are destroyed.

The old terraces of the Thames valley at Swanscombe have for a long time been exploited commercially for gravel and sand, and for years it has been known that they contained many Stone Age tools, washed into them when the geography of England was very different from today. The workmen soon learnt from visiting prehistorians how to recognize the commoner types of stone tool and most of these were preserved as the work progressed, and found their way to museums and private collections. It was, however, definitely a matter of luck that one of Dr. Marston's periodic visits to Swanscombe should have coincided with the uncovering of part of a fossil human skull—a piece of bone which many other visitors to the site might have failed to recognize —and thus lead to the preservation and study of the oldest human fossil so far discovered on English soil.

The Companhia Diamentes de Angola, in the course of their exploitation of old alluvial gravels containing a great wealth of diamonds, had to remove an immense overlying deposit of red wind-blown sand, and it was a matter of luck that the chief geologist to the company, in the person of Mr. J. Janmart, was interested in prehistory and able to recognize stone tools when he saw them, thus leading to the discovery of a most important chapter in the story of the Stone Age cultures of the African continent, in a place where, but for this commercial exploitation of diamonds, little if any evidence would have been found.

It was a matter of considerable luck, too, that in 1926, the steamer in which I was crossing Lake Victoria from Kisumu to Entebbe had to change its sailing schedule and pass Rusinga Island in daylight instead of in darkness. This enabled me to examine the stratified deposits of rock on the island with field-glasses and make a note that the island looked a very promising place to search for fossils. This little incident led to my making my first visit to the island in 1931 and discovering, on my very first day there, some fragmentary fossil fragments of an ape jaw; a discovery which led up to the finding of the famous *Proconsul* skull by my wife on October 2, 1948.

These three typical examples of the part which luck has played and must continue to play in the search for the evidence of the story of man's past, must suffice to make us remember always that the element of chance is very great and that we owe most of our knowledge of our past to this cause.

But it would be wrong to let you think that everything is a matter of luck, for it is not. No amount of luck, in the way in which nature or man exposes the deposits containing the evidence of man's past, would be of any use if there were not people with sufficient knowledge and training to recognize the finds. Moreover, it is not only in geological deposits that the evidence is to be found; many discoveries of fossil human skulls and stone implements are made in the accumulated debris in caves and rock-shelters and at such sites only excavation by persons who have been very carefully trained for the work can result in a proper interpretation of the story that is revealed by the digging of the deposits.

This fact is being more and more impressed upon us as we reconsider some of the work upon which the foundations of prehistory were laid. A great deal of the early work on the Stone Age cultures to be found in caves was carried out in France, in the Dordogne, by people who inevitably—since they were pioneers in prehistory—were not really trained to the work. The results of their work were magnificent, but the interpretation was oversimplified, so that for years it was believed that the sequence of evolution of Stone Age cultures was a simple series of successive stages, whereas, in fact, the story is far from simple.

If we want to make a proper study of man's past in any particular area, one of the first things that has to be done is to study the evidence of what we may call prehistoric geography and prehistoric climate. This can only be done by the aid of geological studies.

Climate and geographical position have always played a most important part in determining where man made his home, where he hunted, and where he lived, just as they do today, and since neither the climate nor yet the geography of the world has remained the same over the long period of time since man first became man, and the still longer period when man's apelike ancestors were slowly evolving to a human status, we must study the world changes of climate and geography before we can appreciate details of the story of man's past history.

There have been a number of major fluctuations in the climate of the world as a whole since the earth was formed, but it is the changes during the last million years or so that are the most important to us, for it was during this period that man was gradually making himself dominant over the rest of the animal kingdom.

Since these changes of world climate manifested themselves in the temperate zones by advances and retreats of the ice-sheets and in tropical and subtropical countries by alternating very much wetter and much drier periods than today, we clearly cannot study man's past without knowing something about the climate of the times. It would be useless to look for living-sites of prehistoric man at a place which —at the particular point of time in which you were interested—was covered by vast glaciers. Nor would it be any better to search in a place which, at the relevant time, was covered by the deep waters of a lake, or was so dry as to be completely waterless.

But equally, a locality which might have been quite uninhabitable at a certain point in the time-scale may have had a really suitable climate for human occupation at a later or an earlier date. Let me illustrate this point by reference to the prehistoric site known as Olorgesailie in Kenya Colony.

Today, the Olorgesailie area is practically a desert, and for the greater part of the year is uninhabited by man, for that reason. But when you begin studying the geological deposits of the area you can see that they are composed in large part of clays and sands and silts and gravels laid down in a lake.

Clearly, if there was ever a big lake in an area that is now desert this must have been at a time when the climate was much wetter than today, so it is first of all necessary to start to make a more detailed study of these old lake deposits, to see what story they have to tell.

Part of the deposits are very fine-grained silts, obviously laid down in calm and fairly deep water; it would be useless to look for Stone Age man's living-sites in these beds, for they were formed under water. But at the top of the silts there is an irregular line separating them from the sands above. What does this mean? The lake must have dwindled so that the silts, laid down in the deep water, were exposed to the sun and wind, and a land surface formed; but probably the lake did not dry up completely, so that this would have been a land surface reasonably near to the waters of the lake while it receded. Such a land surface would have been an excellent place for Stone Age hunters to camp on, near to water for their own needs and with the likelihood that the wild animals of the time would be plentiful near the lake shore, as they are today in Africa by the shores of lakes, where man has not yet destroyed them. This old land surface, then, is worth exploring in more detail, and so you start your search, and if you are lucky—for clearly you cannot excavate the whole land surface—you find, as we did, the clear evidence of a camp site with hundreds of discarded stone implements and the fossilized bones of the animals which Stone Age man killed and ate.

Over this ancient land surface, with its Stone Age campsite, lies a thick layer of water-deposited sand, laid down in shallow water as the level of the lake responded to a fresh oscillation in the climate and started to rise again. The sandy nature of the deposit gradually changes to clay, betokening the presence of deep water again in the area. Above this clay is another irregular line separating it from another series of water-laid deposits. This is another land surface and, as before, it is worth investigating for possible human occupation sites. Actually, at Olorgesailie we found ten different old land surfaces, and on each, in due course, we located one or more campsites of Stone Age man. Thus, the study of the geological deposits revealed the story of climatic changes in the area, as well as evidence of some of the stages of development of the Stone Age culture of that particular part of the world at the period corresponding to the formation of the series of deposits.

I mentioned that the sites of the old camps were marked by "hundreds of discarded stone implements and the fossilized bones of the animals which Stone Age man killed and ate." In finding these fossil bones we were particularly fortunate, for by no means all geological deposits are suitable for the preservation of bones and teeth as fossils, and they are one of the things we need most for the dating of any given geological deposit in order to be able to assign it to its correct position in the time-scale.

In working out the story of the earth's history geologists are dependent to a very considerable extent on the fossil remains of animal and plant life. Such fossil remains do not of course give an absolute date in terms of years, but they do provide an excellent clue to the relative date of one deposit compared with another. I will indicate here very briefly the methods that are used.

We know that evolution has not only taken place in the past but is still taking place, as you can see for yourself if you consider for a moment the history of the dog. The numerous races of present-day dogs, ranging from St. Bernards to Dachshunds, have all been evolved in the last few thousand years from one, or possibly a few, very generalized kinds of dogs which were domesticated by man towards the end of the Stone Age. Of course, this very rapid evolution is unusual and has been greatly accelerated by man's careful selection of breeding stock. If thousands of years hence scientists find deposits containing fossil bones of Dachshunds and Pekingese and, shall we say, merino sheep, in the same deposit as the bones of the otter, rabbit, and fox, they will date the deposit by the creatures which are obviously *new* to the geological sequence and not by the fox or the otter whose bones will also be known as fossils in somewhat older deposits.

So, in studying the past, we can examine the fossil bones of animals which we find in deposits that we wish to date, and can say "here is a fossil representing the straight-tusked elephant," or "this is the tooth of some particular stage in the evolution of the horse," and by this means arrive at a backward limit of dating in the time-scale.

The estimation of the forward limit is not quite so easy, since it must be based upon negative evidence to a considerable extent; except when there is a good stratification and where the overlying deposits can also be dated.

It must also be remembered that in any area where the Stone Age culture sequence has been fairly fully worked out on a stratigraphical basis, it is sometimes possible to use the actual stone implements found at a site as evidence for dating a deposit.

Here I must digress for a moment to stress one very important point. Any conclusions which are based upon one or two specimens only, whether they are fossil bones or Stone Age tools, must be regarded with the gravest doubts, and it is essential to have a large assemblage of specimens—the larger the better—from any geological horizon or level in a cave deposit before drawing conclusions. And the conclusions must be based upon a study of the total assemblage and not by reference only to selected specimens.

This would seem to be such an obvious matter of common sense that it should be unnecessary to state it categorically. But even today, when the study of prehistory has had more than a hundred years in which to develop a code of procedure, it is unfortunately still easy to find examples of single selected specimens being used as a basis for dating purposes and causing erroneous conclusions to be drawn.

Just pause for a moment to consider the contents of the room or the house in which you are reading these words. In all probability there will be some objects such as candlesticks, for instance, which could as well belong to three hundred years ago as to the present day. There will also be many objects whose first appearance in our culture can be dated to the present century—wireless, perhaps, or plastic cups, or stainless steel furnishings. There are also likely to be one or two objects in the house which, in their form and material, are genuine antiques that are not made at all today.

Now clearly, should all this material be buried and preserved, it would be most misleading to use either the antiques or the objects with a wide range of use in time, like the candlesticks, for dating purposes, and it would be upon a consideration of the whole assemblage, including the wireless set and other objects of the present century, that the scientist of the future would be justified in saying "this level dates to about the twentieth century, although it contains several elements from an earlier period."

Whereas the first discovery of an authenticated skull of fossil man was, as we have seen, made a little over a hundred years ago, the story of the discovery of the stone tools which represent part of his material culture dates back to a much earlier period.

So far as we know, the first person who found a Palaeolithic stone implement and actually recognized it as a relic of some culture long antedating the historical period, was John Frere, F.R.S., who in 1791 found a number of hand-axes of the culture which we now call the Acheulean, at Hoxne in Suffolk, and described them as "belonging to a very remote period indeed, even beyond that of the present world."

Prior to this, a pear-shaped stone implement had been found at what was then Gray's Inn Lane in London during 1690, in close association with the tooth of an extinct elephant, but the full significance of this discovery had not been appreciated.

The next important milestone was the demonstration, by Tournal in 1828, that man had been the contemporary of an extinct fauna of the Pleistocene Age in the deposits found in a cave at Bize. A few years later Schmerling confirmed this as a result of his excavations near Liège. But it was not until 1858 and 1859, after the discovery and study of the Neanderthal skull found in 1856 had caused such a sensation, that British scientists began to give serious consideration to the question of the great antiquity of the Stone Age.

It was in these years that a number of leading British scientists visited Abbeville and Amiens to examine for themselves the discoveries made by Boucher de Perthes, who, as early as 1847, had published his first account of the finding of unquestionable stone implements in ancient river gravels and other similar deposits in association with bones of extinct animals. As a result of this visit the British scientists became convinced of the claims that were being made for the antiquity of man, and a paper was read before the Royal Society in 1859, while in 1863 the first monograph on the subject appeared. This was the famous book by Charles Lyell, the geologist, entitled *Geological Evidence of the Antiquity of Man.*

The publication of this book marked a very important step forward in the study of prehistory. From that date onwards new discoveries were made in quick succession, and the study of the Stone Age cultures, based upon an examination of the stratigraphical evidence, began to be seriously undertaken.

By the end of the century a vast amount of material had been accumulated and published, not only in Europe, but also to some extent in other countries such as South Africa and even Java.

During the present century (in spite of the interruption of two world wars) the study of the story of man's past before the dawn of history has advanced so rapidly that there is now practically no country in the world which has not yielded some evidence to help fill in parts of the picture. Naturally, one of the results of this mass of work is that we find that the story is a much more complex one than the earlier workers supposed. Many of the earlier conclusions, based mainly on work in Southwest Europe, have got to be reconsidered and the evidence reinterpreted in the light of discoveries made in other countries and even other continents.

To conclude, I want to try to answer a question which I am very frequently asked. How do remains of Stone Age cultures, and sometimes of the men who made them, come to be preserved in caves and in geological deposits? It is of the greatest importance to understand the answer to this question, for unless we do, we cannot hope to interpret correctly the results obtained by excavation.

Let us for a moment imagine that we can stand back and observe the sequence of events at a rock-shelter some twenty or thirty thousand years ago.

A Stone Age hunter is wandering down the valley in

search of game when he espies a rock-shelter in the side of
the rocky cliff above him. Carefully, and with the utmost
caution, he climbs up to it, fearful lest he may find that it is
occupied by the members of some other Stone Age family
who will resent his intrusion, or possibly even that it is the
lair of a lion or a cave bear. At last he is close enough, and
he sees that it is quite unoccupied, and so he enters and
makes a thorough examination. He decides that it is a
much more suitable habitation than the little shelter where
he and his family are living at present, and he goes off to
fetch them.

Next we see the family arriving and settling into their
new home. A fire is lit either from some embers carefully
nursed and brought from the old home, or else by means of
a simple, wooden fire drill. (We cannot say for certain what
methods Stone Age man used for obtaining fire, but we do
know that from a very early period he did make use of fire,
for hearths are a common feature in almost any occupation
level in caves and rock-shelters.)

Probably some of the family then go off to collect grass
or bracken to make rough beds upon which they will sleep,
while others break branches from bushes and trees in the
near-by thicket and construct a rude wall across the front
of the shelter. The skins of various wild animals are then
unrolled and deposited in the new home, together with such
household goods as they possess.

And now the family is fully settled in, and the day-to-day
routine is resumed once more. The men hunt and trap
animals for food, the women probably help in this and also
collect edible fruits and nuts and roots. Gradually, rubbish
starts to accumulate on the floor; decaying vegetation mingles
with wood ash scraped from the hearth, and mixed with all
this are the bones and teeth of the animals that have served
as food. The stone and bone tools, which comprise the
weapons and domestic implements of the family, break or
become blunt through use, and they are discarded and new
ones made. Blocks of suitable material collected during
hunting expeditions have been brought to the new home, and
from these flakes are knocked off to make new tools. This
process involves the scattering of many waste flakes and chips

over the floor, and these soon become incorporated in the debris in the same way as the tools that have become too blunt for further use. When the weather is fine a great deal of the work is done on the platform outside the shelter, so that deposits accumulate there too.

Years pass, the older members of the family die and—according to custom—are buried in the floor of the shelter; the younger members of the family grow up and marry, and all the time the home continues to be used, so that more and more debris accumulates on the floor. A large part of this debris is perishable material which by the process of decay turns into soil, throughout which imperishable objects of stone and bone are scattered.

Naturally enough, the deposits so formed do not accumulate evenly over the whole floor, and although the floor may have been level to start with (and even this is seldom the case) it very soon ceases to be so.

And so generations pass and a considerable depth of deposit is formed representing an occupation level, and then something happens which results in the shelter being vacated. When this occurs the shelter may perhaps be taken over almost immediately by some other Stone Age family—possibly of a different tribe and with a somewhat different culture—in which case we shall get a somewhat different occupation level superimposed upon the first one. On the other hand, the shelter may remain untenanted for a considerable period of time, in which case dust and leaves and other purely natural material will collect and gradually build up a sterile layer covering the occupation level, until the place is once more selected as a living site.

And so the story goes on; occupation levels alternate with sterile layers, blocks of rock fall from the roof, and slowly but surely the floor level rises.

If the shelter happens to be in a limestone cliff and the site is unoccupied during a period when the climate is very moist, a hard deposit of stalagmite may form over the floor and seal in the underlying deposits. On the other hand, if the shelter is not very high above the level of the river, a spell of heavy floods may result in the partial or complete scouring out of the unconsolidated deposits. Or, alternatively, a layer of water-laid sand may be formed.

Such occurrences and many other events will all leave their traces in the shelter, and if the eventual scientific excavation is carried out with patience and skill the evidence can be recognized and interpreted and the story worked out. If, however, the excavator is not well trained, or if he works too fast, part at least of the evidence will be lost. Above all, the excavator must be very critical, taking care not to confuse facts with his own theoretical interpretation of them, and seizing every opportunity to check and re-check each stage of his work.

Once the facts have been collected, it may be necessary to call in specialists in various branches of science before the data can be fully interpreted. The palaeontologist will have to help identify the various animal bones and teeth and state what conclusions as to geological age and climatic conditions may be drawn from them. The geologist and soil analyst may also be able to give aid in determining climatic conditions from soil samples of the deposits from different levels in the excavation, while the botanist may be able in some cases to identify certain trees and plants from well-preserved pieces of charcoal found in hearths. Even the physicist, by the latest methods of analysis of carbon 14, may be able to help to provide an approximate age from examination of the charcoal.

The stone and bone implements and even the waste flakes will also tell their own story, and so, when all the necessary collaboration has been achieved, the prehistorian will be able to present a reasonably accurate story of the sequence of events in the rock-shelter.

I have already indicated how Stone Age living-sites may come to be sandwiched between geological deposits along the shores of a fluctuating lake, but many other types of geological deposit will also be found to contain stone implements. These, too, if properly studied and understood, will yield very valuable information about Stone Age man and his cultures.

Let us first consider the case of river deposits such as gravels, clays, and sands. These, if they were formed during the period when Stone Age man lived, will often be found to contain stone implements, sometimes in great quantity.

It is not difficult to understand how remains of Stone Age cultures came to be incorporated in river deposits if we think in terms of what is happening today. Who has not stood upon a bridge and, looking down into the water beneath, has seen lying on the gravel in the bed of the stream broken bottles, tin cans, bits of china, bones, and other relics of our present-day culture? All of these objects are now being slowly incorporated in the sands and gravels and clays of the river, and they have reached their present position either because they have been thrown in or else washed in by flood waters.

Stone Age man—especially at certain stages of his history —was particularly fond of living close to the banks of streams and rivers, probably because he had no vessels in which to store and carry water and therefore liked to live as close as possible to his water supply. Living thus—and by analogy with what happens today—it is quite natural that many of his cultural objects as well as the bones thrown away after his meals got washed into the rivers and incorporated in the deposits. Owing to changes of climate and topography, many of these old river deposits of Stone Age date lie, today, either on high-level terraces well above the present river levels, or in sunken channels; whole parts of these old deposits are sometimes washed into the present-day rivers, and in this way cultural material of a much earlier date, that was originally incorporated in the old gravels, gets re-deposited in younger gravels, bringing about a mixture of elements in the newly forming gravels.

Such a mixture of the remains of Stone Age cultures of several periods, in a single level of gravel or sand, is not an unusual phenomenon, and it is only by very careful examination of all the evidence that the story can be sorted out.

Another type of geological deposit which is often found to contain Stone Age man's tools is that formed under glacial conditions. Considerable areas of the zones that at the present time have a temperate climate were, during the Stone Age, covered from time to time by ice-sheets. This was the result of world changes of climate. Deposits formed under glacial conditions often consist of boulder clays and glacial outwash gravels. When an ice-sheet advances over the countryside it tends to plough up all the surface deposits that lie in its path and also to pick up most of this material and carry it forward. If the deposits so ploughed into and picked up already contained Stone Age tools of an earlier period, or if such implements were lying on the surface, they too were carried forward and churned up with the mass of other material. When further changes of climate resulted in the melting of the ice-sheets, all the mass of rubble and rock and earth that had been caught up in the ice was deposited in the form of boulder clays and outwash gravels. Thus it often happens that such glacial deposits contain Stone Age implements, but that does not mean that the men who made them were living in the area while the ice sheets were there. It means rather that they had lived at some period before that particular advance of the ice.

From what I have said, it is clear that ordinary common sense is a very important factor in the interpretation of the past. To this must be added a great deal of scientific knowledge, if we are to obtain a proper picture of the climate, geography, and general environment which existed in the days when Stone Age man lived.

In 1914, a Swedish geologist named Johan Gunnar Andersson went to China to investigate the country's coal and oil resources. He became interested in fossil remains which he encountered during his explorations and gradually shifted his research from geology to archaeology and anthropology. In prehistoric grave sites he unearthed pottery of extraordinary beauty, some of which has been dated as early as 3000 B.C. His finds threw new light on the Neolithic culture of China. They were not, however, his only claim to distinction. Like such archaeologists as Schliemann and such anthropologists as Leakey, he seemed to have a "nose" for important discoveries. It was due to his inspiration that the site of Sinanthropus pekinensis, one of the great exhibits in man's evolutionary history, was excavated. The "feeling that there

lie here the remains of one of our ancestors and it is only a
question of your finding them" that he conveyed to his
collaborator Dr. O. Zdansky was of course based on intimate
knowledge of his subject. It was a "feeling" that was akin
to the moment of inspiration which has characterized the
discoveries of some of the greatest scientists—Archimedes,
Newton, Darwin, and Pasteur.

THE PEKING MAN

J. GUNNAR ANDERSSON

ONE DAY in February 1918 I met in Peking J. McGregor
Gibb, professor of chemistry at the mission university which
at that time bore the somewhat pretentious title of Peking
University. He knew that I was interested in fossils and
consequently he told me that he had just been out at Chou
K'ou Tien, about 50 km. south-west of Peking.

He had there heard of a place called "Chicken Bone
Hill," Chi Ku Shan. It was so called because red clay had
been found there full of the bones of birds. Professor Gibb
had himself visited the place and had brought back to
Peking various fragments of the bone-bearing clay. He was
kind enough to show me these fragments. They consisted of
the characteristic red clay which fills up the cavities in the
limestone in many places in the district of Chou K'ou Tien,
but the remarkable thing about this particular clay was
that it was full of small bones, most of them hollow and
evidently belonging to birds.

Gibb's description was so alluring that I visited the spot
on March 22–23 in the same year.

During our visit we found the bones of a couple of species
of rodents, as well as of one smaller and one larger beast of
prey, but especially numerous bones of birds.

We were much pleased with our discovery, which was the
first of fossil bones. But the bones were small, and belonged,
as it seemed, to common and possibly still surviving forms.

It also seemed probable that the age of the deposit was not great. When, later on in the same autumn, we made the great *Hipparion* discoveries in Honan, our interest in Chicken Bone Hill entirely vanished.

But when Dr. Zdansky came out to China in the early summer of 1921 in order to assist me in the excavation of the *Hipparion* deposits, we agreed that he should first of all journey to Chou K'ou Tien and excavate on Chicken Bone Hill in order to obtain some knowledge of conditions in Chinese country districts.

Just at that time there arrived in Peking the famous mammal palaeontologist, Dr. Walter Granger, from the American Museum of Natural History in New York, in order to take up his duties as Chief Palaeontologist in Dr. Roy Chapman Andrews' great expedition to Mongolia.

Dr. Granger and I agreed to visit Chou K'ou Tien in order to see Dr. Zdansky, and to give Dr. Granger some idea of working conditions in China, while at the same time Dr. Granger very kindly offered to acquaint us with the extraordinarily developed technique of excavations which had been one of the factors in the phenomenal progress of the American vertebrate palaeontologists.

Zdansky had taken up his headquarters in the same little village temple in which I had lived in 1918. Dr. Granger and I installed ourselves with Zdansky and went with him to Chicken Bone Hill, where we pointed out some of the small bones. While we were sitting at our work a man of the neighborhood came and looked at us.

"There's no use staying here any longer. Not far from here there is a place where you can collect much larger and better dragons' bones," said he.

Knowing well that in the matter of search for dragons' bones in China we must never neglect any clue, I immediately began to question the man. His information seemed so reliable that after a few minutes we packed up our kit and followed him in a northerly direction over the limestone hills. It appeared that the new discovery also lay in an abandoned quarry 150 metres west of, and at a higher level than, the railway station at Chou K'ou Tien. In an almost perpendicular wall of limestone, about 10 metres high, which faced north, the man showed us a filled-up fissure in the limestone consisting of pieces of limestone and fragments of bones of larger animals, the whole bound together by sintered limestone. We had not searched for many minutes before we found the jaw of a pig, which showed that we were in the presence of a discovery with much greater possibilities than Chicken Bone Hill. That evening we went home with rosy dreams of great discoveries.

Granger sat that evening and pondered over a toothless jaw which he had found and which I guessed to belong to a stag. The learned palaeontologist would assuredly have laughed at me if he had not been such a far-sighted and kindly man, for this remarkable lower jaw showed such a marked thickening that it was almost circular in section and consequently far from the type of a normal stag's jaw. Now it so happened that in the late autumn of 1918 I had found in red clay on the Huai Lai plain north of Peking well-preserved jaws with the teeth intact, which convinced me that I had to do with a stag with an extreme development of the mysterious phenomenon of bone thickening which the learned call hyperostosis.

The following day broke in brilliant sunshine and we wandered along the straight road from our temple to Lao Niu Kou, as the new place of discovery is called, and which will one day become one of the most sacred places of pilgrimage for investigations into the history of the human race.

The day's harvest exceeded all expectations. Not only did we find the jaws, with all the teeth intact, of the hyperostotic animal, but we were able to confirm that it really was a stag. Rhinoceros teeth, the jaws of a hyena and pieces of jawbone belonging to the bear genus were also some of the finds of the day. When we raised our glasses at the beginning of dinner, our happy trio was able to drink to a certain discovery.

Dr. Zdansky remained several weeks at Lao Niu Kou and continued his digging. He has published the results of his work in an essay "Über ein Säugerknochenlager in Chou K'ou Tien." Zdansky's investigations clearly proved that the Lao Niu Kou find fills a cavity in the Ordovician lime-

IRETON LIBRARY
MARYMOUNT COLLEGE, VA.

stone, and that consequently it is essentially of the same kind as the Chicken Bone Hill, only of much greater dimensions. The perpendicular filling in which we made the first discovery is rather a rootlike branch of the larger cavity, which is seen in the middle of the section.

I give below Dr. Zdansky's measurements, from which it appears that the large central part of the cave was clearly stratified and consisted primarily of clay and clayey sand as well as breccia and yellowish sandstone.

The succession of strata from the top to the bottom is as follows:

SECTION A

8. Breccia of angular sandstone fragments, unstratified. Binding material sandy limestone. Contains land molluscs and pieces of bone.
7. 80 cm. bright red clayey sand with sandstone inlays. Land molluscs.
6. 33 cm. brown clay, slightly banded.
5. 21 cm. dark brown, banded fat clay.
4. 6.5 cm. light yellow clay.

3. 4.5 cm. black-brown fat clay. Bones and occasionally much corroded teeth. Contains flakes of quartz.
2. 15 cm. light yellow sandy clay with numerous bone remains. Contains angular pieces of quartz.
1. Yellow sandstone of unknown thickness. Contains numerous bone remains, bits of limestone and of travertine.

SECTION B

9. Like A 8.
8. 80 cm. red stratified sand.
7. 16 cm. clay deposit, yellow at the bottom.
6. 15 cm. red sandstone.
5. 30 cm. red banded, partially hardened sand.

4. 6 cm. light yellow clay.
3. Like A 3.
2. 17 cm. light yellow sandy clay with numerous bone remains. Contains flakes of quartz.
1. Like A 1.

On studying these descriptions of the two sections the reader will observe that in both cases deposits 2 and 3 contain angular pieces of quartz. During my visit to Chou K'ou Tien in order to follow the progress of Zdansky's work I was especially interested in these pieces of quartz, which had often such sharp edges that they might very well have been used as cutting tools.

I also observed that the limestone beside the cave is streaked with narrow veins of quartz, which are cleft in such a manner that it is quite conceivable that the edged pieces of quartz in deposits 2 and 3 simply fell down from the roof.

This is perhaps the most probable, or at any rate the least sensational, interpretation of the occurrence of the flakes of quartz. But, if we begin to reflect on the origin of the human species we are inevitably forced to the conclusion that the very earliest and extremely simple implements *were not prepared* by the "hominid," but were picked up and selected from the bits of wood and stone which came his way.

In accordance with this compelling conclusion it seemed entirely reasonable that if a hominid had lived in or near the Chou K'ou Tien cave, he would have made use of these flakes of quartz, in order, for example, to cut up the animals which he had succeeded in killing.

This was the train of thought which led me on one of my visits to Zdansky to knock on the wall of the cave deposits and say:

"I have a feeling that there lie here the remains of one of our ancestors and it is only a question of your finding him. Take your time and stick to it till the cave is emptied, if need be."

The Chou K'ou Tien deposits were more difficult than we at first supposed, and Zdansky concluded his excavations in the late summer of 1921, when he had reached a stage when it would have been dangerous, without large scaffoldings, to dig farther into the now overhanging wall of the cave deposits.

But I could never forget the thought of hominid remains in this cave, and thus it happened that Zdansky, at my request, returned to Chou K'ou Tien for further excavations in the summer of 1923. We shall soon come to the result of his search for the expected hominid remains.

When the Crown Prince and Crown Princess of Sweden set out in May 1926 on their journey round the world via North America and the countries of the Far East, they invited Dr. Lagrelius and me to meet them in Peking and to me was entrusted the special mission of arranging the archaeological and art studies of the Crown Prince of China. I then conceived the idea of trying to arrange, among other things, a scientific meeting in Peking at which some of the scholars living there might communicate something of the results they had achieved. What was to me personally of much the greatest interest was a communication from Zdansky that in working on the Chou K'ou Tien material he had found a molar and a premolar of a creature resembling a human being, which he designated merely *Homo sp?* He had dug out the molar himself and identified it at Chou K'ou Tien as belonging to an anthropoid ape. The premolar he had discovered only while cleaning the material in Upsala.

So the hominid expected by me was found.

On October 22 the scientific meeting was held in the auditorium of the Medical High School in Peking. The last contribution to the program of the evening was reserved for me. When, finally, I showed in a lantern picture the hominid teeth discovered by Zdansky, I suggested that this in itself extremely incomplete discovery might come to be the most important result of the whole of our Swedish work in China. I further explained that we had no plan to follow up this result by further investigations, but that we would gladly see a large-scale examination of the Chou K'ou Tien cave organized by the Geological Survey of China, in cooperation with Dr. Black, as representative of the Peking Union Medical College, and with the Rockefeller Foundation.

I now remember with pleasure that the far-reaching importance of this announcement was fully appreciated by the leading scientists of China, such as Dr. Ting, Dr. Wong, Dr. Black, and Dr. Grabau. My proposal to continue work in the field found active support on all sides. Dr. Grabau, who invents such excellent scientific terminology, immediately named the new discovery *The Peking Man,* and it was under this name that this hominid discovery became known throughout the world.

During the first days, nay months, after the communiqué of October 22nd, a shadow of doubt fell upon the hominid discovery at Chou K'ou Tien. The two French scholars, Licent and Teilhard, were present at the reception in the

Peking auditorium, and two days later Teilhard wrote a little note to me, of which I take the liberty of reproducing the brief contents.

DEAR DR. ANDERSSON,

I have reflected much on the photographs which you so kindly showed me and I feel that it would not be right, and still less friendly, to conceal from you what I think of them.

As a matter of fact I am not fully convinced of their supposed human character. Even the rootless assumed premolar, which at first sight seemed most convincing, may be one of the last molars of some carnivore, and the same is true of the other tooth, unless the roots are distinctly four in number.

Even if, as I hope, it can never be proved that the Chou K'ou Tien teeth belong to a beast of prey, I fear that it can never be absolutely demonstrated that they are human. It is necessary to be very cautious, since their nature is undetermined.

I have not seen the specimens, however, and since I place great reliance on Zdansky's palaeontological experience I hope most intensely that my criticism will prove unfounded. I have only wished to be absolutely frank with you.

Sincerely your,
P. TEILHARD.

I need scarcely point out that the French scientist, who is one of the most far-seeing and most delightful men I have ever met, expressed this warning in a spirit of candor and warm friendship, with the sole purpose of checking a too optimistic faith and one which might prove erroneous. I knew only too well that this learned palaeontologist had good reasons for his hesitation, since certain teeth of beasts of prey may, when worn to a certain extent, easily be confused with human teeth. My only reply to this criticism was that I had complete confidence in Zdansky's critical acumen, the more so as he had conducted extensive investigations into the fossil carnivores of China and should thus be proof against the danger suggested by Teilhard.

Dr. Birger Bohlin, who had won his spurs by an especially

fine investigation of the giraffes of the *Hipparion* clay, had undertaken to journey to China in order to direct the new excavations at Chou K'ou Tien.

Work at Chou K'ou Tien began on April 16, 1927, and continued until October 18. As a newcomer to China, Dr. Bohlin experienced to the full the disturbed political conditions of that country. War was raging between Chang Tso Lin and Yen Hsi Shan, and the thunder of the guns was heard for a long time at Chou K'ou Tien. Divisions of troops came and went and occasionally thoughtless youthful soldiers came swinging along with hand grenades to the cave where Bohlin worked. The disturbances round about, however, affected the young Swede very little and work proceeded as usual, though the air buzzed with stories of the movements of troops and attacks of bandits.

The cavity in which the bones had been deposited was now to a large extent laid bare, and it appeared that the cave deposits extended east and west for a distance of about 50 metres, with a breadth north and south of more than 16 metres. The thickness of the deposits varied between 11 and 17 metres, but only a part of it was richly fossil-bearing.

Both the geologist Li and Dr. Bohlin have left brief accounts of this period of their work, during which 3,000 cubic metres of cave deposits were hewn and examined. In this manner the shape of the cave became well known. Both the above-mentioned scientists appear to agree that the cave is a cleft in the limestone which has possibly been widened by the erosive activity of water.

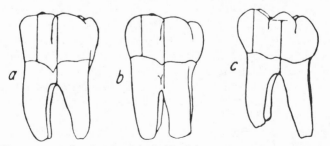

Foremost molar in the left half of lower jaw of a, ten-year-old Chinese child; b, Sinanthropus; c, young chimpanzee. (After Black.)

On October 16, only three days before work for the year ceased, Dr. Bohlin found a hominid tooth, which he conveyed to Peking under very disturbed conditions and delivered to Dr. Black, who in a letter to me dated October 29, 1927, makes the following handsome recognition of the manner in which Bohlin had accomplished his mission:

> Bohlin is a splendid and enthusiastic fellow who refused to allow local difficulties and military crises to affect his work. . . .
>
> On October 19th at half-past six in the evening Bohlin came to my institution in field dress, covered with dust but beaming with pleasure. He had finished the season's work despite the war, and on October 16 he had discovered the tooth. He was himself on the spot when it was taken out of the deposits. Certainly I was overjoyed! Bohlin came to me before he told his wife that he was in Peking. He is indeed a man after my own heart and I hope you will tell Wiman how much I value his assistance in procuring Bohlin for our work in China. . . .
>
> Bohlin is quite certain that he will find more of *Homo pekinensis* when he begins to sift in the laboratory the material he takes home.

This extraordinarily well-preserved and complete tooth has been carefully compared on the one hand with corresponding human teeth and on the other hand with those of the chimpanzee, and it appears that it is more primitive than

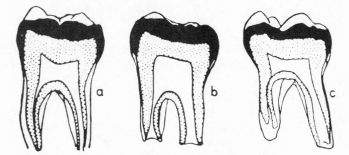

Section of the foremost molar in the left half of the lower jaw of a, ten-year-old Chinese child; b, Sinanthropus; c, chimpanzee. (After Black.)

the former and more specialized than the latter. Dr. Black regards it as certain that in this case also we are dealing with the same species of animal as that which first became known by the two teeth found by Zdansky. The hominid character of this creature was placed beyond all doubt by the new discovery and Black therefore set up a new hominid genus *Sinanthropus*, with the species name of *pekinensis*.

The existence of the Peking Man was hereby fully proved and he was given a scientific name in accordance with the rules of the science.

In the following year, 1928, the excavations at Chou K'ou Tien were resumed, and Dr. Bohlin was assisted this time by W. C. Pei and Dr. C. C. Young, a young palaeontologist who had described the rodents collected by us in China.

This fourth period of work was crowned with much greater success than Dr. Black and his collaborators ever dared to dream of.

In the northeastern corner of the cave there was found, about 10 metres above the deposit in which the tooth had been found in the preceding year, a whole nest of *Sinanthropus* remains. In addition, further discoveries were made on the former site, partly in the cave and partly during the treatment of the material in Peking. More than a score of teeth, of different ages and degrees of wear, as well as parts of skulls of both young and adult individuals, were found. The skulls, however, were embedded for the most part in hard sintered limestone and could therefore not be more closely examined.

The most important of the finds illustrated and described in Black's essay are two fragments of jaws, one belonging to a young and the other to an adult individual. The comparisons which Black drew between these old Pleistocene jawbones and modern Chinese children and a young chimpanzee in the former case and an adult Northern Chinaman and a full-grown orangoutan in the latter, show clearly the position of *Sinanthropus* as being intermediate between modern man and the manlike apes. Especially significant is it that *Sinanthropus*, like the anthropoids (chimpanzee, orangoutan, etc.), lacks the projecting chin which is characteristic of man. Even as regards the structure of incisors and canine teeth the Chou K'ou Tien form shows some anthropoid features. On the whole, however, the arrangement of the teeth is quite like that of man. Black also considers that the *Sinanthropus* corresponds very closely with modern man in size of brain.

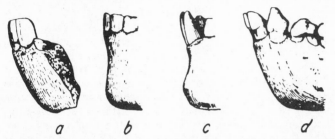

Front portion of lower jaw of a, Sinanthropus; b, a child of the latest Stone-age in China; c, a modern Chinese child; d, a young chimpanzee. (After Black.)

During Zdansky's excavations in 1921 and 1923 only a small part of the upper and outer portions of the cave deposits was examined. But during the great campaign which was begun in 1927, on my initiative, with the support of the Rockefeller Foundation, the field organizers, C. Li, B. Bohlin, C. C. Young and W. C. Pei, excavated during the years 1927–1929, in a total of sixty-four working weeks, 8,800 cubic metres of the bone-bearing deposit, and brought back to Peking 1,845 cases of their collections.

In this way a large part of the old cave was exhausted and toward the end of 1929 a very clear conspectus of the site had been obtained. Inside and in the depths considerable portions of the bone deposits still remained to be investigated.

When the rainy season was over, the search for bones was resumed on September 26 and was concentrated on the bottom cleft. Towards the end of November, when Pei had reached a depth of 22.6 metres below datum level, he struck two open holes at the southern end of the cleft. Into one of them, which he calls cave 2, he could only penetrate by means of a rope. Into cave 1, on the other hand, he could penetrate horizontally, and on December 1 he began to dig out the sediment in that cave. The following day at four o'clock in the afternoon he found an almost complete *Sinanthropus* cranium. It was partially embedded in loose sand and only to a small extent in travertine, for which reason it was possible to detach it without difficulty. [Pei writes:]

> On the morning of December 3 I sent a note to Dr. Wong and Dr. Young containing details of my discovery, and at the same time I telegraphed to Dr. Black.
>
> The skull, situated in a large block of travertine, was first wrapped in a covering of Chinese cotton paper and then in a thick covering of coarse cloth impregnated with flour paste. The weather was so cold that these wrappings had not dried in our comparatively warm rooms even after three days, but on the night of the fifth day I thoroughly dried the block with the help of three chafing dishes. On the morning of the seventh day I left Chou K'ou Tien with the *Sinanthropus* skull and deposited it undamaged at midday at the Cenozoic laboratory.

The travertine enclosing the skull was very hard, and Black was therefore engaged for four months in extremely careful preparatory work before it could be completely laid bare. Happily the sutures between the cranial bones were open, and since the bones were cracked in places, he was able to remove the pieces and to join together all the parietal bones, frontal bones, neck and temple bones. In this manner the inner impression of the skull preserved in the travertine was reserved for future examination and the bones of the cranium could be studied from every point of view before they were joined together into a complete cranium by a final process of preparation.

During the course of 1932 the major part of another skull from the material brought to Peking was prepared, and was designated "Locus D," to distinguish it from the first discovery, which is named "Locus E skull," after the place where it was discovered. Apart from these two crania, which are the best preserved, there were two fragmentary skulls in the 1928 material, one of which was that of a child.

Primarily as a result of the fact that the sutures of the cranium bones are open in the locus E skull, Black has concluded that its owner died between childhood and adolescence. The sex is not definitely determined, but is probably male.

The locus D skull belongs to a young, but full-grown individual, possibly a woman.

The examination of these two *Sinanthropus* crania has enormously extended our knowledge of the earliest history of man. In many characteristics, as, for example, the thick eyebrow arches and the low forehead, the *Sinanthropus* is so closely related to the *Pithecanthropus* of Java that it has sometimes been asked whether the new Chinese species should not rather be connected with Dubois' genus *Pithecanthropus*. Black's extremely exhaustive comparison between these two original hominidae has nevertheless disclosed a contradiction in principle between them. Whereas *Pithecanthropus* is a highly specialized, not to say in certain respects degenerate type, *Sinanthropus* is a remarkable combination of highly original and purely modern features. Black sums up its characteristics by saying that *Sinanthropus* is a generalized and progressive type, closely related to the original type of hominidae which was the prototype not only of the Neanderthal man and the South African fossil human races, but also of the modern *Homo sapiens*.

Lower jaw of Sinanthropus. (After Black.)

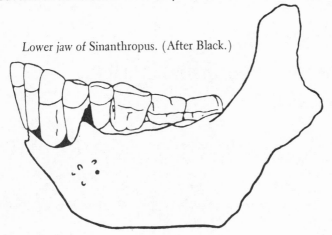

From one deposit there were collected no less than 2,000 quartz fragments and about ten stones of a kind not native to the cave, fine green sandstone, green shale, quartzite of various colors, 3 limonite concretions and two pieces of flint which were found to fit together. Only a very few of these stone fragments show indisputable signs of having been worked upon.

In connection with Pei's most sensational discovery the most eminent expert on the stone technique of the early Stone age, the Abbé Breuil of Paris, was invited to visit Peking and Chou K'ou Tien. During his visit to the East in the autumn of 1931 Breuil fully accepted Pei's view that these objects were indisputably artifacts, and the French scholar considers that some of the horn and bone objects also show traces of having been used as implements.

*In the Introduction to a previous article, it was stated that Dr.
Leakey "has made an intensive study of the Olduvai gorge."
He reports on one of his finds there, how it occurred and why
it was important, in the following article. It is rare
in scientific literature that the scientist actually responsible for
a discovery has been capable of writing so vividly about it.*

THE DISCOVERY OF ZINJANTHROPUS

L. S. B. LEAKEY

THE TEETH were projecting from the rock face, smooth and shining, and quite obviously human.

To my wife Mary and myself, who had long been looking for just such a clue, those bits of fossilized matter represented a priceless discovery, and the end of a twenty-eight-year search.

For there in the rock of that remote, sun-baked gorge in East Africa lay the remains of the most ancient near-man ever found.

In order to understand how the remains of *Zinjanthropus* can be buried in these ancient rocks, let us go back to an imaginary scene by the ancient lake shore about 1¾ million years ago. Rain had fallen for many days and the lake level was rising ominously. Camped by the shore, the little band of primitive humans realized by dawn that they would have to retreat.

Collecting together their few family possessions, the family moved away from the rising floods. Behind them they left the body of a youth who had tried to intrude into their camp during the night, and whose visit had resulted in his death.

Inexorably the lake crept over the campsite, engulfing the body, together with many stone tools abandoned in the flight and the bones of small animals the hunters had eaten. Higher and higher the water rose, depositing a layer of silt over all.

Again and again during what we call pluvial periods— eras of increased rainfall probably coinciding with ice ages farther toward the poles—the lake rose and fell, adding layer on layer of silt and sand on top of the campsite. Finally the water vanished, leaving the body entombed under several hundred feet of sediments that had hardened to rock.

There our story might have ended but for one of those quirks of nature that sometimes seem to do man's work for him.

Some 100,000 years ago—when the bones of our near-man had lain buried for ¾ million years—violent earthquakes convulsed the area, fracturing and reshaping the land on a vast scale. When the tremors had ceased, an immense new chasm had appeared as part of the Great Rift Valley, which stretches from Jordan south through Kenya and Tanganyika.

For thousands of years Africa's sands drifted restlessly, filling an erosion-created side valley. Then what erosion had begun, torrential rains finished. The water, sweeping into the Great Rift, cut through the sands and deepened the channel through the cliffs. This is today's Olduvai Gorge, and it slices precisely through the beds of that long-vanished Stone Age lake.

Olduvai is a fossil-hunter's dream, for it shears 300 feet through stratum after stratum of earth's history as through a gigantic layer cake. Here, within reach, lie countless fossils and artifacts which but for the faulting and erosion would have remained sealed under thick layers of consolidated rock.

I have long believed that it would be at Olduvai that we would find evidence of human life earlier than that represented by Peking Man or Java Man. We now know that this was so, for both *Zinjanthropus* and *Homo Habilis* (discovered subsequently,) are older than Far Eastern man by more than a million years.

Why did I first go to Olduvai Gorge, and what made me so positive it would yield new secrets concerning the development of early man? Olduvai Gorge was discovered in 1911 by a German entomologist named Kattwinkel. The discovery nearly cost him his life: Chasing a butterfly, he almost followed his quarry over a cliff. When he climbed down over the edge, he came upon fossil bones, which he took back with him to Berlin.

German scientists sent an expedition to Olduvai in 1913 under the leadership of my old friend, the late Professor Hans Reck. World War I, however, interrupted the work, and in the postwar years Reck wrote to me in Kenya. He could not resume his initial operations in the gorge. Would I like to take over the exploration?

Early results had been promising. The shores of a vanished inland lake are always likely places to search for evidence of fossil man, since in his earlier stages he had no vessels to carry water and invariably stayed close to an ample source.

I wrote to Reck accepting the offer and made plans for an expedition. Lack of money caused endless delays, and it was not until 1931 that Reck and I finally set out from Nairobi for Olduvai.

The present route via the town of Arusha leads past the rim of the Ngorongoro Crater, then across the part of the Great Rift Valley known as the Balbal Depression to the gorge, at the edge of the Serengeti Plain. The 320-mile journey from Nairobi can nowadays be accomplished in any car in eight hours or so. The first time I went down there it took us seven days by truck and car, using a different driving route. Only a few years ago, the journey needed a Land-Rover and took thirteen or fourteen hours.

There was no lack of wildlife along the way; we saw elephants, giraffes, rhinoceroses, zebras, wildebeests, and smaller game such as Thomson's gazelles and dik-diks, delightful little antelopes only about 14 inches tall. Most of the animals showed scant fear; we could often approach as close to them as 20 feet.

The first night, camped at the edge of the gorge, we met neighbors who have visited us regularly ever since. After darkness fell, I went out to see what was moving around the camp and switched on a large electric torch. In the blackness I was able to pick out the green eyes of eleven lions, some near, some far.

They had come from different parts of the gorge to investigate this invasion of their territory, for these animals are the most curious of all the cat family; they just seem to have to know what is happening. To this day they always greet us on our return to Olduvai, but they have never bothered us. Needless to say, we extend the same courtesy to them.

Not all the animals that visited us over the years were as unobtrusive as our lion neighbors. Giraffes, hyenas, and even rhinos have wandered into our camp. The explanation is simple: water.

From the beginning, lack of water has been the great hardship at Olduvai. Because of the predominance of clay in the soil, excavation during rainy months is difficult. When the rain stops, however, water simply vanishes, and we have to haul every precious drop by trailer from a spring twenty-eight miles away on the rim of the Ngorongoro Crater—a laborious and expensive process. Up to now the cost has limited us to a working season of about seven weeks.

We have tried several ways to overcome this water shortage, sometimes with disastrous results.

One year Mary and I decided to visit the gorge toward

the end of the wet season to avoid having to carry water. It worked beautifully for a week; with runoff from the mountains, we even had running water at the bottom of the gorge for a daily bath. But when the streams dried up, we found ourselves reduced to a single water hole.

Unfortunately for us, two rhinos discovered the hole about the same time, and not content to drink from it, they turned it into a wallow. To those who have never lived on rhino bath water, I can only offer my congratulations. The taste stayed with Mary and me for months afterward.

Another time, when we had a cloudburst, we made funnels out of the tent flaps and collected enough water for everybody to have plenty. We forgot that tent canvas is often treated with copper sulphate for protection against insects. Luckily it made us ill before we drank enough to kill us outright.

During Olduvai's dry spell, the animals often scent the camp's water supply, and this has led to some strange encounters.

One evening as our cook was preparing a meal in the kitchen—merely a fireplace of rocks surrounded by a low brushwood fence—he was interrupted by a faint growl. He glanced up, expecting to see the usual timid hyena sniffing for scraps and found himself face to face with a leopard.

It is hard to say which bolted faster, our screaming cook or the startled leopard, but supper that evening was an understandably sketchy affair.

On another occasion a pair of rhinos ambled into camp and, unnoticed, approached one of my assistants. The near-sighted brutes practically stumbled over him before he gave out a great yell and put them to rout.

Strangely enough, the rhinos are terrified of our two Dalmatians, Sally and Toots. It is a ludicrous picture to see two tons of rhinoceros lumbering across the plain with a fifty-pound dog yapping in hot pursuit.

We have discovered that Toots and Sally are our best protection against animals and snakes. They sense danger long before we do, and this saves us the bother of carrying guns, a definite handicap on an expedition.

That first season at Olduvai convinced me that the gorge

was one vast storehouse of Stone Age relics, a fossil museum such as existed perhaps nowhere else in the world. The animal remains alone were staggering. Since we started digging at Olduvai, we have uncovered fossil remains of 180 different extinct beasts, some of them nightmarish in their size and make-up.

For example there was *Afrochoerus*, a prehistoric pig as big as a rhinoceros. This pig had tusks so gigantic that a German scientist once attributed one to an elephant.

There was *Pelorovis*, a gigantic sheeplike creature that towered six feet on the shoulder and had a horn span of three to four yards, and *Libytherium*, a burly short-necked giraffe with broad antlers like those of the modern moose.

But perhaps the most fantastic and dreadful creature of all was the giant baboon, *Simopithecus jonathani*, named for my son Jonathan, who has spent several seasons with us and who discovered the beast's jaw in 1957. Jonathan's baboon dwarfs a gorilla and, indeed, any primate previously known.

A prize for astonishing discoveries goes to our youngest son, Philip. From time to time in our digging at Olduvai, we had come across bits of fossilized eggshell whose thickness suggested a bird of giant proportions. We theorized that the owner had been a member of the ostrich family, but whether it actually corresponded in size to its enormous eggs we could not tell.

Philip staked out an area for excavation which he guarded with all the pride of a twelve-year-old fossil hunter. Walking across the plot one day, Mary stumbled over a bone barely sticking from the ground. Philip, as proprietor of the site, directed the digging, and together he and Mary began to unearth the specimen.

As more and more of the fossil came to light, they could scarcely believe their eyes. It was a femur—the upper bone of a leg—but what a femur! In size it matched the leg bone of a giraffe. Quickly the two hauled it to where I was working.

"Why, it's a bird," I exclaimed, "but what a giant!"

Now at last the riddle of the eggs was solved. Examination proved that the bird was indeed a giant, a member of the ostrich family. In size it may well have overshadowed the

extinct moa of New Zealand, the largest of which stood
about twelve feet high.

Indeed it became clear that Olduvai was a site such as
none other in all the world. That is why, ever since 1931,
we have gone back again and again, certain that sooner or
later we would find, as we have done, evidence of the earliest men, and perhaps the remains of the men themselves.

To give a clear picture of our work, I should describe
the Olduvai diggings briefly. They are scattered over the
floor and slopes of a gorge, some sites separated from others
by a mile or more.

The earliest fossils—those among which *Zinjanthropus*
came to light—are in what I call Bed I, the bottommost
layer. From 40 to 100 feet above the floor of this stratum,
and representing a later era, lies Bed II. Still higher layers,
of course, record more recent ages.

Our method of searching is simple and, to say the least,
uncomfortable. It consists of crawling up and down the
slopes of the gorge with eyes barely inches from the ground,
stopping at the slightest fragment of a fossil bone or stone
implement and delicately investigating the clue with a fine
brush or a dental pick. All this in heat that sometimes
reaches 110° F.

To nonscientists the procedure seems agonizingly endless
and slow, and it is true that Mary and I often feel we have
spent more of our lives on our hands and knees than on our
feet. Fossil hunting is an exacting business, one that demands patience and endurance above all. Still, the rewards
are great; the gorge has already contributed much to man's
knowledge of his beginnings. And we have made only a
start.

Olduvai has always promised to bear out Charles Darwin's
prophecy, made nearly a century ago, that Africa would be
revealed as the cradle of mankind. In 1931 and 1932 we
were already uncovering crude stone implements from the
dawn of the Palaeolithic Age, predating the stone axes of
the Chellean culture.

I named this well-defined new culture Oldowan, and over
the years we came to learn more and more about its primitive
artisans. But the men themselves, the fossil remains by

which we could reconstruct those dim figures of a distant age, continued to evade us.

The long quest ended on July 17, 1959.

That morning I woke with a headache and a slight fever. Mary was adamant.

"I am sorry," she said, "but you just cannot go out this morning, even though you want to. You're not fit for it, and you'd only get worse. We cannot risk having to go back to Arusha so soon."

I recalled the harrowing drive we had once taken to the hospital there, when one of our staff had suddenly developed appendicitis. Reluctantly I agreed to spend the day in camp.

With one of us out of commission, it was even more vital for the other to continue the work, for our precious seven-week season was running out. So Mary departed for the diggings with Sally and Toots in the Land-Rover, and I settled back to a restless day off.

Some time later—perhaps I dozed off—I heard the Land-Rover coming up fast to camp. I had a momentary vision of Mary stung by one of our resident scorpions or bitten by a snake that had slipped past the dogs.

The Land-Rover rattled to a stop, and I heard Mary's voice calling over and over: "I've got him! I've got him! I've got him!"

Still groggy from the headache, I couldn't make her out. "Got what? Are you hurt?" I asked.

"Him, the man! *Our* man," Mary said. "The one we've been looking for. Come quick. I've found his teeth!"

Magically the headache departed. I somehow fumbled into my work clothes while Mary waited.

As we bounced down the trail in the car, she described the dramatic moment of discovery. She had been searching the slope where I had found the first Oldowan tools in 1931, when suddenly her eye caught a piece of bone lodged in a rock slide. Instantly she recognized it as part of a skull—almost certainly not that of an animal.

Her glance wandered higher, and there in the rock were two immense teeth, side by side. This time there was no question: They were undeniably human. Carefully, she marked the spot with a cairn of stones, rushed to the Land-Rover, and sped back to camp with the news.

The gorge trail ended half a mile from the site, and we left the car at a dead run. Mary led the way to the cairn, and we knelt to examine the treasure.

I saw at once that she was right. The teeth were premolars, and they had belonged to a human. I was sure they were larger than anything similar ever found, nearly twice the width of modern man's.

I turned to look at Mary, and we almost cried with sheer joy, each seized by that terrific emotion that comes rarely in life. After all our hoping and hardship and sacrifice, at last we had found a well-preserved fossil remains of a man-like creature, side by side with tools of the earliest known Stone Age culture.

Somehow we waited until the next day before doing anything further. Des Bartlett, a professional photographer sent by our friend and Nairobi neighbor, film producer Armand Denis, was on his way to Olduvai, and it was essential that we have proper photographs of the teeth just as they had been found.

Then, very gingerly, we began the work of uncovering the find with delicate camel's-hair brushes and dental picks. In the end it took us nineteen days.

We soon discovered that the nearly complete skull—minus only the lower jaw—was imbedded in the soft rock, although expansion and contraction of the rock had cracked the fossil into more than 400 fragments. In order not to lose a single precious scrap, we had to remove and sift tons of scree below the find.

Once we got the skull back to camp, we faced the problem of reassembly, a feat somewhat akin to putting together a complex three-dimensional jigsaw puzzle. The task is now virtually complete, save for the missing lower jaw, and already the skull has begun to tell us a fascinating story.

First of all, how do we know we are dealing with a human being? What distinguished *Zinjanthropus* from *Proconsul africanus,* the small apelike creature of at least twenty-five million years ago, whose skull was found by Mary and me in Kenya in 1948? *Proconsul* already foreshadowed man in a number of ways, but also retained some purely monkey characteristics.

What distinguished *Zinjanthropus* from the ape men—or "near-men" as I prefer to call them—found in the Transvaal in South Africa by anthropologists Robert Broom, Raymond A. Dart, and J. T. Robinson?

To answer these questions, while *Zinjanthropus* has a number of characteristics which distinguish him as a species from the South African near-men, he must as well rank slightly more like man as we know him today than they did. While, at first, we thought of him as a man by definition, although not in his physical appearance, this view can no longer be accepted. It was a view based upon a long-standing definition of man by anthropologists which was man as a maker of tools of a set and regular pattern.

Soon after the discovery of *Zinjanthropus,* we found that another type of early man, also present, might have made the tools. Moreover, as a result of Jane Goodall's study of chimpanzees, we know that apes make simple tools regularly so that the definition of man has had to be revised.

But that is only part of the story. Let us turn to the skull itself and see what it tells us. Oddly enough, the most revealing feature is the one that led to the discovery—the teeth.

Zinjanthropus has the largest molars ever found in a human skull. But what is most important is that only the molars and premolars are extraordinarily large. The incisors and canines—the teeth used for cutting and tearing—are relatively small compared to the huge teeth behind them. Here is the key to our man's way of life, and even to his development as a tool-maker.

When we find such enormous flat-crowned molars, we can be reasonably certain that the owner fed mainly on coarse vegetation. Although broken bones associated with stone tools were found on the living floor where *Zinjanthropus* was discovered, we can no longer be certain that this site was his home, and suspect he was an intruder, and that *Homo habilis* lived here. Consequently, we can no longer discuss the nature of *Zinjanthropus'* animal food.

So much for *Zinjanthropus'* teeth. What about the structure of his skull? In some respects this new Stone Age skull more closely resembles that of present-day man than it does the skulls of the gorilla or of the South African near-men.

The curvature of the cheek region shows a facial architecture comparable to that of present-day man. It suggests a lower jaw with muscle attachments like those which in humans control movements of the tongue and are linked with speech. I shall indeed be surprised if the lower jaw, when we find it, does not exhibit the form characteristic of speaking man.

Another similarity to present-day man is to be found in the mastoid processes, part of the temporal bones behind the ear holes. In our Olduvai fossil near-man these have a shape and size often seen in present-day man but quite unlike those of the gorilla and near-man.

The base of the skull also shows us that this man held his head erect, possibly even more erect than in man's carriage today. To some extent this fact may be linked with a very large and deep lower jaw, which he must have had in harmony with his long face.

With the help of National Geographic artist Peter Bianchi, I have fitted these clues together in a portrait that I believe gives a good picture of *Zinjanthropus*. He is a very odd-looking creature by our standards with his very long face and no brow. This supports a view that he was a near-man, but he is perhaps a little more like man as we know him than were some of his South African cousins.

Human that he is, *Zinjanthropus* clearly stands a long way from the state of development seen in *Homo sapiens* of the present day. For example, the portrait shows a very flat cranium, which probably housed a brain little more than half the size of ours. He had a sagittal crest, a bony ridge crowning the skull, that is seen in certain of the lower primates and some near-men. The same crest appears in carnivores like the lion and hyena. In *Zinjanthropus* it must have developed independently and served as an anchor for his powerful jaw muscles.

I have put the age of death of our particular specimen at eighteen because his wisdom teeth, the third molars, show no signs of wear, while on the other hand the basioccipital suture—a seam between two bones of the skull—is closed, showing that the individual was more than sixteen years old.

There is no riddle of the date of *Zinjanthropus*. The evidence of potassium argon dating, as well as that of glass fission track dating on all the fossil animals found at the same horizon, all point to a date of Lower Pleistocene, around about 1¾ million years ago.

In the present state of our knowledge, we can suggest that *Zinjanthropus* represents a near-man who is contemporary with true man *Homo habilis* at Olduvai. We are no longer certain whether *Zinjanthropus* made the tools found near him, or whether *Homo habilis* was responsible for them, or whether both hominids were tool-makers. Only future discoveries will finally settle this problem.

As to our new near-man's name, the full title is *Zinjanthropus boisei, Zinj* being the ancient Arabic word for eastern Africa, where he was discovered, and *anthropus* of course from the Greek term for man. *Boisei* honors Charles Boise of London, who since 1948 has shown steadfast faith in our work by helping to finance the expeditions to Olduvai. (Our work there, ever since 1931, has been aided by a number of institutions and individual sponsors.)

Earlier I mentioned Bed II at Olduvai, and here in time we shall uncover a sequel to the story of *Zinjanthropus*. For lying somewhere, a mere twenty feet higher in the wall of the gorge than our earliest human, must be a more advanced man, whose slightly improved stone tools enabled him to hunt the giant animals with which his predecessor could not cope.

Already we know this later man used the bola, a weapon consisting of triple stones connected by a thong or vine to be hurled at a quarry with the hope of entangling and disabling it. Primitive Eskimos and Patagonians use modified bolas to this day. The size and weight of the stones at Olduvai indicate their owners were extraordinarily strong, even by present standards.

Since the finding of *Zinjanthropus*, a great deal more work has been done at Olduvai. Many important new discoveries have been made and we hope that much more work will be shown as our expeditions continue to search the gorge. We are working with generous grants from the National Geographic Society Research Committee and discoveries are made at very frequent intervals now. We are convinced that still more light on human evolution will be found.

The exposure of one of the greatest hoaxes in scientific history is described in the following article by a staff member of the Laboratory of Physical Anthropology at Johns Hopkins University. Prior to the work of Weiner, Oakley, and Clark, the Piltdown remains had presented anthropology with one of its major mysteries. If the monistic theory described by Straus was sound, Piltdown man was unlike any of his known relations, living or extinct. He was in fact an abnormality on the human family tree. The acceptance of this anomaly by many anthropologists is an interesting study in the nature of scientific progress. The climate of anthropological theory, in particular the belief that the human brain evolved more rapidly than other parts of the body, contributed to this acceptance. So did the fact that some of the participants were anthropologists of distinction. Most important, the necessary scientific tools for investigation were not available or had not been recognized. The phlogiston theory and the Ptolemaic system are similar false hypotheses which were accepted for decades or centuries.

Although science has frequently followed false paths, chicanery has been relatively rare. It was unquestionably present in the case here under examination. Who was responsible? Weiner, Oakley, and Clark stated that "the distinguished palaeontologists and archaeologists who took part in the excavations were victims." This statement would seem to point to the amateur Dawson as the culprit. As Leakey and others have pointed out, this solution is not entirely satisfactory. The condyle of the jaw, the protuberance which would have articulated with the socket of the skull, was missing, obviously because the articulation could not be counterfeited. Similarly, the first premolar tooth had been destroyed, presumably because the first premolar of an ape and of a human are markedly unlike. The planing down of the teeth was done to

*imitate the wear which would occur in humans but not in
apes. The perpetrator of the hoax was thus intimately
acquainted with the anatomy of both humans and apes and
with the nature of evidence which specialists might accept
or reject. He was also a skillful technician. The question
remains whether Dawson had the requisite knowledge and
capability to carry through the deception.*

THE GREAT PILTDOWN HOAX

WILLIAM L. STRAUS, JR.

WHEN Drs. J. S. Weiner, K. P. Oakley, and W. E. Le
Gros Clark recently announced that careful study had proved
the famous Piltdown skull to be compounded of both recent
and fossil bones, so that it is in part a deliberate fraud, one
of the greatest of all anthropological controversies came to
an end. Ever since its discovery, the skull of "Piltdown man"
—termed by its enthusiastic supporters the "dawn man" and
the "earliest Englishman"—has been a veritable bone of con-
tention. To place this astounding and inexplicable hoax in
its proper setting, some account of the facts surrounding the
discovery of the skull and of the ensuing controversy seems
in order.

Charles Dawson was a lawyer and an amateur antiquarian
who lived in Lewes, Sussex. One day, in 1908, while walking
along a farm road close to nearby Piltdown Common, he
noticed that the road had been repaired with peculiar brown
flints unusual to that region. These flints he subsequently
learned had come from a gravel pit (that turned out to be
of Pleistocene age) in a neighboring farm. Inquiring there
for fossils, he enlisted the interest of the workmen, one of
whom, some time later, handed Dawson a piece of an unusually thick human parietal bone. Continuing his search
of the gravel pit, Dawson found, in the autumn of 1911, another and larger piece of the same skull, belonging to the

frontal region. His discoveries aroused the interest of Sir Arthur Smith Woodward, the eminent palaeontologist of the British Museum. Together, during the following spring (1912), the two men made a systematic search of the undisturbed gravel pit and the surrounding spoil heaps; their labors resulted in the discovery of additional pieces of bone, comprising—together with the fragments earlier recovered by Dawson—the larger part of a remarkably thick human cranium or brain case and the right half of an apelike mandible or lower jaw with two molar teeth in situ. Continued search of the gravel pit yielded, during the summer of 1913, two human nasal bones and fragments of a turbinate bone (found by Dawson), and an apelike canine tooth (found by the distinguished archaeologist, Father Teilhard de Chardin). All these remains constitute the find that is known as Piltdown I.

Dawson died in 1916. Early in 1917, Smith Woodward announced the discovery of two pieces of a second human skull and a molar tooth. These form the so-called Piltdown II skull. The cranial fragments are a piece of thick frontal bone representing an area absent in the first specimen and a part of a somewhat thinner occipital bone that duplicates an area recovered in the first find. According to Smith Woodward's account, these fragments were discovered by Dawson early in 1915 in a field about two miles from the site of the original discovery.

The first description of the Piltdown remains, by Smith Woodward at a meeting of the Geological Society of London on December 18, 1912, evoked a controversy that is probably without equal in the history of paleontological science and which raged, without promise of a satisfactory solution, until the studies of Weiner, Oakley, and Clark abruptly ended it. With the announcement of the discovery, scientists rapidly divided themselves into two main camps representing two distinctly different points of view (with variations that need not be discussed here).

Smith Woodward regarded the cranium and jaw as belonging to one and the same individual, for which he created a new genus, *Eoanthropus*. In this monistic view toward the fragments he found ready and strong support. In addition to the close association within the same gravel pit of cranial fragments and jaw, there was advanced in support of this interpretation the evidence of the molar teeth in the jaw (which were flatly worn down in a manner said to be quite peculiar to man and quite unlike the type of wear ever found in apes) and, later, above all, the evidence of a second, similar individual in the second set of skull fragments and molar tooth (the latter similar to those imbedded in the jaw and worn away in the same un-apelike manner). A few individuals (Dixon, Kleinschmidt, Weinert), moreover, have even thought that proper reconstruction of the jaw would reveal it to be essentially human, rather than simian. Reconstructions of the skull by adherents to the monistic view produced a brain case of relatively small cranial capacity, and certain workers even fancied that they had found evidences of primitive features in the brain from examination of the reconstructed endocranial cast—a notoriously unreliable procedure; but subsequent alterations of reconstruction raised the capacity upward to about 1,400 cc.—close to the approximate average for living men.

A number of scientists, however, refused to accept the cranium and jaw as belonging to one and the same kind of individual. Instead, they regarded the brain case as that of a fossil but modern type of man and the jaw (and canine tooth) as that of a fossil anthropoid ape which had come by chance to be associated in the same deposit. The supporters of the monistic view, however, stressed the improbability of the presence of a hitherto unknown ape in England during the Pleistocene epoch, particularly since no remains of fossil apes had been found in Europe later than the Lower Pliocene. An anatomist, David Waterston, seems to have been the first to have recognized the extreme morphological incongruity between the cranium and the jaw. From the announcement of the discovery he voiced his disbelief in their anatomical association. The following year (1913) he demonstrated that superimposed tracings taken from radiograms of the Piltdown mandible and the mandible of a chimpanzee were "practically identical"; at the same time he noted that the Piltdown molar teeth not only "approach the ape form, but in several respects are identical with them." He concluded that since "the cranial fragments of the Piltdown skull, on the other hand, are in practically all their details essentially human . . . it seems to me to be as inconsequent to refer the mandible and the cranium to the same individual as it would be to articulate a chimpanzee foot with the bones of an essentially human thigh and leg."

In 1915, Gerrit Miller, then curator of mammals at the United States National Museum, published the results of a more extensive and detailed study of casts of the Piltdown specimens in which he concluded that the jaw is actually that of a fossil chimpanzee. This view gradually gained strong support, e.g., from Boule and Ramström. Miller, furthermore, denied that the manner of wear of the molar teeth was necessarily a peculiarly human one; he stated that it could be duplicated among chimpanzees. That some other workers (Friederichs; Weidenreich) have ascribed the jaw to a fossil ape resembling the orangoutan, rather than to a chimpanzee, is unimportant. What is important, in the light of recent events, is that the proponents of the dualistic theory agreed in pronouncing the jaw that of an anthropoid ape, and unrelated to the cranial fragments. Piltdown II remained a problem; but there was some ambiguity about this discovery, which was announced after the death of Dawson "unaccompanied by any direct word from him." Indeed, Hrdlička, who studied the original specimens, felt convinced that the isolated molar tooth of Piltdown II must have come from the original jaw and that there was probably some mistake in its published history.

A third and in a sense neutral point of view held that the whole business was so ambiguous that the Piltdown discovery had best be put on the shelf, so to speak, until further evidence, through new discoveries, might become available. I have not attempted anything resembling a thorough poll of the literature, but I have the distinct impression that this point of view has become increasingly common in recent years, as will be further discussed. Certainly, those best qualified to have an opinion, especially those possessing a sound knowledge of human and primate anatomy, have held largely—with a few notable exceptions—either to a dualistic or to a neutral interpretation of the remains, and hence have re-

jected the monistic interpretation that led to the reconstruction of a "dawn man." Most assuredly, and contrary to the
impression that has been generally spread by the popular
press when reporting the hoax, "Eoanthropus" has remained
far short of being universally accepted into polite anthropological society.

An important part of the Piltdown controversy related to
the geological age of the "Eoanthropus" fossils. As we shall
see, it was this aspect of the controversy that eventually
proved to be the undoing of the synthetic Sussex "dawn
man." Associated with the primate remains were those of
various other mammals, including mastodon, elephant, horse,
rhinoceros, hippopotamus, deer, and beaver. The Piltdown
gravel, being stream-deposited material, could well contain
fossils of different ages. The general opinion, however, seems
to have been that it was of the Lower Pleistocene (some
earlier opinions even allocated it to the Upper Pliocene),
based on those of its fossils that could be definitely assigned
such a date. The age of the remains of "Piltdown man" thus
was generally regarded as Lower Pleistocene, variously estimated to be from 200,000 to 1,000,000 years. To the proponents of the monistic, "dawn-man" theory, this early dating
sufficed to explain the apparent morphological incongruity
between cranium and lower jaw.

In 1892, Carnot, a French mineralogist, reported that the
amount of fluorine in fossil bones increases with their geological age—a report that seems to have received scant attention from palaeontologists. Recently, K. P. Oakley, happening to come across Carnot's paper, recognized the possibilities of the fluorine test for establishing the relative ages of
bones found within a single deposit. He realized, furthermore, that herein might lie the solution of the vexed Piltdown problem. Consequently, together with C. R. Hoskins,
he applied the fluorine test to the "Eoanthropus" and other
mammalian remains found at Piltdown. The results led to
the conclusion that "all the remains of *Eoanthropus* . . . are
contemporaneous"; and that they are, "at the earliest, Middle Pleistocene." However, they were strongly indicated as
being of late or Upper Pleistocene age, although "probably
at least 50,000 years" old. Their fluorine content was the

same as that of the beaver remains but significantly less than that of the geologically older, early Pleistocene mammals of the Piltdown fauna. This seemed to increase the probability that cranium and jaw belonged to one individual. But at the same time, it raised the enigma of the existence in the late Pleistocene of a human-skulled, large-brained individual possessed of apelike jaws and teeth—which would leave "Eoanthropus" an anomaly among Upper Pleistocene men. To complete the dilemma, if cranium and jaw were attributed to two different animals—one a man, the other an ape—the presence of an anthropoid ape in England near the end of the Pleistocene appeared equally incredible. Thus the abolition of a Lower Pleistocene dating did not solve the Piltdown problem. It merely produced a new problem that was even more disturbing.

As the solution of this dilemma, Dr. J. S. Weiner advanced the proposition to Drs. Oakley and Clark that the lower jaw and canine tooth are actually those of a modern anthropoid ape, deliberately altered so as to resemble fossil specimens. He demonstrated experimentally, moreover, that the teeth of a chimpanzee could be so altered by a combination of artificial abrasion and appropriate staining as to appear astonishingly similar to the molars and canine tooth ascribed to "Piltdown man." This led to a new study of the "Eoanthropus" material that "demonstrated quite clearly that the mandible and canine are indeed deliberate fakes." It was discovered that the "wear" of the teeth, both molar and canine, had been produced by an artificial planing down, resulting in occlusal surfaces unlike those developed by normal wear. Examination under a microscope revealed fine scratches such as would be caused by an abrasive. X-ray examination of the canine showed that there was no deposit of secondary dentine, as would be expected if the abrasion had been due to natural attrition before the death of the individual.

An improved method of fluorine analysis, of greater accuracy when applied to small samples, had been developed since Oakley and Hoskins made their report in 1950. This was applied to the Piltdown specimens. The results of these new estimations, based mainly on larger samples, are given in the first and second columns of the accompanying table.

Little elaboration is necessary. The results clearly indicate that whereas the Piltdown I cranium is probably Upper Pleistocene in age, as claimed by Oakley and Hoskins, the attributed mandible and canine tooth are "quite modern." As for Piltdown II, the frontal fragment appears to be Upper Pleistocene (it probably belonged originally to Piltdown I cranium), but the occipital fragment and the isolated molar tooth are of recent or modern age. The foregoing conclusions are supported by evidence concerning the organic content of the specimens, as determined by analysis of their nitrogen content. This method is not as conclusive as fluorine analysis; but its results, given in the third column of the accompanying table, provide additional support for the conclusions ar-

TABLE 1.—Fluorine content, ratio of fluorine to phosphorus pentoxide, and nitrogen content of the bones and teeth of the so-called Piltdown I and Piltdown II skulls, compared with those of various Upper Pleistocene and Recent bones and teeth. (From Weiner, Oakley, and Clark [1], rearranged.)

	% F	$\dfrac{\% F \times 100}{\% P_2O_5}$	% N
Upper Pleistocene:			
Bones (local) (minimum F content)	0.1	0.4	....
Teeth, dentine (minimum F content)	0.1	0.4	....
Bone (London)	....	....	0.7
Equine molar, dentine (Piltdown)	....	....	1.2
Human molar, dentine (Surrey)	....	....	0.3
Recent:			
Neolithic bone (Kent)	....	....	1.9
Fresh bone	....	....	4.1
Chimpanzee molar, dentine	<00.6	<0.3	3.2
Piltdown I:			
Cranium	0.1	0.8	1.4
Mandible, bone	< 0.03	<0.2	3.9
Mandibular molar, dentine	< 0.04	<0.2	4.3
Canine	< 0.03	<0.2	5.1
Piltdown II:			
Frontal bone	0.1	0.8	1.1
Occipital bone	0.03	0.2	0.6
Isolated molar, dentine	< 0.01	<0.1	4.2

rived at by the fluorine-estimation method. In general, as would be expected, the nitrogen content decreases with age; the only specimen that falls out of line is the occipital of Piltdown II.

Weiner, Oakley, and Clark also discovered that the mandible and canine tooth of Piltdown I and the occipital bone and molar tooth of Piltdown II had been artificially stained to match the naturally colored Piltdown I cranium and Piltdown II frontal. Whereas these latter cranial bones are all deeply stained, the dark color of the faked pieces is quite superficial. The artificial color is due to chromate and iron. This aspect of the hoax is complicated by the fact that, as recorded by Smith Woodward, "the color of the pieces which were first discovered was altered a little by Mr. Dawson when he dipped them in a solution of bichromate of potash in the mistaken idea that this would harden them." The details of the staining, which confirm the conclusions arrived at by microscopy, fluorine analysis, and nitrogen estimation, need not be entered into here.

In conclusion, therefore, the *disjecta membra* of the Piltdown "dawn man" may now be allocated as follows: (1) the Piltdown I cranial fragments (to which should probably be added Piltdown II frontal) represent a modern type of human brain case that is in no way remarkable save for its unusual thickness and which is, at most, late Pleistocene in age; (2) Piltdown I mandible and canine tooth and Piltdown II molar tooth are those of a modern anthropoid ape (either a chimpanzee or an orangoutan) that have been artificially altered in structure and artificially colored so as to resemble the naturally colored cranial pieces—moreover, it is almost certain that the isolated molar of Piltdown II comes from the original mandible, thus confirming Hrdlička's earlier suspicion; and (3) Piltdown II occipital is of recent human origin, with similar counterfeit coloration.

Weiner, Oakley, and Clark conclude that "the distinguished palaeontologists and archaeologists who took part in the excavations at Piltdown were the victims of a most elaborate and carefully prepared hoax" that was "so extraordinarily skillful" and which "appears to have been so entirely unscrupulous and inexplicable, as to find no parallel in the history of palaeontological discovery."

It may be wondered why forty years elapsed before the hoax was discovered. Two factors enter here: first, there was no reason at all to suspect the perpetration of a fraud, at least, not until fluorine analysis indicated the relative recency of all the specimens, thus making the association of a human cranium and an anthropoid-ape jaw, either anatomically or geologically, hardly credible; and, second, methods for *conclusively* determining whether the specimens were actual fossils or faked ones, short of their wholesale destruction, were developed only in recent years (it will be recalled that even the fluorine-estimation method used by Oakley and Hoskins a few years ago was inadequate for detecting a significant difference between brain case and jaw). It is of interest to note that Dawson, in his original report, stated:

A small fragment of the skull has been weighed and tested by Mr. S. A. Woodhead, M.Sc., F.I.C., Public Analyst for East Sussex & Hove, and Agricultural Analyst for East Sussex. He reports that the specific gravity of the bone (powdered) is 2.115 (water at 5° C. as standard). No gelatine or organic matter is present. There is a large proportion of phosphates (originally present in the bone) and a considerable proportion of iron. Silica is absent.

This statement obviously refers to the brain case alone; for, in both the title and text of the original report the authors spoke of "skull *and* mandible" (italics mine). One cannot help but wonder what might have come to pass if samples of the jaw and teeth had also been submitted to chemical analysis, even though the present, more refined methods were not then available.

The ready initial acceptance of the Piltdown discovery at its face value, at least by a majority of interested scientists, can probably be attributed to the philosophical climate that invested the problem of human evolution at that time. In September 1912, before the announcement of the discovery of "Piltdown man," the distinguished anatomist Elliot Smith, in an address before the Anthropological Section of the British Association for the Advancement of Science at Dundee,

expressed a prevailing point of view when he developed the
theory that the brain led the way in the evolution of man
and that modification of other parts of the body followed.
Thus the stage was set for the ready acceptance of the Piltdown fragments as constituting a single individual, a "dawn
man" possessing a human cranium housing a human brain,
but with phylogenetically laggard, hence simian, jaws and
teeth. To quote the palaeontologist Sollas:

> The surprise which was first excited by what appeared
> to be a monstrous combination disappears on further re-
> flection. Such a combination had, indeed, been long previ-
> ously anticipated as an almost necessary stage in the course
> of human development. . . . In *Eoanthropus Dawsoni* we
> seem to have realised precisely such a being . . . , one, that
> is, which had already attained to human intelligence but
> had not yet wholly lost its ancestral jaws and fighting
> teeth.

And, as Sir Arthur Keith, perhaps the most vocal champion
of "Eoanthropus," argued in supporting this view:

> . . . before the anthropoid characters would disappear
> from the body of primal man, the brain, the master organ
> of the human body, must first have come into its human
> estate. Under its dominion the parts of the body such as
> the mouth and hands, the particular servants of the brain,
> became adapted for higher uses. Looking at the problem
> from this point of view, we cannot reject the Piltdown
> mandible because as regards the mylo-hyoid ridge it is
> simian and not human in character.

Recent finds of fossil men and other primates, however,
indicate that it is the brain that was the evolutionary laggard
in man's phylogeny; indeed, the studies of Tilly Edinger of
the phylogeny of the horse brain suggest that this may well
be a general rule in mammalian evolution. It was such concepts as this, leading to a change in philosophical climate,
that evoked an increasing skepticism toward the validity of
the monistic interpretation of the Piltdown fragments and led
in turn to what appears to have been the prevailing recent
opinion, namely, that the fragments should, as expressed in

1949 by Le Gros Clark, "be laid aside without further comment until more evidence becomes available." This view, enhanced by the redating of the remains by Oakley and Hoskins, provided the proper psychological setting for the coup de grâce delivered by Weiner, Oakley, and Clark.

As the three latter point out, the solution of the Piltdown enigma greatly clarifies the problem of human evolution. For "Eoanthropus," both morphologically and geologically, just simply did not fit into the picture of human evolution that has gradually been unfolding as the result of palaeontological discoveries throughout the world.

The Piltdown story is a significant one in the history of ideas, more particularly as it bears on the concept of the precise course of human evolution. For, if man's biological history be likened to a book, it is seen to be composed of both blank and written pages and, by those who note them carefully, many if not most of the written ones will be seen to be in the nature of palimpsests—pages that have been rewritten after their original writing has been rubbed out. Of this, the Piltdown affair is a striking demonstration. It is a demonstration, furthermore, that the palimpsest nature of the pages of man's history is not always due directly to new fossil discoveries but can also result from changes in the philosophical climate of the science. That this phenomenon is peculiar to anthropology, however, is seriously to be doubted.

The concept of race has aroused controversy even more bitter than that of evolution. Passion and prejudice have clouded discussion. The idea that certain races are inherently superior or inferior to others has gained wide acceptance. The word itself has become confused with nationality, religion, or language. The result has led to genocide and war. As an inevitable reaction, some students have denied the very existence of race; or conversely have held that there are so many races that attempts at classification become meaningless.

Distinctions in obvious physical characteristics were of course recognized long before anthropology became a science. This science is generally considered to have been founded by Johann

Friedrich Blumenbach (1752–1842) who at the end of the
eighteenth century classified men into five groups—white,
yellow, black, Malayan, and Amerindian. He held that all five
had developed, through environmental causes, from a single
ancestral form. His ideas were widely accepted. Surprisingly,
the classifications he suggested, arrived at before either Darwin
or Mendel, have some features which are markedly similar to
those now generally accepted. About the same period,
Immanuel Kant's Of the Various Races of Men elaborated on
the theme of a single human ancestry, with descendants who
became differentiated largely through climatic influences.
Kant's work was basically philosophic rather than scientific.
There was desultory activity in the field in the first half of the
nineteenth century, but Darwinian theory was the crucial
influence in the development of physical anthropology. As we
have noted, the descent of man became the subject of violent
controversy. The study of races gained new impetus. Techniques in anthropometry were introduced. The science of
craniology and its emphasis on cranial indices received increasing attention. This technique of measurement yielded
important results, but their value was frequently exaggerated.
Sufficient biological insight to assess the evidence was
lacking. Not until the rediscovery about 1900 of the work of
Gregor Mendel was it possible to formulate scientific laws
of heredity. With the discovery of the genes and chromosomes,
the study of phenotypes was supplanted in part by that
of genotypes, but measurement almost for measurement's
sake was by no means abandoned.

A modern scientific view of the subject is here presented
by a well-known American anthropologist. E. Adamson
Hoebel was born at Madison, Wisconsin, in 1906 and received
his Ph.D. at Columbia in 1934. After teaching at New York
University and the University of Utah, he became professor
of anthropology and chairman of the department at the
University of Minnesota in 1954. A writer of distinction, he
is the author of such well-known books as The Law of
Primitive Man, The Cheyenne Indians, and Man in the
Primitive World, from which the following selection is taken.

RACES OF MANKIND

E. ADAMSON HOEBEL

ALL LIVING human beings belong to a single genus and species. This means that in all their major biological characteristics they have more in common than they show in distinguishing differences. It is in this sense that we recognize the commonality of the human race.

At the same time most individuals appear physically different from others in a number of easily discernible traits. This, of course, is even true to some degree within every family of brothers and sisters. If such differences were evenly distributed around the face of the globe, they would merely be noted as representing individual variation among human beings, and that would be that. The fact is, however, that certain distinctive traits tend to cluster in populations that live predominantly in one part of the world or another. It is these populations and the people directly derived from them that we have in mind when we talk about *races*.

The traits that may be noted superficially are such physical manifestations as color of hair, texture of hair, quantity and distribution of hair on the body, eye color, shape of the eyelids, shape of the nose, the lips, and the face in general, color of the skin, body height, and general form.

Anthropometry has been developed over the past century as a technique of measurements for giving more precise expression to such features. It refines to a nice degree all that the layman can see with the unaided eye, and goes on to reduce to measurements many more less obvious features that the inexpert layman is quite unaware of. Thus it provides the raw materials for a scientific beginning to racial identification. But it is only a beginning. Races do not emerge from the welter of measurements until the observer succeeds in classifying all his individuals according to types.

Many popular notions about race go far beyond the facts and rest on folkloristic beliefs. Hence, some anthropologists in overreaction have gone to the extreme of rejecting the whole concept of race as a myth. What we think of as races, however, have been with us for a long time and will continue to be around for some time to come. Therefore, it behooves the student of anthropology to consider scientifically how best to conceive of race and the races of mankind.

A race is a major grouping of interrelated people possessing a distinctive combination of physical traits that are the result of distinctive genetic composition.

The foundation of organic physical structure is the gene. The members of a given race are more like each other in certain physical traits than they are like other human beings because they possess certain genes in common that other populations do not have, or have in greater or lesser quantity. These genes have been distributed among the members of a racial population through interbreeding between its members —or intrabreeding within the population. The population shares a gene pool that is not exactly the same as the gene pool of other populations. Inbreeding is the result of isolation and limited mobility. Isolation among men is the consequence of geographic circumstance *and* social inhibitions.

Space and physiographic features are the primary geographic stimulators of inbreeding. North American Indians did not mate with Australians, because 12,000 miles of ocean separated them. The Polar Eskimos in northwest Greenland were so isolated that, until their illusion was shattered by the arrival of the first Europeans, they thought they were the sole inhabitants of the earth. When we consider that the Polar Eskimos numbered no more than a few hundred individuals, we can realize how close their inbreeding had to be. In fact, in almost any of the smaller primitive tribes (and this includes the majority of all tribal groups) every person is apt to be a genetic relative of every other.

Social isolation, in contrast to geographic isolation, is manmade. Whether we like to admit it or not, human beings in general prefer to associate with their own kind. They incline to be suspicious of differences and to give warm approval to likenesses of themselves. The *consciousness of kind,* which the sociologist Giddings saw as the basis of social groupings, has its counterpart in a *consciousness of difference.* *Endogamy,* or marriage within the group, is a consequence of these two sets of attitudes. The function of endogamy is to regulate marriage in a way that preserves the cultural identity of the group. Its biological effect is to produce intensification of distinctive physical traits through inbreeding. Social distance has the same physical consequence as geographical distance.

The effect of inbreeding is to intensify or narrow the distribution of genetic traits within a population. The physical characteristics of the individuals within the population then reveal a greater degree of standardization than is the case where there is little or no inbreeding. Any unique qualities of genetic composition become more marked, and racial differentiation is thereby enhanced.

This fact has been demonstrated over and over again in animal husbandry.

Among biologists a fundamental principle is that "general anatomical resemblances imply relationship and that detailed similarities of face and form mean that the individuals possessing them have in common all or nearly all of their ancestors." It is assumed in physical anthropology, therefore, that groups of persons who bear distinctive anatomical resemblances are more closely related to each other (inbred) than to others.

The question as to what constitutes a realistic combination of distinctive physical traits is the one that poses the greatest difficulties. What traits legitimately go into the combination and what must be left out?

There is obviously considerable overlapping of single traits among the different races. Only the Negro has a distinctive lip, for instance. This means that a generalized lip form occurs in all other races. Black hair distinguishes the Negro from the blond Nordic but not at all from the multitudinous Mongoloids. Thus the fact that any one of the physical traits found to be characteristic of a race may be found in other races has in itself neither positive nor negative significance. Any suggestion that the presence of a single trait in two different races indicates genetic affinity between the races would be absurd. The fact that certain Melanesians possess "Semitic" noses cannot be used as evidence of Semitic ancestry for those Oceanic Negroes. On the other hand, neither can it be said that the fact of this nose is not an important element in the cluster of distinctive traits that characterizes each of these groups.

The whole concatenation of traits marks the race. Yet an individual person rarely possesses all the traits that characterize his race. If, for purposes of illustration, we say a particular race has twenty-five traits in a distinctive combination, it does not mean that every person who properly is a member of that race possesses all twenty-five traits.

The Swedes, for example, are a notably homogeneous population with unusually distinctive physical traits: flaxen hair, blue eyes, light skin, long heads, etc. Retzius and Furst, in 1898, in measurements of 45,000 Swedish army recruits, found that only 11 per cent possessed *all* the traits that go to make up the distinctive Nordic combination; 29 per cent had all traits except that they were roundheaded. Sixty years ago the statue of an average Harvard undergraduate was produced by sculpting a statue according to the average physical measurements of the Harvard student body. But only one in 1,024 Harvard students would conform to this ideal type.

Should we not conclude from this fact that the racial combination is an imaginative idealization of types that rarely occur in any given individual? Those who would wish away races answer "Yes."

It is a fact that race-conscious persons hold an image of racial types in their heads. The type consists of all the distinctive traits of a race in combination. When these persons associate an individual with a given race, because that individual has one or more of the type traits, they either overlook the presence of nontypical traits or they impute the type traits to the person being considered. Correction of such false perception is a matter of social psychology.

The scientifically oriented observer will make no such error, because he knows that a race is statistically determined on the basis of biologically derived data.

All traditional classifications of race established by physical anthropologists have been in terms of external physical qualities of the order just discussed. What the physical anthropologist has been concerned with until just recently is, therefore, the *phenotype* (Gr. *phainein* to show). Phenotypes look alike. Genetically, however, they may be different. Therefore, a more penetrating analysis of race will seek to isolate the gene qualities that determine the form rather than be content to consider only the form itself. In other words, the question becomes, "What is the genetic composition of the population?"

To undertake the answer to such a question, it is necessary to have an understanding of the basic principles of Mendelian inheritance.

First of all, trait determiners exist in the forms of genes, which are passed to offspring through the germ plasm of the parents. The germ plasm contains rodlike cells, called *chromosomes*. The number of chromosomes contained in the reproductive cells, *gametes* (Gr. *gamete* wife, or *gametes* husband), varies from species to species: in human beings the number is 48, of which 24 come from each parent. Chromosomes may be seen microscopically when properly stained. Genes are submicroscopic structures which have not yet been actually observed. Their existence is scientifically inferred and hypothetically necessary to explain the known facts of heredity. A gene is a biochemical structure that forms a discrete entity. Each gene exerts a specific influence on the development of the organism. How it exercises this influence is at present outside the reach of our knowledge. Whatever the process, it staggers the imagination!

The genius of Gregor Mendel (1822–1884) was to demonstrate that when contrasting pure lines of a plant, such as smooth or wrinkled peas, are crossbred to produce hybrids, the hybrid offspring in almost every instance shows only one of the contrasted characters in its form. Mendel called the prevailing character *dominant* (D) and the apparently suppressed character *recessive* (R). From this comes Mendel's first law of heredity: *a crossing of two different pure lines of the same kind of organism produces dominant-appearing offspring*.

Mendel next demonstrated that when the hybrid offspring

are bred among themselves, the original traits become segregated; i.e., the recessive character reappears in the third generation offspring in one out of four cases. When fertilized only by their own kind, the doubly recessive offspring produce only their own type through all subsequent breedings. The dominant-appearing types, on the other hand, produce one recessive to three dominant-appearing offspring. Of these three, one will produce all dominant offspring, while two will produce dominant and recessive offspring in the 3:1 ratio. From this is derived Mendel's second law: *unit characters (genes) segregate in hereditary transmission.* Put otherwise, unlike genes for the same trait (although the effect of one does not ordinarily show) remain unaltered by their association in the gamete, and they are separated unchanged when passed on to the next generation.

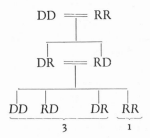

DD ══ RR   (Cross-fertilization of two pure strains of unlike unit characters)

DR ══ RD   (Each offspring receives one D and one R gene)

DD RD   DR RR   (Cross-fertilization of the hybrid generation above produces one pure DD, two mixed DR, and one pure RR)
    3   1

An individual that receives two like genes for a given trait from its parents shows both traits in its appearance, since both genes are the same; it is called a *genotype.* An individual that receives two unlike genes for a given trait from its parents shows only the dominant trait in its appearance; it is called a *phenotype.*

Traditional physical anthropology dealt only with appearances. Because appearance does not reveal the true genetic composition of the majority of individuals at a given moment, and since race is controlled by heredity, obviously anthropologists in the past have been only scratching the surface. They were, as Washburn states, "chiefly concerned with sorting the results of evolution." Today the application of genetic principles to the study of race makes it possible to sort the results more exactly, and even more important, to move toward a more adequate understanding of how races develop and why.

Yet a warning must be raised that a genuinely genetic classification of race is right now more of a potential than a realized fact. Too few human genes have been separated out of the welter that go into human heredity to make it possible to define races clearly on a genetic basis. Estimates indicate the probability of some 10,000 different gene locations on the human chromosome. Since two genes occur on similar loci on the paired chromosomes in a gamete, the possible number of different gene combinations (assuming 10,000 loci is approximately correct) would be $3^{10,000}$. Small wonder that every individual is constitutionally unique! Furthermore, the human body is so complex that few of its parts or functions are controlled by one type of gene alone. This adds to the difficulty of separating out specific genes for racial classification.

The best progress made to date has been through identification of blood-group genes, and through the study of their population distributions.

Almost everyone is today familiar with the existence of the O, A, B, and AB blood types. Blood is classified according to its agglutinative reactions; i.e., as to whether the hemoglobin (red blood corpuscles) clump together when mixed with alien blood. Two classic blood clumpers, A and B, were the first to be isolated. They are antigen A and antigen B. Type O blood is immune to the effect of both antigens; hence it can ordinarily be used in transfusion to any other basic blood type. (O-type persons are universal donors.) Type A can be transfused to Type A and AB, but not to B. Type B can be transfused to Type B and AB, but not to A.

Soon after blood types were discovered, it was noticed that the percentage frequencies of the four types were not the same for different phenotype races. First off, it was observed that most European populations run 40–50 per cent O, 30–40 per cent A, 8–12 per cent B, and 1–6 per cent AB. In sharp contrast, some American Indian tribes revealed almost all O, a little A, and virtually no B. The Utes, for example, run 98 per cent O, 2 per cent A, and zero for B and AB. As against Europeans here is surely a clear-cut hereditary racial difference. Among the Mongoloids of Asia, the samples thus far tested show roughly around 30 per cent of O, A, B, and with a small residue of AB. Local populations within the larger geographic populations just mentioned vary in O, A, B, and AB distributions to some extent, but the major differences tend to run as indicated.

The advantage of blood types as genetic criteria of race is that they are discrete traits. A type is either present or absent in a person. It is not ambiguous like "olive skin" nor continuously variable, as stature. Therefore, the gene distribution for blood types can be precisely calculated—and these distributions vary by populations.

In addition to the classic blood types, numerous other agglutinators have been discovered since 1927. These include the M and N types, the Rh positive and negatives, with several subtypes, the Lewis, Lutheran, Kell, Duffy, and Kidd. Not enough sera have been available as yet for extensive testing of racial populations for all of these.

The A antigens have been found to fall into two subtypes A_1 and A_2. It is significant that the A occurring in American Indians, Asiatics, Pacific Islanders, and Australians is all A_1. This fact reinforces the idea of their common ancestry.

Rh negative genes occur in about 15 per cent of Europeans. They are absent among Asians, Australians, Pacific Islanders, and American Indians who have been tested to date. Once again, the Mongoloid affinity of the American Indian is apparently confirmed.

Beyond blood groupings not much progress has thus far been made in isolating easily identifiable genes for use in racial classifications. One that is peculiarly interesting was discovered twenty-five years ago by A. L. Fox: namely, that which determines the ability to perceive a bitter taste in phenylthiocarbamide (PTC). Dr. Fox was working with this compound in his laboratory when his coworker complained of the bitter taste of the dust it produced in the air. Fox, who could not feel any effect, put crystals directly on his tongue and found them tasteless. The other chemist did likewise, and found them very bitter. This led to putting PTC to the taste of other workers. Some tasted, others failed to taste, the bitter quality.

Follow-up studies showed the tasting ability (T) to be inherited as a Mendelian dominant over nontasting (t). Further studies show that 70 per cent of the population of the United States are T, 30 per cent are t. In terms of gene frequency, this means that 55 per cent of the United States population carry that t gene.[1] Within a sample of Navaho Indians, on the other hand, the proportion of nontasters is only 2 per cent. The frequency of the t gene in this Navaho population is $\sqrt{0.2}$ or 14 per cent. Here is definitely a significant racial difference. Although not enough different populations have as yet been tested for T, t, the indications are, according to Boyd, "that the results for the tasting gene parallel in general what has already been observed for the Rh negative and A_2 genes, that is, that European populations tend to differ rather strikingly from Mongoloid populations. In both situations there is insufficient information about the Africans."

In sum: gene frequency occurrences for various blood types and PTC suggest five major contemporary races similar to those commonly identified by bodily traits (morphological phenotypes). These are the Caucasoid, Negroid, Mongoloid, American Indian, and Australoid. The American Indian is closely linked to the Mongoloid, but the presence of the B agglutin gene among the Mongoloids and its absence among American Indians suggests sufficient racial differentiation on the part of the American Indians since their migration to the New World to warrant a separate racial category in genetic terms. To date, then, known gene frequency distributions validate the racial categories previously established by science. In the future, as more data come in, it is possible that genetic data may lead to further refinement of subracial categories.

Races differentiate within the human species as a result of four factors: (1) gene mutation, (2) natural selection, (3) genetic drift, (4) population mixture.

1.   The frequency of a recessive gene in the gene pool is equal to the square root of the genotypes for the recessive gene in the population: $\sqrt{0.30} = 0.55$.

A *mutation* is a change in the structure of a gene which modifies its influence in bodily development. It is now thoroughly established that mutations are constantly occurring in the gene pools of all living forms. Genes, although highly stable, are not absolutely so. Mutations are not freak occurrences that take place but once and never again. It has been quite definitely established that any mutation of a particular kind recurs again and again with fairly regular probability. Mutations, such as that which produces hemophilia, often result in early death before the individual has a chance to have children. Such mutations have little chance of entering into the permanent gene pool. Yet they are steadily replaced by regularly recurring mutations. As a result there are always a few hemophilics in a given population.

Subsequent to the discovery and use of X rays, it has been demonstrated that exposure of the sex organs to X rays increases at least some mutation rates. Certain chemicals have a like effect.

Mutations are estimated to occur at a possible rate of about 1 to 40,000 instances of a given gene per generation among human beings. If the mutant happens to be recessive, it would have no visible effect whatever on the generation in which it occurs. But if it is not lethal, its effects will show up in homologous genotypes in later generations, in very low frequency. If, on the other hand, the mutation is dominant, it will show its effects immediately on its bearer and on a majority of that person's offspring.

Dominance alone will *not*, however, cause the new trait to spread throughout the population in succeeding generations.

The only possible way in which the new form of a gene may increase the frequency of its occurrence in a gene pool is to step up its frequency of mutation from the original form or to be endowed with increased selective advantage over the old form. Increased selective advantage means that the resultant change in the organism increases its survival value and hence increases the probability that the organism will be able to reproduce itself in greater numbers than otherwise.

Genes that produce heavy skin pigmentation are obviously advantageous to people who live in the tropics. They are disadvantageous for people who live in areas of subnormal sunlight.

Coon, Garn, and Birdsell discuss the functional relation of gross bodily form to hot-dry, hot-damp, and extremely cold environments. The evidence they adduce for selective adaptation to special environments by specific races is impressive.

Races, therefore, differentiate among humanity chiefly through the mechanisms of mutation and subsequent natural selection in relation to specific environments. For a population to become a distinct race, matings must occur within the population with appreciably greater frequency than they do between it and other populations.

It is also possible for an isolated population to experience a change of its original genetic composition without the effect of mutation or natural selection. This is the result of the *Sewell Wright Effect*, named after the great contemporary American geneticist who demonstrated the workings of *genetic drift*, as it is also called.

Suppose a small group of people (or any other organisms, for that matter) migrate to a new territory, subsequently to lose contact with their ancestral group. Suppose, further, that in later generations more groups break off from the descendants of the original immigrants to make their homes elsewhere and they, too, become isolated as a population.

In a situation in which the gene frequency for a given trait is only 15 per cent for the original population, it could easily happen that by sheer chance no more than 5 per cent of the migrants carry the gene. In the gene pool of the emigrant population, the frequency of this gene is automatically reduced by two-thirds. The racial character of the original and the new societies is different by that much. Furthermore, in the absence of intermarriage, mutation, and changes in factors of natural selection, the change would remain constant indefinitely. Now suppose that in the course of time, a handful of dissident or adventurous descendants of the emigrants decides to move on to new territories. There is only a 5 per cent frequency of the gene in the total pool of their parent population. By change, it is possible that none of them may carry the gene. In that event, the gene would drop out of the population entirely. The new population would henceforth be absolutely different from its ancestors in the trait that the gene in question produced.

An obvious factor in the rise of new races is the coming together of racially distinct populations, followed by interbreeding. This process is called *miscegenation*. After interbreeding has progressed sufficiently, the orginally separate gene pools will have fused into one gene pool for the new population. The genes do not blend, because they retain the quality for segregation (Mendel's second law). The proportions of each type of gene in the enlarged gene pool will have altered, however, and the phenotypic appearance of the mixed population can become standardized as a new racial form.

How many races of mankind are there living today? By now it should be evident that there are few or many, depending on where the dividing lines are drawn and the criteria used. Most usages of the term *race* refer to large populations originally or currently dominating a continental land mass or archipelago. In these terms there are six or seven races: Caucasoid, Mongoloid, Negroid, Australoid, African Bushman, Polynesian. If more refined distinctions are drawn, particularly with reference to known gene frequencies as well as external morphology, then there are upwards of thirty living minor racial populations or microgeographic races. There are also unnumbered family lines, closely inbred groups of near relatives within microgeographic races, such as can be found in isolated backwoods areas of the United States or among the members of endogamous kindred in primitive tribes.

Each of the three great races is ordinarily classified into three major subraces as follows:

CAUCASOID	MONGOLOID	NEGROID
Nordic	Asiatic	African
Mediterranean	Oceanic	Oceanic
Alpine	American	Negrito
	Indian	

These, in turn, are sometimes further subdivided, but on this level there is a lack of consensus among anthropologists.

In the typological description of the major races now to be given, attention is paid only to the outstanding distinctive physical traits that characterize the several groups. It must always be remembered that many individual members of the racial group will not look like the description. The blood-group characteristics of the major races should also be brought to mind at this point.

CAUCASOIDS. The white race is not actually white, but relative to other races it is light-colored. Eye color among Caucasoids varies from light blue to dark brown. Hair is ash blond to black, of fine to medium texture; it may be straight, wavy, or curly, but rarely kinky and never woolly. The males tend to grow hair on their chests, arms, legs, and faces as well as on the tops of their heads. The nose is narrow and high, rarely broad or flat. Although the forehead is usually sloping, the face is not prognathous. Chins tend to jut and lips are thin. Stature is medium to tall.

Within the Caucasoid race the Alpines are concentrated in East Central Europe and Asia Minor. Recent migrations have sporadically distributed them in western Europe, North Africa, and North America in particular. They are brachycephalic (cephalic index [C.I.] 83 to 88) and have broad faces with sharp square jaws. They are brunettes through and through; eyes and hair are brown to black; the skin is olive-hued. The nose is well padded with adipose tissue at the tip, and it tends to be broad. The body is usually solid and heavy, rarely exceeding medium stature. Alpine men can grow fine dark beards; and if hair on the chest indicates masculinity, they have more of what it takes than any other Caucasoids.

The Mediterranean is also brunette, but, unlike the stocky Alpine, he is on the average slight of stature. His tendency is to be slight in youth and fat in maturity (this applies to the female also). The race is dolichocephalic (C.I. 72 to 76) with narrow high foreheads unmarked by any protrusion of a supraorbital ridge. Hair is black or dark, usually handsomely wavy and rarely straight. Although luxuriant on the head, it is sparse on the face, limbs, and body. Eyes are brown; the skin is light brown or pale olive. Noses are narrow and high-bridged. Some Britishers are Mediterraneans (especially Welshmen), but the bulk of the Mediterraneans are found in the Iberian Peninsula, Egypt, and Italy, among the Berbers and Arabs of North Africa, and in India and Indonesia.

The mean Nordic (statistically speaking) is low in pigmentation; his hair is blond (from towheaded to light brown); eyes are blue, gray, or hazel. Head form is dolichocephalic; the face is also narrow and angular. Jaws and chin are usually prominent; the nose is narrow and usually high. Hair is sparse on the body, thin on the head, and usually falls out in adult males—a price a man must pay for being a Nordic. In form Nordic hair is straight or wavy but seldom curly. The characteristic Nordic is tall and slender. His body is relatively small, but his legs are long. His chest is usually shallow and flat. Nordics do not have to worry too much about their waists, but there is much evidence in this country that they are not satisfied with themselves as paragons of physical perfection. Numerous males hopefully respond to physical-culture advertisements urging them to develop manly chests with bulging pectoral muscles. The females spend millions of dollars and uncalculated time in attempts to make their hair curly, while both sexes go to great lengths through natural and artificial means to attain the skin color of Mediterraneans.

Nordics predominate in the populations of Scandinavia and the Baltic shores of Germany. Many representatives of this race are found in Britain and its dominions, and among the population of the United States. Nordic enclaves are also found scattered throughout Europe and North Africa.

MONGOLOIDS. The most populous of the present-day races is the Mongoloid. The most outstanding Mongoloid physical trait is the slant eye, more elegantly known to anthropologists as the *internal epicanthic fold*. The infants also have a unique feature in the Mongolian patch: a purplish triangular area of skin at the base of the spine. Mongoloids are midway between Caucasoids and Negroids in pigmentation. Skin color is brown or yellowish-tan. Eyes are brown or dark-brown, and the hair is as black as the Negro's. It is very coarse and straight, growing long on the head and shunning the face and body. Most Mongoloid populations are brachycephalic, but there are exceptions among the American Indians and Eskimos. The malars are broad and high while the nose is squat and low-bridged, thus giving most Mongoloids a flat-faced appearance. In stature they are usually short and squat, due mostly to their short legs, since actually their body trunks are fairly long.

The Mongoloids proper are found in north, central, and southeastern Asia. The American Indians are predominantly Mongoloid and are usually classified as such by most anthropologists. However, they most certainly picked up some Negroid and Caucasoid ancestry long, long ago, before they left the Orient, since non-Mongoloid traits are evident in ancient skeletons and in the features of a number of Central and South American groups, as well as in North America. They also lost the B blood-group genes.

The Mongoloid strain is so strong in the majority of the Malayo-Indonesians that the variety deserves to be linked with the Mongoloid race. Yet it is not submerged in it, since a considerable degree of Mediterranean Caucasoid heredity is obvious. Indonesians, the older population found predominantly in the interiors of the islands of the East Indies, are clearly a Mediterranean offshoot derived in all probability from South India. The Malays, who came into Indonesia within the last several thousand years, picked up a strong Mongoloid strain from immigrants who came into Southeast Asia from South China in recent times. They have given the Mongoloid cast to the present Malayo-Indonesian race.

The result, as it is to be seen in these people, is a short, well-formed population averaging hardly more than 5 feet in stature. Skin color is brownish and eyes are brown. They have black hair with a definite reddish strain in it; where Indonesian elements predominate the hair is wavy and the head long; where Malay traits predominate the hair is usually straight and the cephalic index brachy- to meso-cephalic.

NEGROIDS. There is no justification for speaking of Negroes as the "colored race," since all races are more or less colored. In fact, if black is an absence of color, Negroes may better be called *colorless*. Admittedly Negroes are the possessors of the darkest pigmentation of all mankind; nevertheless, few Negroes are actually black. Most are dark-brown or brownish-black in skin color. Negro hair is prevailingly black, coarse, and wiry, and tightly curled, kinky, or woolly. Negro heads are with few exceptions long and narrow. The occipital region juts out, as does the lower portion of the face, which in appearance is accentuated by the thick, everted mucous membrane that forms the lips. The Negro nose is broad, with flaring alae and a broad, deeply depressed bridge. The hair on the head, though thick, is short in length, while the male beard is sparse and the body is not given to much hair growth. Stature is medium tall; the forearm is long; the legs thin (i.e., the calves do not ordinarily develop thick musculature); feet are low-arched.

The African Negro is the variety most familiar in Europe and the Americas. Originally, he inhabited most of Africa south of the Sahara and Egypt, but the seventeenth to nineteenth centuries saw the forced migration of several million Negroes from the West African Sudan to the New World.

East Africa produces a remarkable subvariety of Negro known as the Nilotic, who outdoes the Nordic in growing long legs on a slender short body to achieve tall stature.

The Oceanic Negro is a denizen of the South Seas, who first came to the attention of more than a handful of Americans when our troops made landings in the Solomons, New Hebrides, New Caledonia, and New Guinea. Physically, Oceanic Negroes are generally similar to African Negroes with these notable exceptions: the hair is more often frizzly and bushy; the supraorbital ridge is pronounced; the nose is prominent, hooked, and depressed at the tip; and the lips are thinner and less everted than the African's.

The pygmy races of the world are all Negroid. This special variety is hence called *Negrito*, or "little Negro." The scattered distribution of these little men indicates great antiquity for the race, which is found in small groups in the depths of the Congo jungle, in the Malay jungles of South-east Asia, in the interiors of New Guinea and the Philippines, and on the Andaman Islands of the Indian Ocean.

The Negritos are very small, averaging less than 4 feet 9 inches. Their skulls are mesocephalic with bulging foreheads, above which sprouts a tightly spiraled crop of close-growing hair. They vary from blackish- to reddish-brown in skin color, but the hair is consistently black. Their noses are exaggeratedly flat and broad, and their facial prognathism is marked. Their little bodies are lightly muscled, and prone to be potbellied. All in all, the physical endowment of the Negrito is so meager that it almost certainly has handicapped him in his precarious struggle for survival against the more powerfully built races of predatory men.

OTHER RACES. The South African Bushman is a Negrito with Mongoloid eye form and Mongoloid skin color. His triangular-shaped face with its protruding cheekbones also reflects Mongoloid characteristics. In spite of the absence of any historical data to support the conclusion, these marked Mongoloid traits indicate an ancient Negrito-Mongoloid cross as the origin of the Bushman race. Archaeological evidence proves that Bushmen have been in South Africa for at least 15,000 years.

The fact that the dark-brown Australoids are called *black-fellows* leads to the easy error of thinking of them as Negroes. They decidedly are not. Their hairiness of head and body and the waviness of their hair indicate a strong probability of archaic Caucasoid relations, such as is predominant in the Ainus.

The Australian aborigine is physically a "low brow." His forehead slopes back from the heaviest supraorbital ridges of any surviving race. His skull is narrow and houses a brain that is notably smaller in volume than that of any other living race. His face juts forward, and his dental arches even more so. His dark-brown eyes are set beside a deeply de-pressed nasal root, below which the broad thick tip of the nose flares up in a great bulb. The whole face is compressed from symphysis to nasion. The Australoid is neither very short nor very tall. Like the Nordic and Nilotic, he grows a slender short body on a pair of pipestem legs. Australia is the land of retarded geological oddities, and Australian man is a slightly retarded representative of *Homo sapiens*.

When the first Mongoloid invaders of Japan landed several thousand years ago, they found an unusual people in possession of the islands. These were the primitive Ainus—a people of swarthy "white" skin, abundantly covered with wavy black hair on head, face, and body. Their eyes were light-brown under heavy browridges similar to the Australian's. Noses, too, were Australoid, only less so. In stature they were short and thickset. The prehistoric Japanese disputed the possession of the islands with these people, gradually crowding them into the northern recesses and at the same time interbreeding to some extent, so that today some Mongoloid traits crop up in what is otherwise a unique race among all the races of mankind.

When it comes to pass at some future date that miscegenation blends all the races of man into one standardized variety, then that variety may reasonably be expected to look somewhat like the polyglot Polynesians. Such a prospect is genuinely gratifying, for rare is the person who dissents from the judgment that they are a handsome and comely people of great ability. Yet the Polynesians are thoroughly mongrelized; predominantly they are Mediterranean Caucasoid (from South India and akin to the Hindus) mixed with Oceanic Negroes and South Asiatic Mongoloids. The race is very similar to the Malayo-Indonesians except that the stronger Mediterranean heredity gives a wavy form to the hair, elongates the face and body, lightens the skin, and produces a high nose. Negroid traits show up in a tendency to fullness of lips. The dominant round-headedness of the Mongoloid characterizes most Polynesians. Hair grows luxuriantly on the head, but, as is to be expected in a Mediterranean-Mongoloid-Negro mixture, it shuns the face and body.

Physical anthropology—one of the two major divisions of anthropology—is itself concerned with a number of diverse areas of investigation. It involves the study of man's ancestors; previous selections have described some aspects of this search. More broadly, it deals with human biology—the science of man as a living organism. The physical anthropologist may thus specialize in the discovery and examination of prehistoric fossils, the measurement of physical traits, classification according to blood types or other genetic variables, or evolutionary changes within the human family. Obviously he must rely heavily on related physical and natural sciences, including palaeontology, primatology, anatomy and physiology, and genetics.

Physical anthropology has had a history of growth similar to those of other scientific disciplines. During the nineteenth century, a dominating concept was that of a hierarchical order of living things. Human beings also were graded, with races like the Hottentots at the bottom and the race to which the anthropologist belonged frequently placed at the top. It was believed that the gap between man and other primates would be filled by the discovery of a "missing link." There was undue emphasis on sheer observation and description, on the collection of facts. Since then physical anthropology has undergone, is still undergoing, a profound reorientation. As Washburn explains, purpose, technique, theory, and interpretation are all involved.

Sherwood L. Washburn is one of the leaders in the reorientation he describes. Born at Cambridge, Massachusetts, in 1911, he studied at Harvard and received his Ph.D. there in 1940. He was assistant professor of anatomy at Columbia from 1939 to 1947 and later became professor of anthropology and head of the department at the University of Chicago, where he studied the evolutionary patterns of man and apes. He is now professor anthropology at the University of California at Berkeley. He has been editor of the American Journal of Physical Anthropology and of the Viking Fund Publications in Anthropology, and is the author of numerous papers on the subject.

THE STRATEGY OF PHYSICAL ANTHROPOLOGY

S. L. WASHBURN

THE STRATEGY of a science is that body of theory and techniques with which it attacks its problems. All sciences have their traditional ways of marshaling and analyzing data, and the effectiveness of a science may be judged by the way its strategy actually solves problems and points the way to new research. For many years physical anthropology changed little and was easy to define. Physical anthropologists were those scientists, interested in human evolution and variation, who used measurements as their primary technique. The main training of a physical anthropologist consisted in learning to make a small number of measurements accurately, and one of the great concerns of the profession has been to get agreement on how these measurements should be taken. The assumption seems to have been that description (whether morphological or metrical), if accurate enough and in sufficient quantity, could solve problems of process, pattern, and interpretation.

It was essential to get a general appreciation of the varieties of primates, including man, before the problems of evolution could be understood. As knowledge of the primates increased, the kinds of problems to be solved became more and more defined. Is man's closest living relative an arboreal ape or a tiny tarsier? By what methods could such a problem be attacked? Should as many characters as possible be compared, or would a few critical ones settle the matter? Should adaptive characters be stressed, or does the solution of the problems of phylogeny lie in nonadaptive features? Does the body evolve as a unified whole, or may different parts change at different times?

The general understanding of the primates and of human races proceeded rapidly and productively in the nineteenth

76

century. The classifications of Flower and Lydekker (1891) and Deniker (1900) are remarkably close to those of today. The principal progress since that time has been in the discovery of fossils, and the quantity and quality of descriptive materials has increased greatly. Many small problems have been clarified, but the main outlines of the classification of the primates were clear more than fifty years ago.

During the last fifty years, although excellent descriptive data were added, techniques improved, and problems clarified and defined, little progress was made in understanding the process and pattern of human evolution. The strategy of physical anthropology yielded diminishing returns, and, finally, application of the traditional method *by experts* gave contradictory results. After more than a century of intensive fact-finding, there is less agreement among informed scientists on the relation of man to other primates than there was in the latter part of the nineteenth century. With regard to race, agreement is no greater, for some recognize a few races based on populations, while others describe a great number, many of which are types and refer to no populations at all.

Difficulties of this sort are by no means confined to physical anthropology but are common in many parts of descriptive zoology. The dilemma arises from continuing the strategy which was appropriate in the first descriptive phase of a science into the following analytic phase. Measurements will tell us which heads are long, but they will not tell us whether longheaded people should be put into one biological category. A photograph may show that a person is fat, but it gives no clue to the cause of the fat, and a grouping of fat people may be as arbitrary as one of longheads.

It is necessary to have a knowledge of the varieties of head form, pigmentation, body build, growth pattern, etc., before the problems of evolution, race, and constitution can be clearly stated. But all that can be done with the initial descriptive information is to gain a first understanding, a sense of problem, and a preliminary classification. To go further requires an elaboration of theory and method along different lines. Having passed through its initial descriptive phase, physical anthropology is now entering into its analytic

stage. Change is forced on physical anthropology partially
by the fact that its own strategy has ceased to yield useful
results but, far more, by the rise of modern evolutionary
theory. The meeting of genetics, palaeontology, and evolutionary zoology created the new systematics (neozoology),
just as the impact of the new evolutionary theory is creating
a new physical anthropology. Anthropologists are fortunate
that their problems are logically and methodologically
similar to those which have been debated and largely solved
in zoology. Therefore, their task is far simpler than that
which confronted taxonomists fifteen years ago. The anthropologist may simply adopt the new evolutionary point
of view, and his task is primarily one of adapting to this
intellectual environment and devising techniques suitable to
his particular needs. The nature and implication of the
changes will be made clearer by considering the contrast
between the old and the new systematically, under the
headings of purpose, theory, technique, and interpretation.
These comparisons will be made briefly in Table 1, and then
each will be considered in some detail. It should be remembered in making the comparisons that the differences are in
degree only and that brief contrasts, especially in a table,
make them appear unduly sharp. As Stewart has rightly
pointed out, the new physical anthropology has evolved from
the old, and there is a real continuity. However, a great
change is taking place in a short time. If this is called
"evolution," it is evolution of a quantum type. It is a burst
of acceleration on the part of a species which had been
quiescent for a long period of time.

Purpose

In commenting on the contrasts between the new and the
old physical anthropology outlined in Table 1, it should be
stressed that the area of interest or ultimate purposes of the
field are the same. The understanding and interpretation
of human evolution remains the objective. However, the
immediate purpose of most scientific investigations will be
but a small step toward the final goal. The investigator will
be concerned with race, constitution, fossil man, or some

similar problem. In the past the primary purpose of the majority of investigations of this sort was classification rather than the interpretation of any part of the phenomenon being investigated.

TABLE 1

OLD	NEW
	Purpose
Primarily classification	Understanding process
Problems solved by classification and correlation	Classification a minor part, and the cause of differences critical
Description of difference enough	
	Theory
Relatively little and unimportant; facts speak for themselves	Theory is critical, and the development of consistent, experimentally verified hypotheses a major objective
	Technique
Anthropometry 80 per cent, aided by morphological comparison	Measurement perhaps 20 per cent, supplemented by a wide variety of techniques adapted to the solution of particular problems
	Interpretation
Speculation	The primary objective of the research is to prove which hypotheses are correct; the major task begins where the old left off

This point can be made clear by examples. It has long been known that browridges vary in size and form. Cunningham gave a classification into which the majority of browridges can be fitted. The classification of browridges by this or similar schemes is a standard part of traditional physical anthropology. But what do the differences mean, and to what are they related? The classification gives no answers to these problems. To say that one fossil has browridges of Type II and another of Type III does not give any information on the significance of the difference, nor does it allow any inference to be made concerning relationship. In general, big browridges are correlated with big faces, but the appearance of size is also dependent on the size and form of the braincase. Microcephals appear to have large ridges, but this is due solely to the small size of the brain. In such an extreme case everyone would interpret the difference as being due to the change in size of the brain, but how much of the difference between the browridge of Java man and modern man is due to the difference in the face, and how much to a difference in the brain? In the literature a phylogeny of browridges is presented. This can be interpreted only if the ridges are sufficiently independent in size and form that tentative conclusions may be drawn from the classification and historical sequence. No one doubts the validity of the descriptive statements, but there is very real doubt that any conclusions can be drawn from this sort of table. This is because the ridge is anatomically complex and because the same general form of ridge may be due to a diversity of different conditions. For example, the central part of the divided type of ridge may be due to a large frontal sinus, acromegaly, a deposit of mechanically unoriented bone, or highly oriented bone. The general prominence of the region may be due to a large face or a small brain; but probably, with faces of equal mass, those associated with long cranial bases and large temporal muscles have larger browridges than those which are associated with shorter bases and larger masseter muscles. The description of the differences between an Australian Aboriginal and a Mongoloid can be done by the traditional methods, but it can be interpreted only if the anatomical causes lying behind the differences are analyzed. The description offers no technical difficulty, but analysis is possible only by the use of a variety of methods which have not been part of the equipment of anthropology.

This example shows the way in which classification was the aim and tool of physical anthropology. As viewed traditionally, if one was interested in browridges, the procedure was to classify the structures and then to draw conclusions on the interrelations of races or fossil men. That is, the classification gave a tool to be used in the analysis of evolution and variation. It was, in this sense, final knowledge. But in a different sense the classification merely outlined the problems to be investigated. No description of the types of browridges gives understanding of the reasons for any of them. The classifications show what kinds exist, under what circumstances they are found, and so pose a series of problems which need investigation. To traditional physical anthropology, classification was an end, something to be used. To the new physical anthropology, classifications merely pose problems, and methods must be devised to solve them.

The traditional reliance on classification as a method of analysis produced two of the characteristics of traditional zoological taxonomy and physical anthropology. 1] If classification is the primary aim and tool, then agreement on method is all-important. Therefore, the efforts of physical anthropologists have been to get agreements on how to take measurements and observations. Introductions to physical anthropology are largely instructions on how to take measurements, with little or no indication of what it is that the measurements are supposed to mean. 2] The second result of the emphasis on classification is that, when difficulties arise, they are met by making the classifications more complicated. This may be illustrated in the study of race. By the early part of the nineteenth century, several simple classifications of races existed, and causal explanations had been offered. Races were due to climate, isolation, etc. In the meantime, classifications of races have become vastly more numerous, and many are extremely complex, but explanations of cause and process have remained much as they were. Dobzhansky points out that the principal task of the anthropologist now should be to try to understand the causes and process of race formation. Dobzhansky's clear and eloquent plea should be read by all anthropologists, and I have only one qualification, or rather explanation. Traditional anthropologists thought that they were dealing with cause and process much more than Dobzhansky thinks they were. The difference really lies in the attitude toward classification. The traditional physical anthropologist thought that classification, if done in sufficient detail, would give the clues to problems of cause and process. Classifications were accompanied by remarks on how they were explained by hybridization, environment, etc. If one believes that classifications alone give understanding, then one will make the classifications more and more complicated, just as anthropologists have been doing. However, if one thinks that classification can do no more than map the results of process, then one will be content with a very rough mapping until the processes have been analyzed. The new physical anthropology is separated from the old, not by any difference in the desire to know causes, but by a very real difference in belief as to the extent to which classification can reveal causes.

Some classification is a necessary first stage in ordering the data in an area of knowledge, but its meaning depends on understanding the processes which produce the variety of form. After the first stage of preliminary description, scientists must turn to problems of process or face an era of futile elaboration of classifications which cannot be interpreted for lack of adequate techniques and theories.

Theory

It is a characteristic of the first stage of a science that theory is not considered important. If classification can solve problems and if it can be reached by marshaling enough facts, then theory need be of little concern. However, as knowledge increases and problems are more precisely formulated, theory becomes of great importance. For a considerable time after the idea of organic evolution had been accepted, comparisons were made without any general theoretical concern, other than that the parts compared should be homologous. Later, anthropology was particularly disturbed by the controversy as to whether deductions concerning relationship should be made on the basis of adaptive or nonadaptive characters. This, in turn, raised the question of whether it was better to compare many features, or whether the comparison of a few critical ones might not give more reliable results. Parallel evolution became recognized as a complicating feature, but, on the whole, physical anthropology continued to operate without any great concern for its theoretical foundations. It should be stressed that this general point of view was characteristic of much of historical zoology, ethnology, and archaeology. Theoretical issues were not absent, but they were not deemed very important, and the major effort went into collecting specimens and data and describing facts. The realization has been growing for some years that facts alone will not settle the problems and that even the collection of the "facts" was guided by a complex body of unstated assumptions.

The necessary guiding theories have been recently set forth by numerous zoologists, and the new zoology states simply that evolution is the history of genetic systems. Changes in isolated populations are due to mutation, selection, and accidents of genetic sampling (drift). The major cause of change is selection, which is a simple word covering a vast number of mechanisms. The implications of this theory for physical anthropology are numerous and complicated. The basic issue may be stated as follows: If evolution is governed primarily by adaptation, the demonstration of the nature and kind of adaptation is the principal task of the anthropologist. Evolution is a sequence of more effective behavior systems. To understand behavior, live animals must be studied first, and then, when fossils are found, the attempt can be made to interpret the differences by a knowledge of the living forms. It is necessary to remember that fossils were alive when they were important. They were the living, adapted forms of their day, and they must be understood in that setting. In so far as the record is fragmentary, the task is full of uncertainty; but this is a difficulty inherent in the kind of material and does not alter the logical problem.

Traditional physical anthropology was based on the study of skulls. Measurements were devised to describe certain features of the bones, and, when the technique was extended to the living, the measurements were kept as close to those taken on the skeleton as possible. From a comparative and classificatory point of view this was reasonable, and for a while it yielded useful results, but it brought the limitations of death to the study of the living. Whereas the new physical anthropology aims to enrich the study of the past by study of the present, to understand bone in terms of function and life, the old tried to reduce the living to a series of measurements designed to describe bones. Similarity in measurements or combinations of measurements was believed to show genetic affinity. Although it is true that humans of similar genotype are metrically similar, it is not true that similar measurements necessarily mean genetic similarity. Boyd has discussed this in detail. However, the point is so important that one example will be given here. Straus has shown that the ilium is approximately the same length in males and females, but the upper part is longer in males, and the lower longer in females. It is only an accident that the two different parts happen to give approximately the same total length. The descriptive statement that the ilium length is the same in male and female is correct and could be proved beyond doubt with elaborate statistics. However, the conclusion that the bones are anatomically or genetically similar would be wrong.

If a measurement is regarded as genetically determined, nonadaptive, and not correlated with others, it might then be used in the comparison of races without further question. This seems to have been the approximate working hypothesis of traditional physical anthropology. However, if traits are anatomically complex, adaptive, and correlated, they will be useful for description, but comparisons will not automatically yield solutions to problems of affinity. Present genetic and evolutionary theory suggests that characters are, for the most part, complex and adaptive, but this does not give information about any particular situation. The theory that the measurements were nonadaptive allowed one to work blindly and with confidence. The traditional measurements, accurately taken and treated with proper statistics, *gave certain answers.* The belief that traits are complex and adaptive means that the metrical comparisons *pose problems,* which must then be investigated by other methods. Measurements tell us that roundheads have become more common, but they do not tell us that roundheads are genetically similar or why roundheads have become more common. From an anatomical point of view, is brachycephalization due to changes in the brain, dura, sutures, or base of the skull? From an evolutionary point of view, is the change due to adaptation or genetic drift? It should be stressed that, although all seem agreed that selection is the most important factor in evolution, there is no agreement on the importance of genetic drift or the extent to which traits of little or no adaptive importance exist or spread.

In the past, investigators have assumed that characters were adaptive or nonadaptive, but this is the very question which needs investigation. Further, it should be stressed that it is not a question of one or the other, but of selective pressures varying from very little to very great. Some characteristic features of a race may be due to drift, others to strong selection, others to mild selection, still others to mixture due entirely to cultural factors. Whether a particular trait or gene frequency is highly adaptive or of little importance can be settled only by research, and the answer will surely differ at different times and places.

Closely related to the idea of nonadaptation is the concept of orthogenesis. If evolution is *not* caused by selection, then the long-term changes must be due to some other cause, and change may be accounted for by some inner irreversible force. This general concept has been very common in anthropology. For example, it has been maintained that, since man's arms are shorter than apes', man could not be descended from an ape, as this would reverse the course of evolution. According to the theory that evolution is adaptive, there is no reason why man's ancestors may not have had much longer arms. When selection changed, arms may have become shorter. (Actually, the difference is small.) According to the irreversible orthogenetic-force theory, man could not be descended from an ape, and a few measurements settle the matter. According to the theory of natural selection, man could be descended from an ape, but the theory does not prove that he was. All it does is indicate the kind of adaptive problem which must be understood before the data of comparative anatomy and the fossil record can be interpreted. Certainly, one of the reasons why the theory of orthogenesis, irreversibility, and the importance of non-adaptive characters was popular is that it allowed conclusions to be drawn by a few rules based on little evidence. The theory of selection offers no simple answers but merely points the direction in which answers must be sought.

Aside from the concept of selection, there are two other aspects of evolutionary theory which are of the utmost importance for anthropology. These are, first, that descriptions should be based on populations and, second, that genes, or traits, may vary independently. Taken together, these two facts mean that the anthropological concept of type is untenable, and refusal to accept this fact is the main reason why some anthropologists have been reluctant to adopt genetic concepts. The implications for anthropology of the concept of population and independence of genes are best understood by the history of the concept of race. In the earlier racial classifications a race was a group of people living in one part of the world who were obviously different from other people in physical characters. Thus the peoples of Europe, Africa south of the Sahara, eastern Asia, Australia, and the Americas were early recognized as races. How the peoples of India should be treated was always a problem, for a variety of reasons which lie beyond the scope of this essay. In the main, this classification is the same as that which Boyd gives on the basis of gene frequencies. Even the difficulty with regard to India is present in Boyd's classification. As knowledge increased, the larger areas were subdivided, and groups such as the Bushmen or Polynesians were recognized. The division of the world into areas occupied by more or less physically distinct groups was completed before 1900. The genetic study of race seems to be substantiating a large part of this general classification of mankind, although parts will surely be changed.

After 1900, to an increasing extent, a fundamentally different kind of "race" came to be used. In this race the group described was not a breeding population but a segment of such a population sorted out by various criteria. This second kind is called "type." Originally, the Australoid race meant the population of aboriginal Australia. By extension, the Australoid type was any skull, whether found in South Africa or America, which had certain morphological features common in the population of Australia. Similarly, the Mongoloid, or Negroid, race applies to groups of populations which have already been found to have genetic individuality. But there is no suggestion that the Mongoloid or Negroid types can be substantiated genetically.

The difficulty with the typological approach has been recognized by many, who pointed out that the more unrelated characters are used for sorting, the more races (types) there will be. Weidenreich objected to adding the blood groups to the traditional anthropological characters, on the ground that this would make the theoretical total of races 92,780! With the typological approach, the more that is known, the more types there will be; but, no matter how much is known, the number of populations remains unchanged. However much is ultimately known about the genetics and anatomy of the Australian aborigines, there are still the same tribes living on the same continent. Populations are reproductive groups which are defined by the ethnologist or archaeologist, or deduced from the way skeletons are found. The intensity of anatomical and genetical investigation does not increase the number of populations.

A "race" is a group of genetically similar populations, and races intergrade because there are always intermediate populations. A "type" is a group of individuals who are identical in those characters (genetic or phenotypic) by which the type was sorted (but *not* in other features!). The race concept and the type concept are fundamentally different, and modern zoological theory is compatible only with the race concept.

If anthropologists should adopt current zoological practice, several of the classifications of human races would be discarded, and the strategy of some schools of thought would be entirely abandoned. However, the change may be less than it appears at first sight. The reason for this is that most physical anthropologists simply were not interested in theory. In the majority of classifications, some of the races refer to populations and others to types. Even the type descriptions usually contain data on the whole series, prior to the type analysis. At present *there is no anthropological theory of race*, but two old, incompatible concepts carried along side by side. One of the primary tasks in developing a new physical anthropology is systematically to apply the modern zoological concept of race, to discard the types, and to put the traditional information into the form in which it will be most useful for the understanding of race formation.

In summarizing the contrast between the old and the new physical anthropology with regard to theory, the main point to emphasize is that the application of a consistent, experimentally verified evolutionary theory is the first task of the physical anthropologist. Since investigators were not interested in theory and since there is great diversity in actual practice, no useful purpose would be served by trying to discuss the implications of the new evolutionary theory in more detail. In the past, all the useful ideas were present in traditional physical anthropology, but so were the useless ones.

Boyd has stressed the break with the past, and Stewart the continuity with the past. Actually, physical anthropology is in a period of rapid transition in which both continuity and great change are important. At such a time disagreements are to be tolerated and major changes of personal opinion expected. For example, in 1940 Boyd criticized anthropologists for using adaptive characters when he maintained that they should use only nonadaptive ones. In 1950 he was equally vehement in his criticism of anthropologists for not seeking to use adaptive traits. At neither time were anthropologists as a profession doing either consistently, and at both times the real issue was to try to demonstrate which traits were adaptive, an issue which can be settled only by research.

Agreement is needed on the following points: (1) physical anthropology needs a consistent, proved, theoretical framework; (2) the necessary evolutionary and genetic theories are available and should be applied to the problems of human evolution; (3) untenable concepts should be abandoned; (4) a time of transition should be *welcomed* in which great differences in personal opinion are to be expected. These differences should be settled by research and not allowed to become personal or national issues.

Technique

A successful scientific strategy depends on theories and techniques adequate to solve problems. As theories change, techniques must alter also, as they exist only to solve problems and not as ends in themselves. Traditional physical anthropology was committed to the view that description alone would solve its problems, and, in practice, description of a very limited kind. The same measurements were applied to the solution of problems of the classification of the primates, relations of fossil men, description of race, human growth, and constitution. The technical training of a physical anthropologist was primarily indoctrination in the measurements of a particular school. In spite of the vast progress in biology, the practices of the physical anthropologist remained essentially the same for over one hundred years, although modified in detail and refined. As pointed out earlier, these techniques were an efficient part of the strategy of a descriptive science. They helped to outline the classification of the primates, fossil men, and races. The problems of interpreting human evolution and variation were clarified, but the traditional techniques failed to solve the problems of process. There are more different theories of man's origin and differentiation now than there were fifty years ago, and in this sense the strategy of physical anthropology failed. This was due partly to the theoretical dilemmas outlined before and partly to inadequacy of the techniques.

Interpretation

The traditional method of interpretation in physical anthropology primarily was speculation. Races, for example, have been attributed to endless mixtures, hormones, minerals, climate, adaptation, isolation, and chance, but little effort has been devoted to proving any of these theories. Similarly, measurements have been claimed to be adaptive or nonadaptive, but detailed proof substantiating either point of view is lacking. Actually, all dimensions of the human body serve functions, and the practical issue is to show what, in an anatomical sense, is being measured and what genetic or environmental factors may modify it. The face as a whole may be highly adaptive, and its main course in human evolution determined by selection, but small differences between races may be due to genetic drift. What is needed is *proof* of adaptation or drift in particular cases.

The point may be made clearer by the example of the nose. It has often been suggested that big noses appear when faces become small. But this theory has many exceptions and gives no idea of the factors actually involved. Since the split-line technique shows that the nasal bones are actually stressed by the forces of mastication, would it be reasonable to suppose that these bones would be bigger if the forces were reduced? If one nasal bone of a rat is removed on the first day of life, the other nasal bone grows to approximately one and a half times normal size. Further comparable removal of interparietal and parietal bones shows that these also grow large if free to do so. It seems to be a general rule that cranial roofing bones will grow bigger if forces normally stopping growth are removed. Schaeffer pictures skulls in which the nasal bones are entirely absent and the roof of the nose is formed by the maxillae. Piecing these lines of evidence together, it appears that the answer is again a question of pattern. Other things being equal, less pressure may result in more growth of nasal bone, but the actual proportions will depend on the interrelations of the size of the nasals, frontal processes of the maxillae, and the pressures.

Instead of relating nose form to selection or climate, it is necessary to insert an intermediate step, the analysis of the nose. Rather than saying that the pygmy's broad nose is an adaptation to the tropics, it may be that the nose is the result of a short face with large incisor teeth. The short face may be correlated with small total size (stature?), and the big teeth need explanation. Not enough is known about the form of the face to be sure that the racial differences of the nose should be correlated with climate at all.

Perhaps the relation of speculation, proof, and the importance of new methods can be best illustrated by theories concerning race mixture. It has become customary in physical anthropology to account for most of the races of the world by mixture. Of the four interrelated causes of difference recognized by zoologists (mutation, selection, drift, and migration), only one has been regarded as the principal source of new varieties of man. The absence of evidence for three primary races has been pointed to by Boyd and numerous others, and it is probably only rarely that mixture has been a major cause of race formation. The differentiation of races, for whatever reasons, must be accounted for on other grounds, as mixture can only make gene frequencies more alike.

If the Indians are a result of Mongoloid and Australian mixture, then they should have high blood group N, and considerable B. Actually they have the least N in the world, and B only among the Eskimo. In other words, the postulated mixture does not explain the facts known about the Indians. The more complicated hypotheses work no better. If Negroids are an important element in the mixture, then Rh⁰ should appear in the Indian, and it does not. If European elements are there, A2 and Rh negative should be present. It is clear that mixture alone will not explain the American Indian blood groups. Drift and/or selection must have operated also to change the gene frequencies, because what is found in the American Indian is something new, not found in the Old World or derivable from Old World frequencies by any mixtures. In spite of all the work that was done by traditional methods, it was possible for competent investigators to hold a number of divergent views as to the origin of the American Indian. The advent of a technique which made it possible to deal with the theories in objective, quantitative terms clearly shows that much of the speculation was unfounded and the role of mixture, as opposed to differentiation, exaggerated. The blood groups provide precise techniques for measuring mixture, provided that the mixture is relatively recent, as Carbon 14 suggests in the case of the American Indian.

In summary, the traditional physical anthropologist thought that his task was finished when he had classified and speculated. This era is past, and there are enough classifications and speculations. Now methods must be developed which will prove which speculations were on the right track. The best of the past should be combined with new techniques to bring proof in the place of speculation.

Conclusion

The attempt has been made to consider under the headings of purpose, theory, technique, and interpretation the changes now taking place in physical anthropology. The strategy of the traditional descriptive investigations has been contrasted with the developing analytic strategy, with its emphasis on theory, process, and experiment. The whole change is precisely parallel to that which has taken place in systematics.

The new strategy does not solve problems, but it suggests a different way of approaching them. The change from the old to the new affects the various parts of physical anthropology very differently. In studies of growth and applied anthropology, where the knowledge of dimensions is directly useful, changing theories make little difference. In evolutionary investigations the theoretical changes are of the greatest importance, and much of the anthropological work on race and constitution is eliminated by the rejection of the concept of type. However, one of the main implications of the new point of view is that there is a far more detailed interrelationship between the different parts of anthropology than under the old strategy. A dynamic analysis of the form of the jaw will illuminate problems of evolution, fossil man, race, growth, constitution, and medical application. The unraveling of the process of human evolution and variation will enrich the understanding of other mammalian groups, whereas the detailed description of a fossil has a much more limited utility. By its very nature, the investigation of process and behavior has a generality which is lacking in purely descriptive studies. The problems of human evolution are but special cases of the problems of mammalian evolution, and their solution will enrich palaeontology, genetics, and parts of clinical medicine.

But some of the problems of human evolution are unique to man. In so far as man has adapted by his way of life, the study of human evolution is inseparably bound to the study of archaeology and ethnology. It is because of the importance of the cultural factor that a separate study of human evolution is necessary. Human migrations, adaptations, mating systems, population density, diseases, and ecology—all these critical biological factors become increasingly influenced by the way of life. If we would understand the process of human evolution, we need a modern dynamic biology and a deep appreciation of the history and functioning of culture. It is this necessity which gives all anthropology unity as a science.

II. **The Study of Man's Culture**

II. The Study of Man's Culture

What are the practical problems faced by the ethnographer, the student of native cultures. He may find himself "alone on a tropical beach close to a native village," with little or no knowledge of the language, viewed with indifference or hostility by the inhabitants. He must insinuate himself into their good graces and somehow obtain the information he requires. How does he go about it and what standards must he set himself? There is perhaps no one better qualified to enlighten us on these matters than Bronislaw Malinowski, one of the founders of modern anthropology. Born at Cracow, Poland, in 1884, he attended the universities there and at Leipzig, and later the London School of Economics. He became interested in primitive civilizations through a reading of Sir James Frazer's The Golden Bough and decided to specialize in the anthropological study of the Western Pacific. In 1913 he published The Family Among the Australian Aborigines. From 1914 to 1918, he made three expeditions to New Guinea, in the course of which he lived two years in the Trobriand Islands, an archipelago off the eastern tip of New Guinea. He writes, "I did my work entirely alone, living for the greater part of the time right in the villages. I therefore had constantly the daily life of the natives before my eyes, while accidental dramatic occurences, deaths, quarrels, village brawls, public and ceremonial events could not escape my notice."

The result of his investigations was a classic in ethnographic study. He made a whole society his laboratory. He emphasized the need for understanding from within, observing natives in all phases of their activities. The natives became something other than curiosities. He collected not only artifacts but also attitudes and ideas.

In 1927, Malinowski joined the faculty of the London School of Economics and later became its first professor of social anthropology. In 1939, he became visiting professor

97

of anthropology at Yale. *His books included* Argonauts of the Western Pacific, *from which the following selection is taken,* The Sexual Life of Savages in Northwest Melanesia, The Dynamics of Cultural Change, *and* Magic, Science and Religion. *He died at New Haven in* 1942.

SUBJECT, METHOD AND SCOPE

BRONISLAW MALINOWSKI

IMAGINE YOURSELF suddenly set down surrounded by all your gear, alone on a tropical beach close to a native village, while the launch or dinghy which has brought you sails away out of sight. Since you take up your abode in the compound of some neighboring white man, trader or missionary, you have nothing to do, but to start at once on your ethnographic work. Imagine further that you are a beginner, without previous experience, with nothing to guide you and no one to help you. For the white man is temporarily absent, or else unable or unwilling to waste any of his time on you. This exactly describes my first initiation into field-work on the south coast of New Guinea. I well remember the long visits I paid to the villages during the first weeks; the feeling of hopelessness and despair after many obstinate but futile attempts had entirely failed to bring me into real touch with the natives, or supply me with any material. I had periods of despondency, when I buried myself in the reading of novels, as a man might take to drink in a fit of tropical depression and boredom.

Imagine yourself then, making your first entry into the village, alone or in company with your white cicerone. Some natives flock round you, especially if they smell tobacco. Others, the more dignified and elderly, remain seated where they are. Your white companion has his routine way of treating the natives, and he neither understands, nor is very much concerned with the manner in which you, as an ethnographer, will have to approach them. The first visit leaves you with a hopeful feeling that when you return alone, things will be easier. Such was my hope at least.

I came back duly, and soon gathered an audience around me. A few compliments in pidgin-English on both sides, some tobacco changing hands, induced an atmosphere of mutual amiability. I tried then to proceed to business. First, to begin with subjects which might arouse no suspicion, I started to "do" technology. A few natives were engaged in manufacturing some object or other. It was easy to look at it and obtain the names of the tools, and even some technical expressions about the proceedings, but there the matter ended. It must be borne in mind that pidgin-English is a very imperfect instrument for expressing one's ideas, and that before one gets a good training in framing questions and understanding answers one has the uncomfortable feeling that free communication in it with natives will never be attained; and I was quite unable to enter into any more detailed or explicit conversations with them at first. I knew well that the best remedy for this was to collect concrete data, and accordingly I took a village census, wrote down genealogies, drew up plans and collected the terms of kinship. But all this remained dead material, which led no further into the understanding of real native mentality or behavior, since I could neither procure a good native interpretation of any of these items, nor get what could be called the hang of tribal life. As to obtaining their ideas about religion, and magic, their beliefs in sorcery and spirits, nothing was forthcoming except a few superficial items of folk-lore, mangled by being forced into pidgin-English.

Information which I received from some white residents in the district, valuable as it was in itself, was more discouraging than anything else with regard to my own work. Here were men who had lived for years in the place with constant opportunities of observing the natives and communicating with them, and who yet hardly knew one thing about them really well. How could I therefore in a few months or a year, hope to overtake or go beyond them? Moreover, the manner in which my white informants spoke about the natives and put their views was, naturally, that of untrained minds, unaccustomed to formulate their thoughts with any degree of consistency and precision. And they were for the most part, naturally enough, full of the biased and prejudged opinions inevitable in the average practical man, whether administrator, missionary, or trader, yet so strongly repulsive to a mind striving after the objective, scientific view of things. The habit of treating with a self-satisfied frivolity what is really serious to the ethnographer; the cheap rating of what to him is a scientific treasure, that is to say, the native's cultural and mental peculiarities and independence—these features, so well known in the inferior amateur's writing, I found in the tone of the majority of white residents.

Indeed, in my first piece of ethnographic research on the South coast, it was not until I was alone in the district that I began to make some headway; and, at any rate, I found out where lay the secret of effective field-work. What is then this ethnographer's magic, by which he is able to evoke the real spirit of the natives, the true picture of tribal life? As usual, success can only be obtained by a patient and systematic application of a number of rules of common sense and well-known scientific principles, and not by the discovery of any marvelous short-cut leading to the desired results without effort or trouble. The principles of method can be grouped under three main headings; first of all, naturally, the student must possess real scientific aims, and know the values and criteria of modern ethnography. Secondly, he ought to put himself in good conditions of work, that is, in the main, to live without other white men, right among the natives. Finally, he has to apply a number of special methods of collecting, manipulating and fixing his evidence. A few words must be said about these three foundation stones of field-work, beginning with the second as the most elementary.

PROPER CONDITIONS FOR ETHNOGRAPHIC WORK. These, as said, consist mainly in cutting oneself off from the company of other white men, and remaining in as close contact with the natives as possible, which really can only be achieved by camping right in their villages. It is very nice to have a base in a white man's compound for the stores, and to know there is a refuge there in times of sickness and surfeit of native. But it must be far enough away not to become a permanent milieu in which you live and from which you emerge at fixed hours only to "do the village." It should not even be near enough to fly to at any moment for recreation. For the native is not the natural companion for a white man, and after you have been working with him for several hours, seeing how he does his gardens, or letting him tell you items of folk-lore, or discussing his customs, you will naturally hanker after the company of your own kind. But if you are alone in a village beyond reach of this, you go for a solitary walk for an hour or so, return again and then quite naturally seek out the natives' society, this time as a relief from loneliness, just as you would any other companionship. And by means of this natural intercourse, you learn to know him, and you become familiar with his customs and beliefs far better than when he is a paid, and often bored, informant.

There is all the difference between a sporadic plunging into the company of natives, and being really in contact with them. What does this latter mean? On the ethnographer's side, it means that his life in the village, which at first is a strange, sometimes unpleasant, sometimes intensely interesting adventure, soon adopts quite a natural course very much in harmony with his surroundings.

Soon after I had established myself in Omarakana (Trobriand Islands), I began to take part, in a way, in the village life, to look forward to the important or festive events, to take personal interest in the gossip and the developments of the small village occurrences; to wake up every morning to a day, presenting itself to me more or less as it does to the native. I would get out from under my mosquito net, to find around me the village life beginning to stir, or the people well advanced in their working day according to the hour and also to the season, for they get up and begin their labors early or late, as work presses. As I went on my morning walk through the village, I could see intimate details of family life, of toilet, cooking, taking of meals; I could see the arrangements for the day's work, people starting on their errands, or groups of men and women busy at some manufacturing tasks. Quarrels, jokes, family scenes, events usually trivial, sometimes dramatic but always significant, formed the atmosphere of my daily life, as well as of theirs. It must be remembered that as the natives saw me constantly every day, they ceased to be interested or alarmed, or made self-conscious by my presence, and I ceased to be a disturbing element in the tribal life which I was to study, altering it by my very approach, as always happens with a newcomer to every savage community. In fact, as they knew that I would thrust my nose into everything, even where a well-mannered native would not dream of intruding, they finished by regarding me as part and parcel of their life, a necessary evil or nuisance, mitigated by donations of tobacco.

Later on in the day, whatever happened was within easy reach, and there was no possibility of its escaping my notice. Alarms about the sorcerer's approach in the evening, one or two big, really important quarrels and rifts within the community, cases of illness, attempted cures and deaths, magical rites which had to be performed, all these I had not to pursue, fearful of missing them, but they took place under my very eyes, at my own doorstep, so to speak. And it must be emphasized whenever anything dramatic or important occurs it is essential to investigate it at the very moment of happening, because the natives cannot but talk about it, are too excited to be reticent, and too interested to be mentally lazy in supplying details. Also, over and over again, I committed breaches of etiquette, which the natives, familiar enough with me, were not slow in pointing out. I had to learn how to behave, and to a certain extent, I acquired "the feeling" for native good and bad manners. With this, and with the capacity of enjoying their company and sharing some of their games and amusements, I began to feel that I was indeed in touch with the natives, and this is certainly the preliminary condition of being able to carry on successful field-work.

But the ethnographer has not only to spread his nets in the right place, and wait for what will fall into them. He must be an active huntsman, and drive his quarry into them and follow it up to its most inaccessible lairs. And that leads us to the more active methods of pursuing ethnographic evidence. The ethnographer has to be inspired by the knowledge of the most modern results of scientific study, by its principles and aims. I shall not enlarge upon this subject, except by way of one remark, to avoid the possibility of misunderstanding. Good training in theory, and acquaintance with its latest results, is not identical with being burdened with "preconceived ideas." If a man sets out on an expedition, determined to prove certain hypotheses, if he is incapable of changing his views constantly and casting them off ungrudgingly under the pressure of evidence, needless to say his work will be worthless. But the more problems he brings with him into the field, the more he is in the habit of molding his theories according to facts, and of seeing facts in their bearing upon theory, the better he is equipped for the work. Preconceived ideas are pernicious in any scientific work, but foreshadowed problems are the main endowment of a scientific thinker, and these problems are first revealed to the observer by his theoretical studies.

As always happens when scientific interest turns towards and begins to labor on a field so far only prospected by the curiosity of amateurs, ethnology has introduced law and order into what seemed chaotic and freakish. It has transformed for us the sensational, wild and unaccountable world of "savages" into a number of well-ordered communities, governed by law, behaving and thinking according to consistent principles. The word "savage," whatever association it might have had originally, connotes ideas of boundless liberty, of irregularity, of something extremely and extraordinarily quaint. In popular thinking, we imagine that the natives live on the bosom of Nature, more or less as they can and like, the prey of irregular, phantasmagoric beliefs and apprehensions. Modern science, on the contrary, shows that their social institutions have a very definite organization, that they are governed by authority, law and order in their public and personal relations, while the latter are, besides, under the control of extremely complex ties of kinship and clanship. Indeed, we see them entangled in a mesh of duties, functions and privileges which correspond to an elaborate tribal, communal and kinship organization. Their beliefs and practices do not by any means lack consistency of a certain type, and their knowledge of the outer world is sufficient to guide them in many of their strenuous enterprises and activities. Their artistic productions again lack neither meaning nor beauty.

It is a very far cry from the famous answer given long ago by a representative authority who, asked what are the manners and customs of the natives, answered, "Customs none, manners beastly," to the position of the modern ethnographer! This latter, with his tables of kinship terms, genealogies, maps, plans and diagrams, proves the existence of an extensive and big organization, shows the constitution of the tribe, of the clan, of the family; and he gives us a picture of the natives subjected to a strict code of behavior and good manners, to which in comparison the life at the Court of Versailles or Escourial was free and easy.

Thus the first and basic ideal of ethnographic field-work is to give a clear and firm outline of the social constitution, and disentangle the laws and regularities of all cultural phenomena from the irrelevances. The firm skeleton of the tribal life has to be first ascertained. This ideal imposes in the first place the fundamental obligation of giving a complete survey of the phenomena, and not of picking out the sensational, the singular, still less the funny and quaint. The time when we could tolerate accounts presenting us the native as a distorted, childish caricature of a human being is gone. This picture is false, and like many other falsehoods, it has been killed by Science. The field ethnographer has seriously and soberly to cover the full extent of the phenomena in each aspect of tribal culture studied, making no difference between what is commonplace, or drab, or ordinary, and what strikes him as astonishing and out-of-the-way. At the same time, the whole area of tribal culture *in all its aspects* has to be gone over in research. The consistency, the law and order which obtain within each aspect make also for joining them into one coherent whole.

An ethnographer who sets out to study only religion, or only technology, or only social organization cuts out an artificial field for inquiry, and he will be seriously handicapped in his work.

Having settled this very general rule, let us descend to more detailed consideration of method. The ethnographer has in the field, according to what has just been said, the duty before him of drawing up all the rules and regularities of tribal life; all that is permanent and fixed; of giving an anatomy of their culture, of depicting the constitution of their society. But these things, though crystallized and set, are nowhere *formulated*. There is no written or explicitly expressed code of laws, and their whole tribal tradition, the whole structure of their society, are embodied in the most elusive of all materials; the human being. But not even in human mind or memory are these laws to be found definitely formulated. The natives obey the forces and commands of the tribal code, but they do not comprehend them; exactly as they obey their instincts and their impulses, but could not lay down a single law of psychology. The regularities in native institutions are an automatic result of the interaction of the mental forces of tradition, and of the material conditions of environment. Exactly as a humble member of any modern institution, whether it be the state, or the church, or the army, is *of* it and *in* it, but has no vision of the resulting integral action of the whole, still less could furnish any account of its organization, so it would be futile to attempt questioning a native in abstract, sociological terms. The difference is that, in our society, every institution has its intelligent members, its historians, and its archives and documents, whereas in a native society there are none of these. After this is realized an expedient has to be found to overcome this difficulty. This expedient for an ethnographer consists in collecting concrete data of evidence, and drawing the general inferences for himself. This seems obvious on the face of it, but was not found out or at least practiced in ethnography till field-work was taken up by men of science. Moreover, in giving it practical effect, it is neither easy to devise the concrete applications of this method, nor to carry them out systematically and consistently.

Though we cannot ask a native about abstract, general rules, we can always enquire how a given case would be treated. Thus for instance, in asking how they would treat crime, or punish it, it would be vain to put to a native a sweeping question such as, "How do you treat and punish a criminal?" for even words could not be found to express it in native, or in pidgin. But an imaginary case, or still better, a real occurrence, will stimulate a native to express his opinion and to supply plentiful information. A real case indeed will start the natives on a wave of discussion, evoke expressions of indignation, show them taking sides—all of which talk will probably contain a wealth of definite views, of moral censures, as well as reveal the social mechanism set in motion by the crime committed. From there, it will be easy to lead them on to speak to other similar cases, to remember other actual occurrences or to discuss them in all their implications and aspects. From this material, which ought to cover the widest possible range of facts, the inference is obtained by simple induction. The *scientific* treatment differs from that of good common sense, first in that a student will extend the completeness and minuteness of survey much further and in a pedantically systematic and methodical manner; and secondly, in that the scientifically trained mind will push the inquiry along really relevant lines, and towards aims possessing real importance. Indeed, the object of scientific training is to provide the empirical investigator with a *mental chart*, in accordance with which he can take his bearings and lay his course.

To return to our example, a number of definite cases discussed will reveal to the ethnographer the social machinery for punishment. This is one part, one aspect of tribal authority. Imagine further that by a similar method of inference from definite data, he arrives at understanding—leadership in war, in economic enterprise, in tribal festivities—there he has at once all the data necessary to answer the questions about tribal government and social authority. In actual fieldwork, the comparison of such data, the attempt to piece them together, will often reveal rifts and gaps in the information which lead on to further investigations.

From my own experience, I can say that, very often, a problem seemed settled, everything fixed and clear, till I began to write down a short preliminary sketch of my results. And only then, did I see the enormous deficiencies, which would show me where lay new problems, and lead me on to new work.

The collecting of concrete data over a wide range of facts

is thus one of the main points of field-method. The obligation is not to enumerate a few examples only, but to exhaust as far as possible all the cases within reach; and, on this search for cases, the investigator will score most whose mental chart is clearest. But, whenever the material of the search allows it, this mental chart ought to be transformed into a real one; it ought to materialize into a diagram, a plan, an exhaustive, synoptic table of cases. The method of reducing information, if possible, into charts or synoptic tables ought to be extended to the study of practically all aspects of native life. All types of economic transactions may be studied by following up connected, actual cases, and putting them into a synoptic chart, again, a table ought to be drawn up of all the gifts and presents customary in a given society, a table including the sociological, ceremonial, and economic definition of every item. Also, systems of magic, connected series of ceremonies, types of legal acts, all could be charted, allowing each entry to be synoptically defined under a number of headings. Besides this, of course, the genealogical census of every community, studied more in detail, extensive maps, plans and diagrams, illustrating ownership in garden land, hunting and fishing privileges, etc., serve as the more fundamental documents of ethnographic research.

A genealogy is nothing else but a synoptic chart of a number of connected relations of kinship. Its value as an instrument of research consists in that it allows the investigator to put questions which he formulates to himself *in abstracto*, but can put concretely to the native informant. As a document, its value consists in that it gives a number of authenticated data, presented in their natural grouping. A synoptic chart of magic fulfills the same function. As an instrument of research, I have used it in order to ascertain, for instance, the ideas about the nature of magical power. With a chart before me, I could easily and conveniently go over one item after the other, and note down the relevant practices and beliefs contained in each of them. The answer to my abstract problem could then be obtained by drawing a general inference from all the cases.

The procedure of concrete and tabularized presentation of data ought to be applied first to the ethnographer's own credentials. That is, an ethnographer who wishes to be trusted must show clearly and concisely, in a tabularized form, which are his own direct observations, and which the indirect information that form the bases of his account.

To summarize the first, cardinal point of method, I may say each phenomenon ought to be studied through the broadest range possible of its concrete manifestations; each studied by an exhaustive survey of detailed examples. If possible, the results ought to be tabulated into some sort of synoptic chart, both to be used as an instrument of study, and to be presented as an ethnological document. With the help of such documents and such study of actualities the clear outline of the framework of the natives' culture in the widest sense of the word, and the constitution of their society, can be presented. This method could be called *the method of statistic documentation by concrete evidence.*

Needless to add, in this respect, the scientific field-work is far above even the best amateur productions. There is, however, one point in which the latter often excel. This is, in the presentation of intimate touches of native life, in bringing home to us these aspects of it with which one is made familiar only through being in close contact with the natives, one way or the other, for a long period of time. In certain results of scientific work—especially that which has been called "survey work"—we are given an excellent skeleton, so to speak, of the tribal constitution, but it lacks flesh and blood. We learn much about the framework of their society, but within it, we cannot perceive or imagine the realities of human life, the even flow of everyday events, the occasional ripples of excitement over a feast, or ceremony, or some singular occurrence. In working out the rules and regularities of native custom, and in obtaining a precise formula for them from the collection of data and native statements, we find that this very precision is foreign to real life, which never adheres to any rules. It must be supplemented by the observation of the manner in which a given custom is carried out, of the behavior of the natives in obeying the rules so exactly formulated by the ethnographer, of the very exceptions which in sociological phenomena almost always occur.

If all the conclusions are solely based on the statements of informants, or deduced from objective documents, it is of course impossible to supplement them in actually observed data of real behavior. And that is the reason why certain works of amateur residents of long standing, such as educated traders and planters, medical men and officials, and last, but not least, the few intelligent and unbiased missionaries to whom ethnography owes so much, surpassed in plasticity and in vividness most of the purely scientific accounts. But if the specialized field-worker can adopt the conditions of living described above, he is in a far better position to be really in touch with the natives than any other white resident. For none of them lives right in a native village, except for very short periods, and everyone has his own business, which takes up a considerable part of his time. Moreover, if, like a trader or a missionary or an official he enters into active relations with the native, if he has to transform or influence or make use of him, this makes a real, unbiased, impartial observation impossible, and precludes all-round sincerity, at least in the case of the missionaries and officials.

Living in the village with no other business but to follow native life, one sees the customs, ceremonies and transactions over and over again, one has examples of their beliefs as they are actually lived through, and the full body and blood of actual native life fills out soon the skeleton of abstract constructions. That is the reason why, working under such conditions as previously described, the ethnographer is enabled to add something essential to the bare outline of tribal constitution, and to supplement it by all the details of behavior, setting and small incident. He is able in each case to state whether an act is public or private; how a public assembly behaves, and what it looks like; he can judge whether an event is ordinary or an exciting and singular one; whether natives bring to it a great deal of sincere and earnest spirit, or perform it in fun; whether they do it in a perfunctory manner, or with zeal and deliberation.

In other words, there is a series of phenomena of great importance which cannot possibly be recorded by questioning or computing documents, but have to be observed in their full actuality. Let us call them *the imponderabilia of actual life*. Here belong such things as the routine of a man's work-

ing day, the details of his care of the body, of the manner of
taking food and preparing it; the tone of conversational and
social life around the village fires, the existence of strong
friendships or hostilities, and of passing sympathies and dis-
likes between people; the subtle yet unmistakable manner in
which personal vanities and ambitions are reflected in the
behavior of the individual and in the emotional reactions of
those who surround him. All these facts can and ought to be
scientifically formulated and recorded, but it is necessary that
this be done, not by a superficial registration of details, as is
usually done by untrained observers, but with an effort at
penetrating the mental attitude expressed in them. And that
is the reason why the work of scientifically trained observers,
once seriously applied to the study of this aspect, will, I believe, yield results of surpassing value. So far, it has been
done only by amateurs, and therefore done, on the whole, indifferently.

Indeed, if we remember that these imponderable yet all-
important facts of actual life are part of the real substance of
the social fabric, that in them are spun the innumerable
threads which keep together the family, the clan, the village
community, the tribe—their significance becomes clear. The
more crystallized bonds of social grouping, such as the definite ritual, the economic and legal duties, the obligations, the
ceremonial gifts and formal marks of regard, though equally
important for the student, are certainly felt less strongly by
the individual who has to fulfill them. Applying this to ourselves, we all know that "family life" means for us, first and
foremost, the atmosphere of home, all the innumerable small
acts and attentions in which are expressed the affection, the
mutual interest, the little preferences, and the little anti-
pathies which constitute intimacy. That we may inherit from
this person, that we shall have to walk after the hearse of the
other, though sociologically these facts belong to the definition of "family" and "family life," in personal perspective of
what family truly is to us, they normally stand very much in
the background.

In the same way, in studying the conspicuous acts of tribal
life, such as ceremonies, rites, festivities, etc., the details and
tone of behavior ought to be given, besides the bare outline

of events. The importance of this may be exemplified by one instance. Much has been said and written about survival. Yet the survival character of an act is expressed in nothing so well as in the concomitant behavior, in the way in which it is carried out. Take any example from our own culture, whether it be the pomp and pageantry of a state ceremony, or a picturesque custom kept up by street urchins, its "outline" will not tell you whether the rite flourishes still with full vigor in the hearts of those who perform it or assist at the performance or whether they regard it as almost a dead thing, kept alive for tradition's sake. But observe and fix the data of their behavior, and at once the degree of vitality of the act will become clear.

As to the actual method of observing and recording in field-work these *imponderabilia of actual life and of typical behavior*, there is no doubt that the personal equation of the observer comes in here more prominently, than in the collection of crystallized, ethnographic data. But here also the main endeavor must be to let facts speak for themselves. If in making a daily round of the village, certain small incidents, characteristic forms of taking food, of conversing, of doing work are found occurring over and over again, they should be noted down at once. It is also important that this work of collecting and fixing impressions should begin early in the course of working out a district.

In observing ceremonies or other tribal events, it is necessary, not only to note down those occurrences and details which are prescribed by tradition and custom to be the essential course of the act, but also the ethnographer ought to record carefully and precisely, one after the other, the actions of the actors and of the spectators. Forgetting for a moment that he knows and understands the structure of this ceremony, the main dogmatic ideas underlying it, he might try to find himself only in the midst of an assembly of human beings, who behave seriously or jocularly, with earnest concentration or with bored frivolity, who are either in the same mood as he finds them every day, or else are screwed up to a high pitch of excitement, and so on and so on.

Again, in this type of work, it is good for the ethnographer sometimes to put aside camera, note book and pencil, and to join in himself in what is going on. He can take part in the natives' games, he can follow them on their visits and walks, sit down and listen and share in their conversations. I am not certain if this is equally easy for everyone—perhaps the Slavonic nature is more plastic and more naturally savage than that of Western Europeans—but though the degree of success varies, the attempt is possible for everyone.

Finally, let us pass to the third and last aim of scientific field-work, to the last type of phenomenon which ought to be recorded in order to give a full and adequate picture of native culture. Besides the firm outline of tribal constitution and crystallized cultural items which form the skeleton, besides the data of daily life and ordinary behavior, which are, so to speak, its flesh and blood, there is still to be recorded the spirit—the natives' views and opinions and utterances. For, in every act of tribal life, there is, first, the routine prescribed by custom and tradition, then there is the manner in which it is carried out, and lastly there is the commentary to it, contained in the natives' mind. A man who submits to various customary obligations, who follows a traditional course of action, does it impelled by certain motives, to the accompaniment of certain feelings, guided by certain ideas. These ideas, feelings, and impulses are molded and conditioned by the culture in which we find them, and are therefore an ethnic peculiarity of the given society. An attempt must be made therefore, to study and record them.

But is this possible? Are these subjective states not too elusive and shapeless? And, even granted that people usually do feel or think or experience certain psychological states in association with the performance of customary acts, the majority of them surely are not able to formulate these states, to put them into words. This latter point must certainly be granted, and it is perhaps the real Gordian knot in the study of the facts of social psychology Without trying to cut or untie this knot, that is, to solve the problem theoretically, or to enter further into the field of general methodology, I shall make directly for the question of practical means to overcome some of the difficulties involved.

First of all, it has to be laid down that we have to study here stereotyped manners of thinking and feeling. As sociologists, we are not interested in what A or B may feel *qua* individuals, in the accidental course of their own personal experiences—we are interested only in what they feel and think *qua* members of a given community. Now in this capacity, their mental states receive a certain stamp, become stereotyped by the institutions in which they live, by the influence of tradition and folk-lore, by the very vehicle of thought, that is, by language. The social and cultural environment in which they move forces them to think and feel in a definite manner. Thus, a man who lives in a polyandrous community cannot experience the same feelings of jealousy as a strict monogynist, though he might have the elements of them.

So, the third commandment of field-work runs: Find out the typical ways of thinking and feeling, corresponding to the institutions and culture of a given community, and formulate the results in the most convincing manner. What will be the method of procedure? The best ethnographical writers have always tried to quote *verbatim* statements of crucial importance. They also adduce terms of native classification; sociological, psychological and industrial *termini technici,* and have rendered the verbal contour of native thought as precisely as possible. One step further in this line can be made by the ethnographer who acquires a knowledge of the native language and can use it as an instrument of inquiry. In working in the Kiriwinian language, I found still some difficulty in writing down the statement directly in translation which at first I used to do in the act of taking notes. The translation often robbed the text of all its significant characteristics—rubbed off all its points—so that gradually I was led to note down certain important phrases just as they were spoken, in the native tongue. As my knowledge of the language progressed, I put down more and more in Kiriwinian, till at last I found myself writing exclusively in that language, rapidly taking notes, word for word, of each statement. No sooner had I arrived at this point, than I recognised that I was thus acquiring at the same time an abundant linguistic material, and a series of ethnographic documents which ought to be reproduced as I had fixed them, besides being utilized in the writing up of my account.

Our considerations thus indicate that the goal of ethnographic field-work must be approached through three avenues:

1] *The organization of the tribe, and the anatomy of its culture* must be recorded in firm, clear outline. The method of *concrete, statistical documentation* is the means through which such an outline has to be given.

2] Within this frame, the *imponderabilia of actual life*, and the *type of behavior* have to be filled in. They have to be collected through minute, detailed observations, in the form of some sort of ethnographic diary, made possible by close contact with native life.

3] A collection of ethnographic statements, characteristic narratives, typical utterances, items of folk-lore and magical formulae has to be given as a *corpus inscriptionum,* as documents of native mentality.

These three lines of approach lead to the final goal, of which an ethnographer should never lose sight. This goal is, briefly, to grasp the native's point of view, his relation to life, to realize *his* vision of *his* world. We have to study man, and we must study what concerns him most intimately, that is, the hold which life has on him. In each culture, the values are slightly different; people aspire after different aims, follow different impulses, yearn after a different form of happiness. In each culture, we find different institutions in which man pursues his life-interest, different customs by which he satisfies his aspirations, different codes of law and morality which reward his virtues or punish his defections. To study the institutions, customs, and codes or to study the behavior and mentality without the subjective desire of feeling by what these people live, or realizing the substance of their happiness—is, in my opinion, to miss the greatest reward which we can hope to obtain from the study of man.

For Malinowski's tropic beach, substitute the Cuchumatán Highlands in Guatemala; for a tribe of Melanesian islanders the descendants of an ancient Mayan civilization; for a Polish-born and European-educated anthropologist, a young American recently graduated from Harvard. The problem and its solution remain the same. In La Farge's words, "If you really believe that these people are your full equals, after a long period of doubt, of suspicion, of watching for the fraud or the ulterior motive behind your attitude, will come a surprised, grateful, warm response and solid loyalty." Malinowski's discussion of what the anthropologist must look for and how he must go about finding it are here illustrated in actual practice.

Oliver La Farge, who describes the incident in which he himself participated, was a member of a distinguished American family, the son of Christopher La Farge, the architect. He was to achieve distinction in three separate fields. He was a well-known ethnologist, serving with scientific expeditions in Arizona, Mexico, and Guatemala. He was the author of a number of books of high literary excellence, including Laughing Boy, a novel which was awarded the Pulitzer Prize, and Raw Material, from which the following selection was taken. He was also one of the foremost champions of the rights of the American Indian. From 1930 to 1932 he served as director of the Eastern Association on Indian Affairs; from 1933 to 1937 as president of the National Association on Indian Affairs; and from 1937 to 1942 as president of its successor, the American Association on Indian Affairs. He died in 1963, at the age of sixty-two.

THE PERFECT CIRCLE

OLIVER LA FARGE

YOU COULD LOSE yourself in the great spaces of the Navajo country. You could do this literally and die of thirst, or spiritually and forget that the white world existed, like water backed too high against a levee, all around the reservation. The life of the Indians seemed little changed except in surface matters of materials for clothing, wagons, some tools; the white man dwindled to a merchant from whom at rare intervals the people secured these goods; here in the canyons and mountains the Navajo way was immutable, secure, a complete refuge.

Bart Hayes and I were young, curious, and unwashed. I rode a skinny little black mare with more fire in her than one had any right to expect. His horse was various bright shades of pink, it was oddly constructed, and at one glance an observer could satisfy himself that the animal had all his ribs. Our outfit—cooking equipment, bedding, grub, grain, the other shirt—was wrapped in a canvas wagon-cover and tied with a squaw hitch onto an albino pack horse with blue eyes. Lorenzo Hubbell, the great trader of Oraibi, had lent us thirty dollars on our faces, but there was nothing to buy. When we ran short on grub we ran short on grub and that was that. We didn't need to buy as a matter of fact because there were plenty of Indians around. We had discovered why the traders did not get lonely.

At one camp they told us that there was to be a dance, so we stayed, eating out of the local stew-pots, to see more Navajos riding in than we had ever seen together before. Our hostess warned us to put our stuff inside the hogaan as newcomers, not knowing we were friends, might steal something.

At one end of the dance area, close enough to the bonfire to be comfortably warm after the night had taken on an edge, there was a big log. I sat on the end of it next to a middle-aged, grim-looking Indian, a man with the broad cheekbones, strong nose, and firm mouth of the true Apache type. You would say he was a formidable customer. Beyond him his wife was all but faceless in her blanket, watching the dance. The man had something under his blanket at which he looked from time to time. By and by he spoke to another, elderly Indian standing near him. The second Indian bent down to look, they both spoke softly and smiled. Then he spoke to a man behind him and the process was repeated. At length, after eyeing me a couple of times, pride was too much for him and he turned to me.

"Shoh," he said, "look how it sleeps."

He opened the blanket enough to let me see a baby, screwed up tight in sleep.

"It sleeps," he said, "very much it sleeps."

"Yes, very much it sleeps."

It was small and pink with a brown overcast, its features were more neatly cut, it was more attractive than white babies.

"How many its returning snows?" I asked.

"Nine moons."

"A boy? A girl?"

"A girl."

The man's smile was lovely. The Navajo behind us leaned forward to join our admiring. The father repeated softly, "Very much it sleeps," and touched its face gently with one finger. I did the same. We smiled at each other. The baby half-woke and let out a trial cry. Its mother turned, spoke sharply, the man closed his blanket and settled to watch the dance looking like any husband caught off base, the other Indian and I felt sheepish.

Hastiin Asola said we should camp at his niece's place. He had not seen her in some time. Hastiin Asola was a friendly old man with a taste for small, rather dirty jokes. He found us diverting. He was gray-haired, impressive, and had the back, waist, and arms of a boy. We rode up to the hogaan near sundown. Navajo-style, the old man did not speak but sat leaning over his saddle, at first with his face gravely neutral although there was humor visible behind it, then with his smile slowly breaking through. The woman followed much the same procedure, and then there was that brief pause which is one of the pleasantest things about Indian politeness. Whether one loves or hates, one's spirit must always adjust to the impact of another person's presence, wherefore simple considerateness dictates that one pause a moment to let adjustment take place.

She rose with a cry of pleasure and they shook hands beaming. There was a brief greeting, then she said, "Don't dismount, save yourselves trouble." She handed us two water-bottles and a small keg and told us where to find the spring, remarking that it was a long haul on foot but easy for horsemen. It was an informal reception.

She took us for granted after that; her husband when he came was amused that she had sent white men on her errand and he was entertained by us. The atmosphere was such that the children, two little girls, were not afraid of our strangeness and for the first time we had the same relationship with them we might have had with nicely brought up little girls at home.

Bart and I slept near where the sheep were bedded down. We aroused their eternal curiosity, and waking in the night we would see their foolish, grave, white faces ringing us all around in the moonlight. It didn't bother us much. We were heartily tired, we had only a vague idea of where we were, we didn't care. We had achieved something close to total immersion.

My second expedition outside the United States, in 1927, was to the Jacalteco Indians of the Cuchumatán Highlands in Guatemala. With me went Douglas Byers, now head of the Andover Museum. Byers had been with me in Arizona, he was an ideal companion for a long, difficult assignment, he seemed about to become a banker, and I was in hopes of seducing him back into anthropology.

Casual information which Frans Blom and I had picked up when we passed through Jacaltenango in 1925 proved to us that here in secret there was a rich and rare survival of the ancient Mayan religion. To learn about that I came back with Byers.

The Highland Maya of Guatemala live in what can best be called townships, using the word in a New England sense. The townships are areas with legally determined boundaries, often secured to the tribe by royal grants of considerable age. (Jacaltenango holds its territories from Ferdinand VII.) Within the township is a village which is the seat of government, with the Town Hall, jail, church, market and other institutions. Two *alcaldes* and a number of *regidores,* or councilmen, democratically elected at least in theory, form the local government under the supervision of one or more officials representing the federal government. The Jacalteco tribe numbers about seven thousand, of whom the greater part lives all year or for part of the year in the village of Jacaltenango, leaving it at intervals to cultivate their fields in the outlying sections. Within the township they enjoy a measure of self-government, freedom to follow their customs, free enterprise, freedom in the small things of everyday life, which has been extended only recently to our Indians. Here for the first time I came to know a tribe of Indians whose future was not inevitable, steadily approaching ruin and disaster. The native culture had changed, was changing, and would continue to change until at long last it merged with the general Latin-American pattern but there would be no destruction, only adaptation and absorption proceeding gently. Although the Guatemalan Indian was a conquered man, meek before his conquerors, socially despised, subject to a special and unequal justice, exploited in many ways, and full of hatred, I felt that were I a native of one of our own tribes I would sooner move down here and face all the difficulties and humiliations than remain to await the deadly end prescribed for me. Here at least I could share in the American dream, that my son might become President. Here it had happened.

One descended upon the village from the high backbone of the Cuchumatanes, firs, pines, and tall cedars above on the crest, more great evergreens across the gorge a couple of miles away, alongside the trail manifold patches of corn and wheat on slopes so steep that falling would be a genuine hazard of farming. The houses, hundreds of them, sprawled over the delta-like hanging valley, straw-thatched huts scattered higgledy-piggledy with the big, white church and municipal buildings at the center, here and there the deep green of coffee groves or the yellow color of bananas. The valley was open to the west, falling off at the edge of the village in a cliff, then below the cliff the land dropped away, ridged and rugged, a thousand feet and another thousand and another, down to the Mexican border ten leagues away. Far beyond the Sierra Madre rose again, a jumbled, blue formation over which the red sunsets formed. Late afternoon light came yellow over the houses, in its bath the smoke seeped through the thatched roofs so that each house carried a trailing, sunshot nimbus. There were wild, white roses along the trail; in the village, hibiscus by the doorways.

Here were seven thousand people of whom I knew virtually nothing. I had done a little work among related tribes the other side of the border. I had heard tales that, pressed hard enough, the men of these tribes will kill to protect their gods. I knew what one could see in passing through. The men were slender, small, golden-skinned, neatly made. They wore a heavy, black wool tunic over white cotton shirts and trousers, kept their hair short, occasionally carried blowguns. The women were handsome, they too were slender, their long skirts of green cotton with an all-over blue and white design wrapped in a narrow sheath, showed that, unlike our Indians, they did not spread as they grew older. They wound their dark hair in a crown around their heads with wide ribbons of native weave, rich and lustrous in color.

As one looked down over the steep edge of the trail one could see in front of the church the great cross, seventy-two feet high, slender, gray-weathered, skeletal. Its base I knew was a crude, square altar containing a number of fire pits. In the dusk I had seen a file of some six men go to that altar. Instead of the ordinary tunics they wore long ponchos of black wool, on their heads and also over their shoulders like stoles were kerchiefs with a striped design, predominantly dark red. They carried long staves. They had gone quickly and quietly to the base of the cross and prayed there while the clouds of *copal* incense billowed up from the fires they kindled. The dull flames of the pitchwood licked into the base of the rising smoke. Then they had risen and moved on to another part of the village, quiet, intense, oblivious.

These things I knew. We were riding down to face a strange personality and attempt the ridiculous task of persuading it that two young men, unknown to it, alien in race, should be accepted by it to the inner limits of confidence. This was my big chance, this if it succeeded would wipe out past failures, it would forestall the drudgery of getting a Ph.D. It would say something important to me about myself. The tales one had heard of that personality were strange and streaked with violence. The horses continued moving steadily, mechanically, down upon the village. I felt the gun under my leg and wondered if I should need it, I speculated upon failure.

The religion of Jacaltenango existed upon four levels. There was, first, formal Christianity, public and shared with the Ladinos—the small group of Spanish-speaking people who had settled in the village. Then there were Mayan practices so publicly carried on that it would be absurd to attempt to conceal them. These were *practices:* clearly observable, external performances and little more. Then there was that part of the old religion which was known to every Indian but jealously guarded from white men. This included the major myths and most of what a man had to know in ordinary times in order to ensure the well-being of himself and his family, but even in the course of an ordinary year a lay man would not be able to fulfill all his religious needs unaided. Lastly, there was the completely esoteric part known only to the priests, without which no prayer could be offered for the community as a whole, no major ceremonies conducted, no serious personal crisis met. Penetration of this fourth sector was made more difficult by the fact that it was divided into specialties according to the divine gifts or the training of the practitioners, so that there was no one man who knew everything, although there were a few who understood the whole structure and had a general grasp of the specialties they themselves could not practice, as was necessary if the whole pattern of ritual and prayer was to be coordinated.

A few local white men had from time to time picked up scattered information concerning the fourth level. Many of them, from living side by side with the Indians, from daily contact and observation, and the casual talk of friends, had a sketchy, general idea of the layman's practices. But complete initiation of a white man was unthinkable. Items might leak out so that in the course of thirty or forty years one had learned a good deal, but no Indian would sit down and deliberately give a white man a coherent account of his beliefs. In fact, white men *were not capable* of receiving such knowledge just as only certain Indians were capable, by innate gift, of induction into the esoteric part.

Further, the Indians did not like the Ladinos. And the Ladinos, with their sense of racial superiority, from time to time did things which violated the native religion, sometimes obliviously, sometimes out of mere curiosity or in a mood of idle, coarse humor. We rated, of course, as Ladinos, and the idea of telling us anything secret was so unheard of that it would be necessary to open new channels in the Indians' brains before such a thing could be contemplated.

I suppose ethnologists work in many different ways. I know, for instance, that most are in the habit of hiring informants. I have always suspected this method except where one finds, as among the Navajos, a positive desire to have the secret things recorded in books. Then it is fair enough to compensate a man for sitting down with you and working hard to achieve something you both desire.

I have very seldom paid an informant except for the making of linguistic lists. My method has been to hire men for normal, unsurprising work and then lead them into telling me what they know as a friendly matter undertaken almost without realizing it. This is not easy to do but the results are more trustworthy and in the end one gets much further. Of course one pays medicine-men the fees they would expect from other Indians, and even allows oneself to be grossly overcharged—ten cents for a service ordinarily worth a nickel.

The process is heartbreakingly slow; in other ways, too, it is close to heartbreaking, close to intolerable. First, to stick to this case which is typical, we had to establish ourselves in the minds of the Jacaltecos as something entirely outside of their previous experience and therefore of their established rules. We had to open their minds to the previously unthinkable rules. It was no use playing Indian. Byers was blond, tall, humorous—the last a characteristic to which they responded eagerly. I may be dark-haired and my skin tan deeply, but among these little Mongoloids there was no hope of my becoming an Indian. No, we had to be Ladinos. Then, we had to be a kind of Ladino they had never met before, we had to be utterly and totally new.

The main means of this is sincere democracy, a genuine belief in the brotherhood of man, and an unsurprised respect for all the tribe's customs, prejudices, and manners. Courtesy comes automatically out of this. If you really believe that these people are your full equals, after a long period of doubt, of suspicion, of watching for the fraud or the ulterior motive behind your attitude, will come a surprised, grateful, warm response and solid loyalty.

But it's a long period, during which your delicate tentatives meet nothing but rebuff—or, if you're skillful, the signs that if you pushed further you would meet rebuff. Nothing happens, nothing opens up, and all this time the secret, inner men, who are nobody's fools, are thinking and worrying about you and hardening their hearts against you.

He has asked questions of the young men. Yesterday Shuwan heard Kash Pelip, who works for him, telling him part of the story of How the Sun Rose. What is he after? Why has he come all the way from New York, a country which they say is even further than Germany, to disturb us here? What evil does he portend? We see him look at us as we go to pray at the altars of the guardians, what is he trying to do with his looking? He is a strange, new kind of a man and we are afraid of him, and it might be well to send him a message that he must not try to enter the House of the Prayermakers, he must not ask questions of the Prayermakers. Let us pray about him, let us ask the gods a question what we should do about him.

The unease runs through the village. The Prayermakers, seeing you at a distance as they go on their rounds, turn to look at you, speak to each other, and then pass on. A Knower, seeing you on the road, turns aside and detours to avoid passing you.

You let another rumor go out. Not only did Kash tell the man about How the Sun Rose, but the man already knew the story, a little different, but he had heard of it. Perhaps he knows something, perhaps he has some power. He is not like other Ladinos at all. Perhaps he has knowledge.

Week after week and nothing happening. In all this time you cannot be yourself. You cannot make enemies. You may know that a certain old man is a moocher and a fraud, but he has his position in the community and you cannot throw him out on his ear as you would wish. You are feeling in the dark along a blank wall, looking for a crevice, you may never stop feeling even for an instant, and you have no idea in what place, at what moment, the crevice will appear.

Therefore you can have no normal relation with anyone. This is irritating with casual acquaintances and people you dislike. The requirement to be everybody's friend, always a good fellow, a complete politician, builds up in you a deep longing to root an Indian, any Indian, violently in the tail.

But it is much worse with your friends. You like these men and they have learned to like you. They are trusting you increasingly. Everything they say, their most casual remarks, their actions, must always be sifted in your mind. God only knows where the lead may be. You prostitute your friendships, and that is a nightmare. Throw in a touch or two of malaria, a few attacks of dysentery, but do not allow them to deflect your constant, steady attention to business. Why in God's name does anyone want to be an ethnologist?

When the pressure gets too heavy you have, in that country, the relief of saddling up and going to visit some small ruin you have been told of. The travel is refreshing, and no diplomacy is needed to clear away brush and draw a plan. A spell of skilled work with the inanimate is delightful. And then, of course, the men you have brought with you become more closely allied to you, you camp and eat together, sit over the fire, there is some legend about this place, and away from the village tongues are loosened. By golly, you have brought your torment right along with you.

Luck enters into every enterprise. What you are trying to do is to be ready for the break that must come sometime, but the waiting is dreadfully long. In the end, not through your skill but by an accident, you find the crevice. Then, to shift metaphors, the dam breaks. Then, if you have handled yourself rightly, you and a number of Indians become allied in the enterprise of putting the heart of their life down on paper. If your malaria gets bad at that time it's tough luck. Eat quinine till your ears ring, have a stiff drink, but don't let the process drop.

All of this is fairly directly contrary to escapism. You have made a major escape from the problems of your own world to those of an alien and somewhat simpler one, but now escape has been so perfected that it begins to become endowed with many of the drawbacks of reality. You have been robbed of sentimentalization; you have to make hard, accurate judgments of your men, you have to consider all factors, economy, relation to white men, good and ugly customs, stupidities, meanness, nobilities, for just exactly what they are. You may bathe yourself in this Indian world, but you

cannot go on pretending about it. Every factor which forms
or malforms its character must be directly and fully faced.

In return you acquire a form of power as you achieve a fair
degree of knowledge while retaining a perception which is
impossible for the people themselves. For instance: one of
the cornerstones of the esoteric religion is the process of divination or soothsaying, carried on by specialists called
Knowers. The most important Knower is called The Shower
of the Road. He is one of two or three key men in the entire
hierarchy. He does not merely "answer questions," through
his deep knowledge of ritual and communication with the
gods he dictates major religious and, I believe, civic policies,
prescribes prayers and rites, determines whether or not a
man is fit to receive or retain priestly office. I had a natural
desire to meet this man, and I discovered a Ladino who was
on fairly friendly terms with him and to whom he had once
let fall a few items of information—nothing much, for The
Shower of the Road's knowledge is as esoteric as Hell.

I arranged to go to him to ask a question about a lost
object, which gave me a chance to observe the process of
soothsaying. It was thrilling to discover that what he was
doing was the ancient, priestly process which the first
Spanish conquerors had described in an incomplete way
and which archaeologists had partly reconstructed, not
entirely correct. From what I saw and heard in those few
minutes I knew that in fact there did exist here a survival
of the ancient lore such as had never before been found.
Here was antiquity still alive and functioning, archaeology
on the hoof. I wanted more of this man.

He thought otherwise. After I left he became frightened
and fled me. The door slammed shut again.

Putting together everything I had picked up from laymen,
what I had seen, and what archaeology knew, I had a fair
idea of how a divination worked. I can't exactly reconstruct
that incomplete idea now because later, in another village, I
became a qualified Knower myself, but I can describe the
general system as far as it relates to this story. There are
twenty powerful gods who rule the days in turn, much as if
on Monday we worshiped the moon and it ruled us, on
Tuesday, Tue, on Wednesday, Wodin, and so forth. Archaeol-

ogists refer to these characters as "day-names", they are
not, they are gods. This gives a "week" or twenty days. In
addition, days are counted by numbers up to thirteen, the
two systems revolving as do our weeks and days of the
month only in reverse proportion. Thus if we start with a day
ruled by Imish, god of the soil, it also has the number one.
The numbers go on to thirteen then start at one again, so that
when we come to the end of the list with Ahau ruling (he
has too many powers to list here), the number is seven, then
comes Imish with eight to start over again. At the end of
two hundred and sixty days Imish will come in conjunction
with one again.

Each of these gods has his own character, some good,
some bad. The numbers also have their qualities. The soothsayer takes a number of seeds at random from a pile and
throws them on a cloth. Then, starting with the god and
number of the current day (that combination is the true
day-name), he counts forward according to the number of
seeds. Their arrangement will indicate that certain names
and numbers reached on the way are important, others unimportant.

He may make one cast, one count, and give an answer, or
he may cast over and over again, either because the answer
is unclear or because he hopes for a pleasanter one.

I suspected then what I know now, that there was a wide
range for interpretation in this system. You seldom get a
simple case of the ace of spades meaning death. You are
more likely to get a bad god, say Chabin, who relates to
death, with a pretty good number like four, and then have
Cheh of the animals turn up with a neutral number, which
can mean death or sickness to an animal or death or accident
because of an animal, or might be overbalanced by Watan,
the farmer's friend and one of the strongest gods coming
along with a very good number such as thirteen. The soothsayer's predisposition is most important.

For various reasons it became increasingly important for
me to get through to The Shower of the Road. I had begun
to acquire the reputation of being "one who knows something," which means someone initiated in some part of the
esoteric knowledge, and hence "a man of clear heart," which

is a person innately qualified to receive knowledge and therefore possessing some power. And fortunately the Ladino who
was my link with The Shower had a deep belief in the reality
of all forms of Indian magic, however little he might think of
their religion. So I tried a gamble.

I told my Ladino friend in the most impressive way I
could that he was to take a message to The Shower and to
use my exact words. He was to tell The Shower to bring out
his seeds, to make his prayer, and to ask his question of the
gods. I, of my knowledge, would tell him in advance what
the answer would be. I knew that the gods would not lie,
I was perfectly confident of the gods. They would tell him
to receive me and tell me what I wanted to know. They
would tell him that I was a man of clear heart, and that I
ought to know these things.

The Ladino was astounded. He believed me. It had been
a good act. And it worked. Since then I've pulled the trick
twice more, once in rather a serious crisis, and it's worked
each time. I've done it with a little more confidence since
I learned to use the native phrases and to have the message
conveyed so that it sounded like one priest sending word to
another; still, I hope I don't have to try it too often.

The old man received me with the Ladino interpreting.
He was a nice, sincere old man with a fine, wrinkled face. He
was deeply interested in his lore, he had an alert mind and
had done some speculating about the mathematical laws
governing the calendar and other such things. He was prepared to talk now, and his confidence increased as he saw
that I was not entirely ignorant and that my attitude was
reverent. Now we met a new obstacle. The Ladino was a
hopelessly incompetent interpreter. Not only was his grasp
of Jacalteca extremely limited, but he was one of those
dummies whom no amount of explanation can cure of ren-
dering five minutes of careful explanation as "He says,
'Yes.'" Also, his presence was a deterrent in itself, since I
might be a man of clear heart, but he was just an amiable
alien.

Antel, The Shower, had no Spanish. I had the kind of
Jacalteca one might be expected to pick up in three months
during which I had made some effort to learn. We were

treating of serious matters which it was blasphemous to convey incorrectly; we both became interested. And between us this dope destroyed rather than aided communication.

I worded a rather long, careful question. I heard the interpreter render it in four words. I cut in and stated the question again, begging him to translate it in full. He pretty nearly did. The answer was nearly as long, and was returned to me as "No." We tried that again, and failed. The trouble was that the man didn't understand the full of what Antel had said. I think I understood as much as he did.

Digging into my brain for all the Jacalteca I could summon, I asked the next question for myself. Antel hesitated. Then a lovely look of relief came over his face in the candlelight, and he answered me *in halting Spanish*. The interpreter was astonished, so was I. It was a beautiful tribute, the laying aside of a shield, an advantage he had guarded for years. We worked together from there on, helping each other, piecing the two languages together in co-operation in order to deal fitly with sacred things. Of all my work among Indians, this remains the highest moment.

In a previous article, Sherwood L. Washburn presented a new look at physical anthropology. In the following article Claude Lévi-Strauss offers a similar commentary on the cultural branch of the science. In a number of ways the ill winds of two world wars provided valuable aid to anthropology. In many theaters, the techniques of anthropology were put to practical use in enlisting the cooperation of primitive peoples. In these same theaters, the anthropologist was offered new opportunities for study. As a result, there is hardly a culture on earth which now is completely isolated from the investigator. There is another aspect of the situation. Aboriginal tribes have tended to go in one of two directions. If unable to adjust to civilization, they face extinction. If Westernized, their culture can no longer be studied in its pure form. Moreover, even semi-civilized tribes often become hostile to anthropological investigation. Therein lies the crisis in modern anthropology.

One of the world's greatest anthropologists here examines

*this modern dilemma. Claude Lévi-Strauss is an authority on
the tribes of Central Brazil, where he has led a number of
scientific expeditions. He was professor of sociology at the
University of São Paulo from 1935 to 1939, and is now
professor of social anthropology at the Collège de France in
Paris. Among his books is* Tristes Tropiques, *translated into
English under the title* A World on the Wane, *which elabo-
rates on one of the points he makes in the following article.*

TODAY'S CRISIS IN ANTHROPOLOGY

CLAUDE LÉVI-STRAUSS

THE IMPORTANT PLACE social anthropology holds in contemporary thinking may seem paradoxical to many people.
It is a science very much in vogue: witness not only the
fashion for films and books about travel, but also the interest
of the educated public in books on anthropology.

Towards the end of the nineteenth century people were
apt to look to the biologist in their quest for a philosophy
of man and the world, and then later to the sociologist, the
historian, and even the philosopher.

But for the past several years anthropology has come to
play the same role, and today it too is expected to provide
us with deep reflections on our world and a philosophy of
life and hope.

It is in the United States that this approach to anthropology seems to have begun. As a young nation intent on
creating a humanism of its own, America broke with
traditional European thinking. It saw no reason why the
civilizations of Greece and Rome should be admired to the
exclusion of all others merely because in the Old World
of the Renaissance, when mankind came to be considered
the most proper and necessary study of man, there were
the only two civilizations sufficiently known.

Since the nineteenth century and especially the twentieth,

practically every human society on our planet has become accessible to study. Why then limit our interests? And indeed, when we contemplate humanity in its entirety we cannot fail to recognize the fact that for 99/100 of mankind's existence, and over most of the inhabited globe, there have been no customs, no beliefs, no institutions which do not fall within the province of anthropological study.

This was strikingly emphasized during the last war with the struggle waged on a worldwide scale. Even the most obscure and remote corners of our planet were suddenly catapulted into our lives and consciousness and took on three-dimensional reality. These were the lands where the last "savage" peoples on earth had sought safety in isolation —the far north of America, New Guinea, the hinterlands of southeast Asia, and certain islands in the Indonesian archipelago.

Since the war many names, once charged with mystery and romance, have remained on our maps but now they designate landing spots for long-distance jet liners. Under the impact of aviation and with increase in world population our planet has shrunk in size, and improved communications and travel facilities permit us no longer to close our eyes or remain indifferent to other peoples.

Today there is no fraction of the human race, no matter how remote and retarded it may still appear, which is not directly or indirectly in contact with others, and whose feelings, ambitions, desires and fears do not affect the security and prosperity and the very existence of those to whom material progress may once have given a feeling of ascendancy.

Even if we wanted to, we could no longer ignore or shrug off with indifference, say, the last head-hunters of New Guinea, for the simple reason that *they* are interested in us. And surprising though it may be, the result of our contacts with them means that both they and we are now part of the same world, and it will not be long before we are all part of the same civilization.

For even societies with the most widely divergent patterns of thought and whose customs and mores took thousands of years to evolve along isolated paths, impregnate one another once contact is established. This occurs in many, devious ways; sometimes we are clearly aware of them, often we are not.

As they spread throughout the world, the civilizations which (rightly or wrongly) felt that they had reached the height of development, such as Christianity, Islamism, Buddhism, and on a different level the technological civilization which is now bringing them together, are all tinged with "primitive" ways of life, "primitive" thinking and "primitive" behavior which have always been the subject of anthropological research. Without our realizing it the "primitive" ways are transforming these civilizations from within.

For the so-called primitive or archaic peoples do not simply vanish into a vacuum. They dissolve and are incorporated with greater or lesser speed into the civilization surrounding them. At the same time the latter acquires a universal character.

Thus, far from diminishing in importance, primitive peoples concern us more with each passing day. To take only one example, the great civilization the West is justly proud of and which has spread its roots across the inhabited globe, is everywhere emerging as a "hybrid." Many foreign elements, both spiritual and material, are being absorbed into its stream.

As a result, the problems of anthropology have ceased to be a matter of specialists, limited to scholars and explorers; they have become the direct and immediate concern of every one of us.

Where, then, lies the paradox? In reality there are two —insofar as anthropology is chiefly concerned with the study of "primitive" peoples. At the moment when the public has come to recognize its true value, we may well ask whether it has not reached the point where it has nothing more left to study.

For the very transformations which are spurring a growing theoretical interest in "primitives" are in fact bringing about their extinction. This is not really a new phenomenon. As early as 1908, when he inaugurated the chair of Social Anthropology at the University of Liverpool, Sir James

Frazer (author of the monumental *Golden Bough*) dramatically called the attention of governments and scholars to this very problem. Yet we can hardly compare the situation half a century ago with the large-scale extinction of "primitive" peoples which we have witnessed since then.

Let me cite a few examples. At the beginning of white settlement in Australia, the Aborigines numbered 250,000 individuals. Today no more than 40,000 are left.

Official reports describe them herded in reserves or clustered near mining centers where in the place of their traditional wild food-gathering parties they are reduced to sneak-scavenging in rubbish heaps outside the mining shacks. Other aborigines, who had retreated deep into the forbidding desert, have been uprooted by the installation of atomic explosion bases or rocket launching sites.

Protected by its exceptionally hostile environment, New Guinea, with its several million tribesmen, may well be the last great sanctuary of primitive society on earth. But here too, civilization is making such rapid inroads that the 600,-000 inhabitants of the central mountains, who were totally unknown a mere twenty years ago, are now providing labor contingents for the building of roads. And it is no rarity today to see road signs and milestones parachuted into the unexplored jungle!

But with civilization have come strange diseases, against which "primitives" have no natural immunization and which have wrought deadly havoc in their ranks. They are succumbing rapidly to tuberculosis, malaria, trachoma, leprosy, dysentery, gonorrhea, syphilis, and the mysterious disease known as *kuru*. The result of primitive man's contact with civilization, though not actually introduced by it, *kuru* is a genetic deterioration which inevitably ends in death and for which no treatment or remedy is known.

In Brazil, 100 tribes became extinct between 1900 and 1950. The Kaingang, from the State of São Paulo, numbering 1,200 in 1912, were no more than 200 in 1916, and today have dwindled to 80.

The Munduruku were 20,000 in 1925—in 1950 they numbered 1,200. Of the 10,000 Nambikwara in 1900, I could trace only a thousand in 1940. The Kayapo of the

River Araguaya were 2,500 in 1920 and 10 in 1950. The Timbira, 1,000 in 1900 and 40 in 1950.

How can this rapid decimation be explained? Foremost, by the introduction of Western diseases against which the Indian's body had no defense. The tragic fate of the Urubu, an Indian tribe from northeastern Brazil, is typical of many others. In 1950, only a few years after they were discovered, they contracted the measles. Within a few days, out of the population of 750 there were 160 deaths. An eyewitness has left this stark description:

"We found the first village abandoned. All the inhabitants had fled, convinced that if they ran far away they would escape the sickness which they believed was a spirit attacking the villages.

"We discovered them in the forest, halted in their flight. Exhausted and shivering with fever in the rain, nearly all of them had fallen victim to the disease. Intestinal and pulmonary complications had so weakened them that they no longer had strength to seek food.

"Even water was lacking, and they were dying as much from hunger and thirst as from the disease. The children were crawling about on the forest floor trying to keep the fires alight in the rain and hoping to keep warm. The men lay burning and paralyzed by fever; the women indifferently thrust away their babes seeking the breast."

But in addition to infectious diseases, vitamin and other nutritional deficiencies are also an important problem. Motor-vascular disorders, eye lesions and dental decay, unknown to primitive man when he lived according to his ancient ways, make their appearance when he is confined to villages and must eat food which does not come from his native forest. Then, even the old and tried traditional remedies, such as charcoal dressings for severe burns, prove useless. And simple diseases to which tribesmen have long been accustomed become extraordinarily virulent.

The decimation of the Indians is due to other, less direct, causes, such as the collapse of the social structure or pattern of living. The Kaingang of São Paulo, already mentioned, lived by a series of strict social rules with which every anthropologist is acquainted. The inhabitants of each village were divided into two groups on the principle that the men from the first group could marry only women from the second group and vice versa.

When their population diminished, the foundations permitting their survival collapsed. Under the rigid system of the Kaingang, it was no longer possible for every man to find a wife and many had no choice but celibacy unless they resigned themselves to mating within their own group—which to them was incest, and even then their marriage had to be childless. In such cases a whole population can disappear within a few years.

Bearing this in mind, need we be surprised that it is more and more difficult not only to study the so-called primitive peoples but even to define them satisfactorily. In recent years, a serious attempt has been made to revise existing thinking regarding protective legislation in the countries facing this problem.

Neither language nor culture nor the conviction of belonging to a group are valid as criteria for a definition. As enquiries of the International Labor Organization have emphasized, the notion of *indigenous* people is being superseded by the concept of *indigence*.

But this is only one half of the picture. There are other parts of the world where tens and hundreds of millions of people live who were traditionally the subject of anthropology. These populations are increasing rapidly in Central America, the Andes, southeast Asia and Africa. But here, too, anthropology faces a crisis. Not because the populations are dying out but because of the nature of the people involved.

These peoples are changing and their civilizations are gradually becoming Westernized. Anthropology, however, has never yet included the West within its competence or province. Furthermore, and even more important, there is a growing opposition in these regions to anthropological enquiries. Instances have occurred where regional museums of "Anthropology" have been forced to change their names and can only continue disguised as "Museums of Popular Art and Tradition."

In the young states which have recently obtained independence, economists, psychologists and sociologists are warmly welcomed by universities. The same can hardly be said of the anthropologist.

Thus it would almost seem that anthropology is on the point of falling victim to a dual conspiracy. On the one hand are the peoples who have ceased physically to lend themselves to study by simply vanishing from the face of the earth. On the other are those who, far from dead, are living a great population "explosion," yet are categorically hostile to anthropology for psychological and ethical reasons.

There is no problem about how to meet the first of these crises. Research must be speeded up and we must take advantage of the few years that remain to gather all the information we can on these vanishing islands of humanity. Such information is vital for, unlike the natural sciences, the sciences of man cannot originate their own experimentation.

Every type of society, or belief or institution, every way of life, constitutes a ready-made experiment the preparation of which has taken thousands of years and as such is irreplaceable. When a community disappears, a door closes forever locking away knowledge which is unique.

That is why the anthropologist believes that it is essential, before these societies are lost and their social customs destroyed, to create sharper observation techniques, rather like the astronomer who has brought electronic amplifiers into play to capture the weakening signals of light from distant stars racing away from us.

The second crisis in anthropology is much less serious in the absolute since there is no threat of extinction to the civilizations concerned. But it is much more difficult to deal with out of hand. I wonder whether it would help matters if we tried to dispel the distrust of the people who were formerly the anthropologist's field-work by proposing that our research should henceforth no longer be "one way only." Might not anthropology find its place again if, in exchange for our continued freedom to investigate, we invited African or Melanesian anthropologists to come and study us in the same way that up to now only we have studied them?

Such an exchange would be very desirable, for it would enrich the science of anthropology by widening its horizons, and set us on the road to further progress. But let us have no illusions—this would not resolve the problem, for it does not take into consideration the deep motives underlying the former colonized peoples' negative attitude to anthropology. They are afraid that under the cloak of an anthropological interpretation of history what they consider to be intolerable inequality will be justified as the desirable *diversity* of mankind.

If I may be permitted a formula which, coming from an anthropologist, can have no derogatory connotation even as pure scientific observation, I would say that Westerners will never (except in make-believe) be able to act the role of "savages" opposite those whom they once dominated. For when we Westerners cast them in this role they existed for us only as *objects*—whether for scientific study or political and economic domination. Whereas we, who in their eyes are responsible for their past fate, now appear to them inevitably as directing forces and therefore it is much harder for them to look at us with an attitude of detached appraisal.

By a curious paradox, it was undoubtedly a feeling of sympathy that prompted many anthropologists to adopt the idea of pluralism (this asserts the diversity of human cultures and concomitantly denies that certain civilizations can be classified as "superior" and others as "inferior." Yet these very anthropologists—and indeed all anthropology—are now accused of denying this inferiority merely to conceal it, and hence of contributing more or less directly to its continued existence.

If, therefore, anthropology is to survive in the modern world, there can be no disguising that it must be at the price of much deeper changes than a mere enlarging of the circle (very restricted it is true up to now) by the rather childish formula of offering to lend our toys to the newcomers provided they let us go on playing with theirs.

Anthropology must transform its very nature and must admit that, logically and morally, it is almost impossible to continue to view societies as *scientific objects*, which the scientist may even wish to preserve, but which are now *collective subjects* and claim the right to change as they please.

The modification of anthropology's subject matter also implies modifications in its aims and methods. And these fortunately appear quite feasible, for our branch of science has never defined its purposes in the absolute but rather as a relationship between the observer and his subject. And it has always agreed to change whenever this relationship has been modified.

Doubtless, the property of anthropology has always been to investigate on the spot or "from within." But only because it was impossible to investigate at a distance or "from without." In the field of the social sciences, the great revolution of our times is that whole civilizations have become conscious of their existence, and having acquired the necessary means to do so through literacy, have embarked on the study of their own past and traditions and every unique aspect of their culture which has survived to the present day.

Thus, if Africa, for instance, is escaping from anthropology, it will not so easily escape from science. In place of the anthropologist—that is the outside analyst, working from the outside—study of the continent will be in the hands of African scientists, or foreigners who will use the same methods as their African colleagues.

They will no longer be anthropologists but linguists, philologists, historians of facts and ideas. Anthropology will gladly accept this transition to richer, more subtle methods than its own, confident that it has fulfilled its mission by keeping alive so much of the great riches of humanity on behalf of scientific knowledge, so long as it was the only branch of science able to do so.

As to the future of anthropology itself, it seems to lie now at the far extreme and the near extreme of its traditional positions. At the far extreme, in the geographical sense first, since we must go further and further afield to reach the last of the so-called primitive populations, and they are getting fewer and fewer; but in the far extreme in its logical meaning too, since we are now interested in the essentials.

On the near extreme, in the sense that the collapse of the material foundations of the last primitive civilizations has made their intimate experiences one of our last fields of investigation in place of the weapons, tools and household objects that have disappeared. But also because as Western civilization becomes more complex with each passing day and spreads across the whole of the earth, it is already beginning to show signs of the sharp differences which anthropology has made it its business to study but which it could formerly do only by comparing dissimilar and widely separated cultures.

Here, no doubt, lies the permanent function of anthropology. For if there exists, as anthropologists have always affirmed, a certain "optimum diversity" which they see as a permanent condition of human development then we may be sure that divergencies between societies and groups within societies will disappear only to spring up again in other forms.

Who knows if the conflict between the old and new generations, which so many countries are now experiencing, may not be the ransom that must be paid for the growing homogenization of our social and material culture? Such phenomena seem to be pathological but anthropology has always been characterized by its ability to explain and justify forms of human behavior which men found strange and could not understand.

In this way anthropology at every phase has helped to enlarge the currently held and always too constricting view of humanity. To picture the disappearance of anthropology, one would have to conjure up a civilization where all men— no matter what corner of the globe they inhabited, and whatever their way of life, their education, their professional activities, their age, beliefs, sympathies and aversions— were, to the very roots of their consciousness, totally intelligible to all other men.

Whether one deplores it, approves it, or merely states it as a fact, technical progress and the development of communications hardly seem to be leading us to this end. And as long as the ways of thinking or of acting of some men perplex other men, there will be scope for meditation on these differences; and this, in a constantly renewing form, will be the abiding province of anthropology.

III. **Aspects of Culture**

III. Aspects of Culture

In the general Introduction to this volume, it was noted that examination of the customs of other peoples helps us place our own in proper perspective. In our society, murder is a heinous crime. In certain others, and under identical circumstances, it is considered not only praiseworthy but even obligatory. In advanced societies, reverence for a deity is usually held to be one of the elements of responsible citizenship; in more primitive cultures, the god or gods are often derided or punished. No aspect of the social structure offers more striking divergences than family life. It is fairly well-known that in Western civilization, polygyny is a crime, while in others it is a mark of wealth and position. It is less well-known that certain societies require a man to act in loco parentis not to his own children but to those of his sister. There are other intricacies of family structure which have escaped the attention of all but professional anthropologists. Some of them are discussed in the following article.

Despite many divergences in pattern, the family seems to be a well-nigh universal element in the social structure of mankind, even in those "with sexual and educational customs very remote from our own." Are such divergent patterns, which may seem surprising or shocking to the unaccustomed reader, less advanced, less "civilized" than ours? Do they indicate immorality or amorality? Or do they in fact play a necessary role in the integrated activities of the societies of which they are a part? These are among the questions discussed in the following article.

THE FAMILY

CLAUDE LÉVI-STRAUSS

THE WORD Family is so plain, the kind of reality to which it refers is so close to daily experience that one may expect to be confronted in this chapter with a simple situation. Anthropologists, however, are a strange breed; they like to make even the "familiar" look mysterious and complicated. As a matter of fact, the comparative study of the family among many different peoples has given rise to some of the most bitter arguments in the whole history of anthropological thought and probably to its more spectacular reversal.

During the second half of the nineteenth century and the beginning of the twentieth, anthropologists were working under the influence of biological evolutionism. They were trying to organize their data so that the institutions of the simpler people would correspond to an early stage of the evolution of mankind, while our own institutions were related to the more advanced or developed forms. And since, among ourselves, the family founded on monogamic marriage was considered as the most praiseworthy and cherished institution, it was immediately inferred that savage societies —equated for the purpose with the societies of man at the beginning of its existence—could only have something of a different type. Therefore, facts were distorted and mis-interpreted; even more, fanciful "early" stages of evolution were invented, such as "group marriage" and "promiscuity" to account for the period when man was still so barbarous that he could not possibly conceive of the niceties of the social life it is the privilege of civilized man to enjoy. Every custom different from our own was carefully selected as a vestige of an older type of social organization.

This way of approaching the problem became obsolete

when the accumulation of data made obvious the following fact: the kind of family featured in modern civilization by monogamous marriage, independent establishment of the young couple, warm relationship between parents and off-spring, etc., while not always easy to recognize behind the complicated network of strange customs and institutions of savage peoples, is at least conspicuous among those which seem to have remained on—or returned to—the simplest cultural level. Tribes like the Andamanese of the Indian Ocean Andaman Islands, the Fuegians of the southernmost tip of South America, the Nambikwara of central Brazil, and the Bushmen of South Africa—to quote only a few examples —live in small, semi-nomadic bands; they have little or no political organization and their technological level is very low since, in some of them at least, there is no knowledge of weaving, pot-making, and even sometimes hut-building. Thus, the only social structure worth speaking of among them is the family, mostly monogamous. The observer work-ing in the field has no trouble identifying the married couples, closely associated by sentimental bonds and eco-nomic cooperation as well as by the rearing of children born from their union.

There are two ways of interpreting this pre-eminence of the family at both ends of the scale of development of hu-man societies. Some writers have claimed that the simpler peoples may be considered as a remnant of what can be looked at as a "golden age," prior to the submission of man-kind to the hardships and perversities of civilization; thus, man would have known in that early stage the bliss of monogamic family only to forgo it later until its more recent Christian rediscovery. The general trend, however, except for the so-called Vienna school, has been that more and more anthropologists have become convinced that familial life is present practically everywhere in human societies, even in those with sexual and educational customs very remote from our own. Thus, after they had claimed for about fifty years that the family, as modern societies know it, could only be a recent development and the outcome of a slow and long-lasting evolution, anthropologists now lean toward the opposite conviction, i.e., that the family, consisting of a more or less durable union, socially approved, of a man, a woman, and their children, is a universal phenomenon, present in each and every type of society.

These extreme positions, however, suffer equally from oversimplification. It is well known that, in very rare cases, family bonds cannot be claimed to exist. A telling example comes from the Nayar, a very large group living on the Malabar coast of India. In former times, the warlike type of life of the Nayar men did not allow them to found a family. Marriage was a purely symbolical ceremony which did not result in a permanent tie between a man and a woman. As a matter of fact, married women were permitted to have as many lovers as they wished. Children belonged exclusively to the mother line, and familial as well as land authority was exercised not by the ephemeral husband but by the wife's brothers. Since land was cultivated by an inferior caste, subservient to the Nayar, a woman's brothers were as completely free as their sister's temporary husband or lovers to devote themselves to military activities.

Now, the case of the Nayar has been frequently misunderstood. In the first place, they cannot be considered as a vestige of a primitive kind of social organization which could have been very general, in the past, among mankind. Quite to the contrary: the Nayar exhibit an extremely specialized and elaborate type of social structure and from that point of view, they do not prove very much.

On the other hand, there is little doubt that the Nayar represent an extreme form of a tendency which is far more frequent in human societies than is generally acknowledged.

There are a large number of human societies which, although they did not go quite as far as the Nayar in denying recognition to the family as a social unit, have nevertheless limited this recognition by their simultaneous admission of patterns of a different type. For instance, the Masai and the Chagga, both of them African tribes, did recognize the family as a social unit. However, and for the same reason as among the Nayar, this was not true for the younger class of adult men who were dedicated to warlike activities and consequently were not allowed to marry and found a family. They used to live in regimental organizations and were permitted, during that period, to have promiscuous relations with the younger class of adult girls. Thus, among these peoples, the family did exist side by side with a promiscuous, nonfamilial type of relations between the sexes.

For different reasons, the same type of dual pattern prevailed among the Boróro and several other tribes of central Brazil, the Muria, and other tribes of India and Assam, etc. All the known instances could be arranged in such a way as to make the Nayar appear only as the more consistent, systematic and logically extreme case of a situation which may eventually reappear, at least in embryonic form, in modern society.

This was well shown in the case of Nazi Germany, where a similar cleavage was beginning to appear in the family unit: on the one hand, the men dedicated to political and warlike activities, with a great deal of freedom resulting from their exalted position; and on the other hand, women with their "3K" functional assignment: *Küche, Kirche, Kinder,* i.e., kitchen, church, and children. One might very well conceive that, had the same trend been maintained for several centuries, this clear-cut division of functions between men and women, together with the accompanying differentiation of their respective status, could very well have led to a type of social organization where the family unit would receive as little recognition as among the Nayar.

During recent years anthropologists have taken great pains to show that, even among people who practice wife-lending, either periodically in religious ceremonies or on a statutory basis (as where men are permitted to enter into a kind of institutional friendship entailing wife-lending among members), these customs should not be interpreted as survivals of "group marriage" since they exist side by side with, and even imply, recognition of the family. It is true enough that, in order to be allowed to lend one's wife, one should first get one. However, if we consider the case of some Australian tribes as the Wunambal of the northwestern part of the continent, a man who would not lend his wife to her other potential husbands during ceremonies would be considered as "very greedy," i.e. trying to keep for himself a privilege intended by the social group to be shared between numerous persons equally entitled to it. And since that attitude toward sexual access to a woman existed along with the official dogma that men have no part in physiological procreation (therefore doubly denying any kind of bond between the husband and his wife's children), the family becomes an economic grouping where man brings the products of his hunt and the woman those of her collecting and gathering. Anthropologists, who claim that this economic unit built up on a "give and take" principle is a proof of the existence of the family even among the lowest savages, are certainly on no sounder basis than those who maintain that such a kind of family has little else in common than the word used to designate it with the family as it has been observed elsewhere.

The same relativistic approach is advisable in respect to the polygamous family. The word polygamy, it should be recalled, refers to polygyny, that is, a system where a man is entitled to several wives, as well as to polyandry, which is the complementary system where several husbands share one wife.

Now it is true that in many observed cases, polygamous families are nothing else than a combination of several monogamous families, although the same person plays the part of several spouses. For instance, in some tribes of Bantu Africa, each wife lives in a separate hut with her children, and the only difference with the monogamous family results from the fact that the same man plays the part of husband to all his wives. There are other instances, however, where the situation is not so clear. Among the Tupi-Kawahib of central Brazil, a chief may marry several women who may be sisters, or even a mother and her daughters by former marriage; the children are raised together by the women, who do not seem to mind very much whether they nurse their own children or not; also, the chief willingly lends his wives to his younger brothers, his court officers, or to visitors. Here we have not only a combination of polygyny and polyandry, but the mix-up is increased even more by the fact that the co-wives may be united by close consanguineous ties prior to their marrying the same man. In a case which this writer witnessed, a mother and daughter, married to one man, were together taking care of children who were, at the same time, stepchildren to one woman and, according to case, either grandchild or stepbrother to the other.

As to polyandry proper, it may sometimes take extreme forms, as among the Toda where several men, usually brothers, share one wife, the legitimate father of the children being the one who has performed a special ceremony and who remains legal father of all the children to be born until another husband decides to assume the right of fathership by the same process. In Tibet and Nepal, polyandry seems to be explained by occupational factors of the same type as those already stated for the Nayar: for men living a semi-nomadic existence as guides and bearers, polyandry provides a good chance that there will be, at all times, at least one husband at hand to take care of the homestead.

If the legal, economic, and sentimental identity of the family can be maintained even in a polygynous or a polyandrous setup, it is not sure that the same would be true when polyandry exists side by side with polygyny. As we have already seen, this was to some extent the case among the Tupi-Kawahib, since polygynous marriages existed, at least as a chief's privilege, in combination with an elaborate system of wife-lending to younger brothers, helpers, and visitors from different tribes. Here one might argue that the bond between a woman and her legal husband was more different in degree than in kind from a gamut of other bonds which could be arranged in order of decreasing strength: from rightful, semi-permanent lovers to occasional ones. However, even in that case, the children's status was defined by the legal marriage, not by the other types of unions.

We come closer to the so-called "group marriage" when we consider the modern evolution of the Toda during the nineteenth century. They had originally a polyandrous system, which was made possible through the custom of female infanticide. When this was prohibited by the British administration, thus restoring the natural sex-ratio, the Toda continued to practice polyandry; but now instead of several brothers sharing one wife, it became possible for them to marry several. As in the case of the Nayar, the types of organization which seem remotest to the conjugal family do not occur in the more savage and archaic societies but in the relatively recent and extremely sophisticated forms of social development.

Therefore, it becomes apparent why the problem of the family should not be approached in a dogmatic way. As a matter of fact, this is one of the more elusive questions in the whole field of social organization. Of the type of organization which prevailed in the early stages of mankind, we know very little, since the remnants of man during the Upper Palaeolithic Period of about 50,000 years ago consist principally of skeletal fragments and stone implements which provide only a minimum of information on social customs and laws. On the other hand, when we consider the wide diversity of human societies which have been observed since, let us say, Herodotus' time until present days, the only thing which can be said is as follows: monogamic, conjugal family is fairly frequent. Wherever it seems to be superseded by different types of organizations, this generally happens in very specialized and sophisticated societies and not, as was previously expected, in the crudest and simplest types. Moreover, the few instances of nonconjugal family (even in its polygamous form) establish beyond doubt that the high frequency of the conjugal type of social grouping does not derive from a universal necessity. It is at least conceivable that a perfectly stable and durable society could exist without it. Hence the difficult problem: if there is no natural law making the family universal, how can we explain why it is found practically everywhere?

In order to try to solve the problem, let us try first to define the family, not by integrating the numerous factual observations made in different societies nor even by limiting ourselves to the prevailing situation among us, but by building up an ideal model of what we have in mind when we use the word *family*. It would then seem that this word serves to designate a social group offering at least three characteristics: 1] it finds its origin in marriage; 2] it consists in husband, wife, and children born out of their wedlock, though it can be conceived that other relatives may find their place close to that nuclear group; and 3] the family members are united together by a] legal bonds, b] economic, religious, and other kinds of rights and obligations, c] a precise network of sexual rights and prohibitions, and a varying and diversified amount of psychological feelings such as love, affection, respect, awe, etc. We will now proceed to a close examination of several aspects in the light of the available data.

As we have already noticed, marriage may be monogamous or polygamous. It should be pointed out immediately that the first kind is not only more frequently found than the second, but even much more than a cursory inventory of human societies would lead to believe. Among the so-called polygamous societies, there are undoubtedly a substantial number which are authentically so; but many others make a strong difference between the "first" wife who is the only true one, endowed with the full right attached to the marital status, while the other ones are sometimes little more than official concubines. Besides, in all polygamous societies, the privilege of having several wives is actually enjoyed by a small minority only. This is easily understandable, since the number of men and women in any random grouping is approximately the same with a normal balance of about 110 to 100 to the advantage of either sex. In order to make polygamy possible, there are definite conditions which have to be met: either children of a given sex are voluntarily destroyed (a custom known to exist in a few rare cases, such as female infanticide among the Toda already referred to), or special circumstances account for a different life expectancy for members of both sexes, as among the Eskimo and some Australian tribes where many men used to die young because their occupations—whale-hunting in one case, warfare in the other—were especially dangerous. Or else we have to look for a strongly hierarchical social system, where a given class: ancients, priests and sorcerers, rich men, etc., is powerful enough to monopolize with impunity more than their share of the womenfolk at the expense of the younger or the poorer people. As a matter of fact, we know of societies—mostly in Africa—where one has to be rich to get many wives (since there is a bride-price to pay), but where at the same time the increase in wives is a means to increase wealth, since female work has a definite economic value.

However, it is clear that the systematic practice of polygamy is automatically limited by the change of structure it is likely to bring up in the society.

Therefore, it is not necessary to wonder a great deal about the predominance of monogamic marriage in human societies. That monogamy is not inscribed in the nature of man is sufficiently evidenced by the fact that polygamy exists in widely different forms and in many types of societies; on the other hand, the prevalence of monogamy results from the fact that, unless special conditions are voluntarily or involuntarily brought about, there is, normally, about just one woman available for each man. In modern societies, moral, religious, and economic reasons have officialized monogamous marriage (a rule which is in actual practice breached by such different means as premarital freedom, prostitution, and adultery). But in societies which are on a much lower cultural level and where there is no prejudice against polygamy, and even where polygamy may be actually permitted or desired, the same result can be brought about by the lack of social or economic differentiation, so that each man has neither the means, nor the power, to obtain more than one wife and where, consequently, everybody is obliged to make a virtue of necessity.

If there are many different types of marriage to be observed in human societies—whether monogamous or polygamous, and in the last case, polygynous, polyandrous, or both; and whether by exchange, purchase, free-choice or imposed by the family, etc.—the striking fact is that everywhere a distinction exists between marriage, i.e., a legal, group-sanctioned bond between a man and a woman, and the type of permanent or temporary union resulting either from violence or consent alone. This group intervention may be a notable or a slight one, it does not matter. The important thing is that every society has some way to operate a distinction between free unions and legitimate ones. There are several levels at which that distinction is made.

In the first place, nearly all societies grant a very high rating to the married status. Wherever age-grades exist, either in an institutional way or as noncrystallized forms of grouping, some connection is established between the younger adolescent group and bachelorhood, less young and married without children, and adulthood with full rights, the latter going usually on par with the birth of the first child. This threefold distinction was recognized not only among many primitive tribes but also in peasant western Europe, if only for the purpose of feasts and ceremonies, as late as the early twentieth century.

What is even more striking is the true feeling of repulsion which most societies have toward bachelorhood. Generally speaking it can be said that, among the so-called primitive tribes, there are no bachelors, simply for the reason that they could not survive. One of the strongest field recollections of this writer was his meeting, among the Boróro of central Brazil, a man about thirty years old: unclean, ill-fed, sad, and lonesome. When asked if the man were seriously ill, the natives' answer came as a shock: what was wrong with him? —nothing at all, he was just a bachelor. And true enough, in a society where labor is systematically shared between man and woman and where only the married status permits the man to benefit from the fruits of woman's work, including delousing, body painting, and hair-plucking as well as vegetable food and cooked food (since the Boróro woman tills the soil and makes pots), a bachelor is really only half a human being.

This is true of the bachelor and also, to a lesser extent, of a couple without children. Indeed they can make a living, but there are many societies where a childless man (or woman) never reaches full status within the group, or else, beyond the group, in this all-important society which is made up of dead relatives and where one can only expect recognition as ancestor through the cult, rendered to him or her by one's descendants. Conversely, an orphan finds himself in the same dejected condition as a bachelor. As a matter of fact, both terms provide sometimes the strongest insults existing in the native vocabulary. Bachelors and orphans can even be merged together with cripples and witches, as if their conditions were the outcome of some kind of supernatural malediction.

The interest shown by the group in the marriage of its members can be directly expressed, as it is the case among us where prospective spouses, if they are of marriageable age, have first to get a license and then to secure the services of an acknowledged representative of the group to celebrate their union. Although this direct relationship between the individuals, on the one hand, and the group as a whole, on the other, is known at least sporadically in other societies, it is by no means a frequent case. It is almost a universal feature of marriage that it is originated, not by the individuals but by the groups concerned (families, lineages, clans, etc.), and that it binds the groups before and above the individuals. Two kinds of reasons bring about this result: on the one hand, the paramount importance of being married tends to make parents, even in very simple societies, start early to worry about obtaining a suitable mate for their offspring and this, accordingly, may lead to children being promised to each other from infancy. But above all, we are confronted here with that strange paradox to which we shall have to return later on, namely, that although marriage gives birth to the family, it is the family, or rather families, which produce marriage as the main legal device at their disposal to establish an alliance between themselves. As New Guinea natives put it, the real purpose of getting married is not so much to obtain a wife but to secure brothers-in-law. If marriage takes place between groups rather than individuals, a large number of strange customs become immediately clearer. For instance, we understand why in some parts of Africa, where descent follows the father's line, marriage becomes only final when the woman has given birth to a male child, thus fulfilling its function of maintaining her husband's lineage. The so-called *levirate* and *sororate* should be explained in the light of the same principle: if marriage is binding between two groups to which the spouses belong there can be without contradiction a replacement of one spouse by his brothers or by her sisters. When the husband dies, the levirate provides that his unmarried brothers have a preferential claim on his widow (or, as it is sometimes differently put, share in their deceased brother's duty to support his wife and children), while the sororate permits a man to marry preferentially in polygamous marriage his wife's sisters, or—when marriage is monogamous—to get a sister to replace the wife in case the latter remains childless, has to be divorced on account of bad conduct, or dies. But whatever the way in which the collectivity expresses its interest in the marriage of its members, whether through the authority vested in strong consanguineous groups, or more directly, through the intervention of the State, it remains true that marriage is not, is never, and cannot be a private business.

We have to look for cases as extreme as the Nayar, already described, to find societies where there is not, at least, a temporary *de facto* union of the husband, wife, and their children. But we should be careful to note that, while such a group among us constitutes the family and is given legal recognition, this is by no means the case in a large number of human societies. Indeed, there is a maternal instinct which compels the mother to care for her children and makes her find a deep satisfaction in exercising those activities, and there are also psychological drives which explain that a man may feel warmly toward the offspring of a woman with whom he is living, and the development of which he is witnessing step by step, even if he does not believe (as is the case among the tribes who are said to disclaim physiological paternity) that he had any actual part in their procreation. Some societies strive to reinforce these convergent feelings: the famous *couvade*, the custom according to which a man is made to share in the inabilities (either natural or socially imposed) of the woman in confinement, has been explained by some as an attempt to build up a welded unit out of these otherwise not too homogeneous materials.

The great majority of societies, however, do not show a very active interest in a kind of grouping which, to some of them at least (including our own), appears so important. Here too, it is the groups which are important, not the temporary aggregate of the individual representatives of the group. For instance, many societies are interested in clearly establishing the relations of the offspring with the father's group on the one hand, and with the mother's group on the other, but they do it by differentiating strongly the two kinds of relationships. Territorial rights may be inherited through one line, and religious privileges and obligations through the other. Or else, status from one side, magical techniques

from the other. Innumerable examples could be given from
Africa, Australia, America, etc. To limit oneself to just one,
it is striking to compare the minute care with which the
Hopi Indians of Arizona traced different types of legal and
religious rights to the father's and to the mother's lines, while
the frequency of divorce made the family so unstable that
many fathers did not actually share the same house as their
children, since houses were women's properties and, from
the legal point of view, children followed the mother's line.

This brittleness of the conjugal family, which is so common among the so-called primitive peoples, does not prevent
them from giving some value to conjugal faithfulness and
parental attachment. However, these are moral norms and
they should be contrasted strongly with the legal rules which
in many cases only acknowledge formally the relationship
of the children with either the father's or the mother's lines
or, when both lines are formally recognized, do so for wholly
different types of rights and/or obligations. Extreme cases
have been recorded such as the Emerillon, a small tribe of
French Guiana now reduced to about fifty persons. Here,
according to recent informants, marriage is so unstable that,
during a lifetime, everybody has a good chance to get married to everybody of the opposite sex and the tribe is said
to use special names for children, showing from which one of
at least eight consecutive marriages they may be the offspring. This is probably a recent development which should
be explained on the one hand by the smallness of the tribe
and, on the other, by the unstable conditions under which it
has lived for the past century. However, it shows that conditions may exist where the conjugal family is hardly recognizable.

Instability accounts for the above examples; but some
others may stem from quite opposite considerations. In
most of contemporary India and in many parts of western
and eastern Europe, sometimes as late as the nineteenth
century, the basic social unit was constituted by a type of
family which should be described as *domestic* rather than
conjugal: ownership of the land and of the homestead, parental authority and economic leadership were vested in the
eldest living ascendant, or in the community of brothers

issued from the same ascendant. In the Russian *bratsvo*, the south-Slavic *zadruga*, the French *maisnie*, the family actually consisted of the elder or the surviving brothers, together with their wives, married sons with their wives and unmarried daughters, and so on down to the great-grandchildren. Such large groups, which could sometimes include several dozen persons living and working under a common authority, have been designated as *joint families* or *extended families*. Both terms are useful but misleading, since they imply that these large units are made up of small conjugal families. As we have already seen, while it is true that the conjugal family limited to mother and children is practically universal, since it is based on the physiological and psychological dependency which exists between them at least for a certain time, and that the conjugal family consisting of husband, wife, and children is almost as frequent for psychological and economical reasons which should be added to those previously mentioned, the historical process which has led among ourselves to the legal recognition of the conjugal family is a very complex one: it has been brought about only in part through an increasing awareness of a natural situation. But there is little doubt that, to a very large extent, it has resulted from the narrowing down to a group, as small as can be, the legal standing of which, in the past of our institutions, was vested for centuries on very large groups. In the last instance, one would not be wrong in disallowing the terms joint family and extended family. Indeed, it is rather the conjugal family which deserves the name of: *restricted family*.

We have just seen that, when the family is given a small functional value, it tends to disappear even below the level of the conjugal type. On the contrary, when the family has a great functional value, it becomes actualized much above that level. Our would-be universal conjugal family, then, corresponds more to an unstable equilibrium between extremes than to a permanent and everlasting need coming from the deepest requirements of human nature.

To complete the picture, we have finally to consider cases where the conjugal family differs from our own, not so much on account of a different amount of functional value, but rather because its functional value is conceived in a way qualitatively different from our own conceptions.

As will be seen later on, there are many peoples for whom the kind of spouse one should marry is much more important than the kind of match they will make together. These people are ready to accept unions which to us would seem not only unbelievable, but in direct contradiction with the aims and purposes of setting up a family. For instance, the Siberian Chukchee were not in the least abhorrent to the marriage of a mature girl of let us say about twenty, with a baby-husband two or three years old. Then, the young woman, herself a mother by an authorized lover, would nurse together her own child and her little husband. Like the North American Mohave, who had the opposite custom of a man marrying a baby girl and caring for her until she became old enough to fulfill her conjugal duties, such marriages were thought of as very strong ones, since the natural feelings between husband and wife would be reinforced by the recollection of the parental care bestowed by one of the spouses on the other. These are by no means exceptional cases to be explained by extraordinary mental abnormalities. Examples could be brought together from other parts of the world: South America, both highland and tropical, New Guinea, etc.

As a matter of fact, the examples just given still respect, to some extent, the duality of sexes which we feel is a requirement of marriage and raising a family. But in several parts of Africa, women of high rank were allowed to marry other women and have them bear children through the services of unacknowledged male lovers, the noble woman being then entitled to become the "father" of her children and to transmit to them, according to the prevalent father's right, her own name, status, and wealth. Finally, there are the cases, certainly less striking, where the conjugal family was considered necessary to procreate the children but not to raise them, since each family did endeavor to retain somebody else's children (if possible of a higher status) to raise them while their own children were similarly retained (sometimes before they were born) by another family. This happened in some parts of Polynesia, while "fosterage," i.e., the custom whereby a son was sent to be raised by his mother's brother, was a common practice on the Northwest Coast of America as well as in European feudal society.

During the course of centuries we have become accustomed to Christian morality, which considers marriage and setting up a family as the only way to prevent sexual gratification from being sinful. That connection has been shown to exist elsewhere in a few scattered instances; but it is by no means frequent. Among most people, marriage has very little to do with the satisfaction of the sexual urge, since the social setup provides for many opportunities which can be not only external to marriage, but even contradictory to it. For instance, among the Muria of Bastar, in central India, when puberty comes, boys and girls are sent to live together in communal huts where they enjoy a great deal of sexual freedom, but after a few years of such leeway they get married according to the rule that no former adolescent lovers should be permitted to unite. Then, in a rather small village, each man is married to a wife whom he has known during his younger years as his present neighbor's (or neighbors') lover.

On the other hand, if sexual considerations are not paramount for marriage purposes, economic necessities are found everywhere in the first place. We have already shown that what makes marriage a fundamental need in tribal societies is the division of labor between the sexes.

Like the form of the family, the division of labor stems more from social and cultural considerations than from natural ones. Truly, in every human group, women give birth to children and take care of them, and men rather have as their specialty hunting and warlike activities. Even there, though, we have ambiguous cases: of course men never give birth to babies, but in many societies, as we have seen with the couvade, they are made to act as if they did. And there is a great deal of difference between the Nambikwara father nursing his baby and cleaning it when it soils itself, and the European nobleman of not long ago to whom his children were formally presented from time to time, being otherwise confined to the women's quarters until the boys were old enough to be taught riding and fencing. Conversely, the young concubines of the Nambikwara chieftain disdain domestic activities and prefer to share in their husband's adventurous expeditions. It is by no means unlikely that a similar custom, prevailing among other South American tribes, where a special class of women, half wantons and half helpers, did not marry, but accompanied the men on the warpath, is at the origin of the famous legend of the Amazons.

When we turn to activities less basic than child-rearing and war-making, it becomes still more difficult to discern rules governing the division of labor between the sexes. The Boróro women till the soil while among the Zuñi this is a man's work; according to tribe, hut building, pot making, weaving, may be incumbent upon either sex. Therefore, we should be careful to distinguish the *fact* of the division of labor between the sexes which is practically universal, from the *way* according to which different tasks are attributed to one or the other sex, where we should recognize the same paramount influence of cultural factors, let us say the same *artificiality* which presides over the organization of the family itself.

Here, again, we are confronted with the same question we have already met with: if the natural reasons which could explain the division of labor between the sexes do not seem to play a decisive part, as soon as we leave the solid ground of women's biological specialization in the production of children, why does it exist at all? The very fact that it varies endlessly according to the society selected for consideration shows that, as for the family itself, it is the mere fact of its existence which is mysteriously required, the form under which it comes to exist being utterly irrelevant, at least from the point of view of any natural necessity. However, after having considered the different aspects of the problem, we are now in a position to perceive some common features which may bring us nearer to an answer than we were at the beginning of this chapter. Since family appears to us as a positive social reality, perhaps the only positive social reality, we are prone to define it exclusively by its positive characteristics. Now it should be pointed out that whenever we have tried to show what the family is, at the same time we were implying what it is not, and the negative aspects may be as important as the others. To return to the division of labor we were just discussing, when it is stated that one sex must perform certain tasks, this also means that the other sex is forbidden to do them. In that light, the sexual division of labor is nothing else than a device to institute a reciprocal state of dependency between the sexes.

The same thing may be said of the sexual side of the family life. Even if it is not true, as we have shown, that the family can be explained on sexual grounds, since for many tribes, sexual life and the family are by no means as closely connected as our moral norms would make them, there is a negative aspect which is much more important: the structure of the family, always and everywhere, makes certain types of sexual connections impossible, or at least wrong.

Indeed, the limitations may vary to a great extent according to the culture under consideration. In ancient Russia, there was a custom known as *snokatchestvo* whereby a father was entitled to a sexual privilege over his son's young wife; a symmetrical custom has been mentioned in some part of southeastern Asia where the persons implied are the sister's son and his mother's brother's wife. We ourselves do not object to a man marrying his wife's sister, a practice which English law still considered incestuous in the mid-nineteenth century. What remains true is that every known society, past or present, proclaims that if the husband-wife relationship, to which, as just seen, some others may eventually be added, implies sexual rights, there are other relationships equally derived from the familial structure, which make sexual connections inconceivable, sinful, or legally punishable. The universal prohibition of incest specifies, as a general rule, that people considered as parents and children, or brother and sister, even if only by name, cannot have sexual relations and even less marry each other. In some recorded instances —such as ancient Egypt, pre-Columbian Peru, also some African, southeast Asian, and Polynesian kingdoms—incest was defined far less strictly than elsewhere. Even there, however, the rule existed, since incest was limited to a minority group, the ruling class (with the exception of perhaps, ancient Egypt where it may have been more common); on the other hand, not every kind of close relatives were permitted as spouse: for instance it was the half-sister, the full-one being excluded; or, if the full-sister was allowed, then it should be the elder sister, the younger one remaining incestuous.

The space at our disposal is too short to demonstrate that, in this case as previously, there is no natural ground for the custom. Geneticists have shown that while consanguineous marriages are likely to bring ill effects in a society which has consistently avoided them in the past, the danger would be much smaller if the prohibition had never existed, since this would have given ample opportunity for the harmful hereditary characters to become apparent and be automatically eliminated through selection: as a matter of fact, this is the way breeders improve the quality of their subjects. Therefore, the dangers of consanguineous marriages are the outcome of the incest prohibition rather than actually explaining it. Furthermore, since very many primitive peoples do not share our belief in biological harm resulting from consanguineous marriages, but have entirely different theories, the reason should be sought elsewhere, in a way more consistent with the opinions generally held by mankind as a whole.

The true explanation should be looked for in a completely opposite direction, and what has been said concerning the sexual division of labor may help us to grasp it. This has been explained as a device to make the sexes mutually dependent on social and economic grounds, thus establishing clearly that marriage is better than celibacy. Now, exactly in the same way that the principle of sexual division of labor establishes a mutual dependency between the sexes, compelling them thereby to perpetuate themselves and to found a family, the prohibition of incest establishes a mutual dependency between families, compelling them, in order to perpetuate themselves, to give rise to new families. It is through a strange oversight that the similarity of the two processes is generally overlooked on account of the use of terms as dissimilar as *division*, on the one hand, and *prohibition* on the other. We could easily have emphasized only the negative aspect of the division of labor by calling it a prohibition of tasks; and conversely, outlined the positive aspect of incest-prohibition by calling it the principle of division of marriageable rights between families. For incest-prohibition simply states that families (however they should be defined) can only marry between each other and that they cannot marry inside themselves.

We now understand why it is so wrong to try to explain the family on the purely natural grounds of procreation, motherly instinct, and psychological feelings between man and woman and between father and children. None of these would be sufficient to give rise to a family, and for a reason simple enough: for the whole of mankind, the absolute requirement for the creation of a family is the previous existence of two other families, one ready to provide a man, the other one a woman, who will through their marriage start a third one, and so on indefinitely. To put it in other words: what makes man really different from the animal is that, in mankind, a family could not exist if there were no society; i.e., a plurality of families ready to acknowledge that there are other links than consanguineous ones, and that the natural process of filiation can only be carried on through the social process of affinity.

How this interdependency of families has become recognized is another problem which we are in no position to solve because there is no reason to believe that man, since he emerged from his animal state, has not enjoyed a basic form of social organization, which, as regards the fundamental principles, could not be essentially different from our own. Indeed, it will never be sufficiently emphasized that, if social organization had a beginning, this could only have consisted in the incest-prohibition since, as we have just shown, the incest-prohibition is, in fact, a kind of remodeling of the biological conditions of mating and procreation (which know no rule, as can be seen from observing animal life), compelling them to become perpetuated only in an artificial framework of taboos and obligations. It is there, and only there, that we find a passage from nature to culture, from animal to human life, and that we are in a position to understand the very essence of their articulation.

As Taylor has shown almost a century ago, the ultimate explanation is probably that mankind has understood very early that, in order to free itself from a wild struggle for existence, it was confronted with the very simple choice of "either marrying-out or being killed-out." The alternative was between biological families living in juxtaposition and endeavoring to remain closed, self-perpetuating units, overridden by their fears, hatreds, and ignorances, and the systematic establishment, through the incest-prohibition, of links of intermarriage between them, thus succeeding to build, out of the artificial bonds of affinity, a true human society, despite, and even in contradiction with, the isolating influence of consanguinity. Therefore we may better understand how it came to be that, while we still do not know exactly what the family is, we are well aware of the prerequisites and the practical rules which define its conditions of perpetuation.

The so-called primitive peoples have, for that purpose, very simple and clever rules which the tremendous increase in size and fluidity of modern society makes it sometimes difficult for us to understand.

In order to insure that families will not become closed and that they will not constitute progressively as many self-sufficient units, we satisfy ourselves with forbidding marriage between near relatives. The amount of social contacts which any given individual is likely to maintain outside his or her own family is great enough to afford a good probability that, on the average, the hundreds of thousands of families constituting at any given moment a modern society will not be permitted to "freeze" if one may say so. On the contrary, the greatest possible freedom for the choice of a mate (submitted to the only condition that the choice has to be made outside the restricted family) insures that these families will be kept in a continuous flow and that a satisfactory process of continuous "mix-up" through intermarriage will prevail among them, thus making for a homogeneous and well-blended social fabric.

Conditions are quite different in the so-called primitive societies: there, the global figure of the population is a small one, although it may vary from a few dozen up to several thousands. Besides, social fluidity is low and it is not likely that many people will have a chance to get acquainted with others, during their lifetime, except within the limits of the village, hunting territory, etc., though it is true that many tribes have tried to organize occasions for wider contacts, for instance, during feasts, tribal ceremonies, etc. Even in such cases, however, the chances are limited to the tribal group, since most primitive peoples consider that the tribe is a kind of wide family, and that the frontiers of mankind stop together with the tribal bonds themselves.

Given such conditions, it is still possible to insure the blending of families into a well-united society by using procedures similar to our own, i.e., a mere prohibition of marriage between relatives without any kind of positive prescriptions as to where and whom one should correctly marry. Experience shows, however, that this is only possible in small societies under the condition that the diminutive size of the group and the lack of social mobility be compensated by widening to a considerable extent the range of prohibited degrees. It is not only one's sister or daughter that, under such circumstances, one should not marry, but any women with whom blood relationship may be traced, even in the remotest possible way. Very small groups with a low cultural level and a loose political and social organization, such as some desert tribes of North and South America, provide us with examples of that solution.

However, the great majority of primitive peoples have devised another method to solve the problem. Instead of confining themselves to a statistical process, relying on the probability that certain interdictions being set up, a satisfactory equilibrium of exchanges between the biological families will spontaneously result, they have preferred to invent rules which every individual and family should follow carefully, and from which a given form of blending, experimentally conceived of as satisfactory, is bound to arise.

Whenever this takes place, the entire field of kinship becomes a kind of complicated game, the kinship terminology being used to distribute all the members of the group into different categories, the rule being that the category of the parents defines either directly or indirectly the category of the children, and that, according to the categories in which they are placed, the members of the group may or may not get married. The study of these rules of kinship and marriage has provided modern anthropology with one of its more difficult and complicated chapters. Apparently ignorant and savage peoples have been able to devise fantastically clever codes which sometimes require, in order to understand their workings and effects, some of the best logical and even mathematical minds available in modern civilization. Therefore, we will limit ourselves to explaining the crudest principles which are the more frequently met with.

One of these is, undoubtedly, the so-called rule of cross-cousin marriage, which has been taken up by innumerable tribes all over the world. This is a complex system according to which collateral relatives are divided into two basic categories: "parallel" collaterals, when the relationship can be traced through two siblings of the same sex, and "cross" collaterals, when the relationship is traced through two siblings of opposite sex. For instance, my paternal uncle is a parallel relative and so is my maternal aunt; while the maternal uncle on the one hand, the paternal aunt on the other, are cross-relatives. In the same way, cousins who trace their relationship through two brothers or two sisters, are parallel-cousins; and those who are connected through a brother and a sister are cross-cousins. In the generation of the nephews, if I am a man, my brother's children will be my parallel-nephews while my sister's children are my cross-nephews.

Now, the startling fact about this distinction is that practically all the tribes which make it claim that parallel relatives are the same thing as the closest ones on the same generation level: my father's brother is a "father," my mother's sister a "mother"; my parallel-cousins are like brothers and sisters to me; and my parallel-nephews like children. Marriage with any of these would be incestuous and is consequently forbidden. On the other hand, cross-relatives are designated by special terms of their own, and it is among them that one should preferably find a mate. This is true to the extent that quite frequently, there is only one word to mean both "cross-cousin" and "spouse." What can be the reason for this claim, exactly similar among hundreds of different tribes in Africa, America, Asia, Oceania, that one should not marry, under any pretense, a father's brother's daughter, since that would amount to marrying one's sister, while the best conceivable spouse consists of a mother's brother's daughter, namely a relative, who on purely biological grounds, is exactly as close as the former?

There are even tribes which go a step further in these refinements. Some think that it is not cross-cousins who should marry, but only cross-cousins once removed (i.e. children of cross-cousins); others, and this is by far the most frequent case, are not satisfied with the simple distinction between cross- and parallel-cousins; they subdivide the cross-cousins themselves into marriageable and nonmarriageable ones. For instance, although a mother's brother's daughter is, according to the above definitions, a cross-cousin in the same sense as a father's sister's daughter, there are in India, living side by side, tribes which believe that one of them, only different according to case, makes a suitable spouse, death being preferable to the sin of marrying the other.

All these distinctions (to which others could be added) are fantastic at first sight because they cannot be explained on biological or psychological grounds. But, if we keep in mind what has been explained in the preceding section, i.e., that all the marriage prohibitions have as their only purpose to establish a mutual dependency between the biological families, or, to put it in stronger terms, that marriage rules express the refusal, on the part of society, to admit the exclusive existence of the biological family, then everything becomes clear. For all these complicated sets of rules and distinctions are nothing but the outcome of the processes according to which, in a given society, families are set up against each other for the purpose of playing the game of matrimony.

Let us consider briefly the rules of the game. Since societies try to maintain their identity in the course of time, there should be first a rule fixing the status of the children in respect to that of their parents. The simplest possible rule to that end, and by far the most frequently adopted, is the generally called rule of *unilineal descent,* namely that children get the same status of either their father (patrilineal descent) or their mother (matrilineal descent). It can also be decided that the status of both the father and the mother are taken into consideration, and that they should be combined to define a third category in which the children will be put. For instance, a child of a father belonging to the status A and of a mother belonging to the status B, would himself belong to a status C; and the status will be D if it is the father who is B and the mother who is A. Then, C and D will marry together and procreate children either A or B according to the sex orientation, and so on indefinitely. Everybody with some leisure time may devise rules of this kind, and it will be surprising indeed if some tribe, at least, cannot be found where each rule is actually being applied.

The rule of descent being defined, the second question is to know in how many exogamous groups the society in consideration is being divided. An exogamous group is one inside of which intermarriage is forbidden and which, consequently, requires at least another exogamous group with whom it may exchange its sons and/or daughters for marriage purposes. Among ourselves, there are as many exogamous groups as restricted families, that is, an extremely high number, and it is this high number which allows us to rely on probability. In primitive societies, however, the figure is usually much smaller, on the one hand because the group itself is a small one, and on the other hand because the familial ties go much further than is the case among us.

Our first hypothesis will be the simpler one: that of unilineal descent and of two exogamous groups, A and B. Then, the only solution will be that men of A marry women of B, and men of B marry women of A. A typical case will be that of two men, respectively A and B, exchanging their sisters so that each one may get a wife. The reader has just to take a pencil and a sheet of paper to build up the theoretical genealogy which will be the outcome of such a set-up. Whatever the rule of descent, siblings and parallel-cousins will always fall in the same category, while cross-cousins of whatever kind will fall in opposite categories. Therefore, only cross-cousins (if we are playing the game with 2 to 4 groups) or children of cross-cousins (if we are playing with 8 groups, for 6 provide an intermediary case) will meet the initial rule that spouses should belong to opposite groups.

So far, we have considered groups tied up in pairs: 2, 4, 6, 8. They can only come in even numbers. What, now, if the society is made up of an odd number of exchanging groups? With the preceding rule, there will be a group which will remain alone by itself, without a partner with whom to set up an exchange relationship. Hence, the need for additional rules which can be of use whatever the number of elements, either even or odd.

There are two ways to meet the difficulty. Exchange can either remain simultaneous and become indirect, or remain direct at the expense of becoming consecutive. The first type will be when group A gives its daughters as wives to group B, B to C, C to D, D to n . . . and finally n to A. When the cycle is completed, every group has given a woman and has received one, though it has not given to the same group as that from which it has received. In that case, pencil and paper will show that parallel-cousins always fall in one's own group, the same as brothers and sisters, and cannot consequently be married according to rule. As to cross-cousins, a new distinction will appear: the female cross-cousin on the mother's side (i.e., the mother's brother's daughter) will always fall in the marriageable group (A to B, B to C, etc.), while that on the father's side (father's sister's daughter) will fall in the opposite group (that is, the one to which my group gives wives, but from which it does not receive any: B to A, C to B, etc.).

The alternative would be to keep the exchange direct, though in consecutive generations: for instance, A receives a wife from B, and returns to A the daughter born from that marriage to become the spouse of a man A of the following generation. If we keep our groups arranged in a series: A, B, C, D, n . . . , the general set-up will be, then, that any group, let us say C, at one generation gives to D and receives from B; at the following generation, C repays B and gets its own return from D, and so on indefinitely. Here again the patient reader will find out that cross-cousins are being distinguished in two categories, but this time in a reverse way: for a man, the correct mate will always be the father's sister's daughter, the mother's brother's daughter being always in the "wrong" category.

These are the simplest cases. All over the world there are still kinship systems and marriage rules for which no satisfactory interpretation has as yet been brought forward; such are the Ambrym system in the New Hebrides, the Murngin of northwestern Australia, and the whole North American complex known as the Crow-Omaha kinship system. It is fairly certain that to explain these and other sets of rules, however, one will have to proceed as we have shown here, namely to interpret kinship systems and marriage rules as embodying the rule of that very special kind of game which consists, for consanguineous groups of men, in exchanging women among themselves, that is, building up new families with the pieces of earlier ones, which should be shattered for that purpose.

The female reader, who may be shocked to see womankind treated as a commodity submitted to transactions between male operators, can easily find comfort in the assurance that the rules of the game would remain unchanged should it be decided to consider the men as being exchanged by women's groups. As a matter of fact, some very few societies, of a highly developed matrilineal type, have to a limited extent attempted to express things that way. And both sexes can be comforted from a still different (but in that case slightly more complicated) formulation of the game, whereby it would be said that consanguineous groups consisting of both men and women are engaged in exchanging together bonds of relationships.

The important conclusion to be kept in mind is that the restricted family can neither be said to be the element of the social group, nor can it be claimed to result from it. Rather, the social group can only become established in contradistinction, and to some extent in compliance, with the family, since in order to maintain the society through time, women should procreate children, benefit from male protection while they are engaged in confinement and nursing, and, since precise sets of rules are needed, to perpetuate throughout the generations the basic pattern of the social fabric. However, the primary social concern regarding the family is not to protect or enhance it: it is rather an attitude of diffidence, a de-nail of its right exist either in isolation or permanently; restricted families are only permitted to live for a limited period of time, either long or short according to case, but under the strict condition that their component parts be ceaselessly displaced, loaned, borrowed, given away, or returned, so that new restricted families may be endlessly created or made to vanish. Thus, the relation between the social group as a whole and the restricted families which seem to constitute it is not a static one, like that of a wall to the bricks it is built with. It is rather a dynamic process of tension and opposition with an equilibrium point extremely difficult to find, its exact position being submitted to endless variations from time to time and from society to society. But the word of the Scriptures: "You will leave your father and mother" provides the iron rule for the establishment and functioning of any society.

Society belongs to the realm of culture, while the family is the emanation, on the social level, of those natural requirements without which there could be no society and indeed no mankind. As a philosopher of the sixteenth century has said, man can only overcome nature by complying with its laws. Therefore, society has to give the family some amount of recognition. And it is not so surprising that, as geographers have also noticed with respect to the use of natural land resources, the greatest amount of compliance with the natural laws is likely to be found at both extremes of the cultural scale: among the simpler peoples as well as among the more highly civilized. Indeed, the first ones are not in a position to afford paying the price of too great a departure, while the second have already suffered from enough mistakes to understand that compliance is the best policy. This explains why, as we have already noticed, the small, relatively stable, monogamic restricted family seems to be given greater recognition, both among the more primitive peoples and in modern societies, than in what may be called (for the sake of the argument), the intermediate levels. However, this is nothing more than a slight shift of the equilibrium point between nature and culture, and does not affect the general picture given in this chapter. When one travels slowly and with great effort, halts should be long and frequent. And when one is given the possibility to travel often and fast, he or she should also, though for different reasons, expect to stop and rest frequently. The more roads there are, the more crossings there are likely to be. Social life imposes on the consanguineous stocks of mankind an incessant traveling back and forth, and family life is little else than the expression of the need to slacken the pace at the crossroads and to take a chance to rest. But the orders are to keep on marching. And society can no more be said to consist of families than a journey is made up of the stopovers which break it down into discontinuous stages. They are at the same time its condition and its negation.

Linguistics, the study of languages, their origins, development, and laws, represents a complex and difficult branch of scholarship. The basic science has been subdivided into such specialties as phonetics, etymology, morphology, and semantics. There is an enormous literature on comparative linguistics, on the difference between spoken and written language, on dialects and argot, on marginal languages like pidgin English, and on attempts to invent a universal language like Esperanto or basic English. The great dictionaries, of which the Oxford Dictionary is an example, are the repositories of information which has been collected over a span of centuries.

That part of linguistics, and it is large, which has to do with the relationship between language and culture and society is a division of anthropology. Without language, as Hoijer explains, there would be no civilization, no body of knowledge, and only the most rudimentary banding together of human beings into cooperative groups. ". . . there is no group of men anywhere, today or in the past, who lack this important aspect of culture." How did language originate; what is the relationship between specific languages and specific cultures; how do languages undergo change in differing degrees and at differing rates? These are among the questions which engage the student of linguistics and which are discussed in the following article.

Born at Chicago in 1904, Harry Hoijer obtained his Ph.D. at the University of Chicago in 1931 and became an instructor in anthropology there. In 1940 he joined the faculty of the

University of California in Los Angeles, in 1948 became professor of anthropology and in 1949 chairman of the department
of anthropology and sociology. He is a past President of the
Linguistic Society of America.

LANGUAGE

HARRY HOIJER

LANGUAGE IS so much a part of our daily activities that
some of us may come to look upon it as a more or less automatic and natural act like breathing or winking. Of course, if
we give the matter any thought at all, we must realize that
there is nothing automatic about language. Children must be
taught their native tongue, and the necessary training takes
a long time. Language is not something that is inherited; it is
an art that can be passed on from one generation to the next
only by intensive education.

It is difficult to realize the enormously important role that
language plays in our social behavior. What would a society
without language be like? It would of course have no writing
or other means of communication by words, for all these are
ultimately dependent on spoken speech. Our means of learning would therefore be greatly restricted. We should be
obliged, like the animals, to learn by doing or by observing
the actions of others. All of history would disappear, for
without language there would be no way of re-creating past
experiences and communicating them to others. We should
have no means of expressing our thoughts and ideas to others
or of sharing in the mental processes of our fellowmen. Indeed, it is very likely that we should not think at all. Many
psychologists maintain that thought itself requires the use of
language, that the process of thinking is really talking things
over with ourselves.

A society lacking language would be incapable of engaging in any but the simplest of co-operative enterprises. An in-

dividual or group of individuals would have no way of planning such activities, of explaining them to others, or of directing the actions of the participants in cooperative enterprises toward the common goal. Each individual would be to a large extent dependent on his own strength and ability since he would lack the means of securing the help of others.

Most important, a society lacking language would have no means of assuring the continuity of behavior and learning necessary to the creation of culture. Human society, without culture, would be reduced to the level of present-day ape societies. Apes have a bodily structure very like our own. Like humans, they learn readily from experience and by observing and imitating the actions of others. A number of experimenters have shown that apes not only learn to use tools but also invent them. Despite, however, the fact that individual apes learn easily and, as individuals, show remarkable progress in the acquisition of knowledge, apes as a species have never developed a culture.

There are two reasons for this. Lacking language, the apes have no way of continuing in word and thought their separate experiences in the use of tools and techniques. When an ape has disposed of a problem the knowledge he has derived from that experience remains static. He may remember it when and if another problem of the same sort arises, but he does not in between times mull over his knowledge and devise means of applying it to further problems. Man does. His overt experiences with practical problems are, like those of the ape, separate and distinct. But because man possesses language, he can continue his problem-solving activities beyond the actual physical experience and so develop, in thought and discussion, new applications of his knowledge and improved means of solving problems. In short, by reason of language, man's experiences are continuous, not discontinuous as among apes, and so show far more rapid development.

Secondly, man's possession of language enables him to share the experiences and thoughts of his fellows and to recreate his personal experiences for their benefit. An ape's knowledge, acquired through experience and observation, is his alone, except in so far as he can demonstrate it in physical activity so that it may be acquired by another ape. No matter how skillful an ape may become in the use of tools and techniques, his offspring will be obliged to begin their learning as he began his, by experience and observation. The learned ape cannot communicate his knowledge and so enable his successors to build upon it. Culture among men reveals progress. Each generation takes over, by word of mouth and tradition, the accumulated knowledge of their predecessors, adds its own contributions as drawn from its experiences and observations, and passes the whole on to succeeding generations. This cumulative aspect, which differentiates human cultures from the kind of knowledge current in animal societies, is made possible by language.

The Antiquity of Language

Studies of the skeletal and cultural remains of ancient man have shown that the first human beings came into being about one million years ago. Man's early cultures were very simple and crude and we know only a portion of their material remains, the tools and implements made of materials tough enough to withstand the passage of time. It is highly significant, however, that these early traces of man's cultures reveal a cultural continuity through time. As we study the several chronological phases of culture in any given area of the world, there is revealed a slow but steady advance both in the number of tools made and in the complexity of their manufacture. The men of successive generations did not begin anew each generation to fashion their cultures but built upon the techniques which had been discovered in the past and transmitted to them by their ancestors.

The fact that the history of man's cultures shows a continuous and cumulative development extending from their earliest beginnings to the present means of course that man has possessed language as long as he has possessed culture. Language must be as old as the oldest of man's cultural artifacts; it began when culture began and has developed continuously ever since.

This inference as to the age of language is amply borne out by other observations which may be made on modern languages. First, it is clear that all human societies have possessed a language for as long as we have known them; there is no group of men anywhere, today or in the past, who lack this important aspect of culture. Secondly we may also observe that modern languages are very numerous and exceedingly diverse. The precise number of distinct languages spoken today cannot even be estimated, but we know that there are several thousand. Some of these are historically related to one another; that is, they are clearly derived from a single earlier tongue. Languages so derived are said to belong to the same linguistic family or stock, and there are hundreds of such stocks in the world today. Most of these stocks show no resemblance whatsoever to each other, because, as we may almost certainly assume, all traces of common origin have long since disappeared.

The universality of language and the amazing diversity of modern idioms can only mean that language is very old. Studies of languages known for centuries through the medium of written records reveal that languages change with relative slowness. Thus, though English and German have certainly been separate languages for well over 2000 years, they still retain many obvious similarities in both vocabulary and grammar which point clearly to their common origin. The enormous diversity of modern languages, then, must have taken a very long time to achieve.

A third and final evidence as to the antiquity of language is found in the fact that known languages, ancient or modern, cannot be classed in terms of their level of development. There are neither primitive languages nor highly developed ones, if we take into account only their structural features.

Thus, all the languages we know possess a well-defined system of distinctive speech sounds. These are finite in number, are carefully distinguished from one another, and are put together to form words, phrases, and sentences in accordance with definite rules. In this respect, there is no real difference between the languages of people who possess very simple and crude cultures and those of the highly civilized peoples of Europe and America.

Similarly, all human groups, regardless of the crudity of their culture, have a vocabulary sufficiently detailed and comprehensive to meet every need likely to arise. Languages vary, of course, in the size of their vocabularies, but this variation is cultural, not linguistic. The language of a people having a relatively simple or undeveloped culture may have a smaller vocabulary than one belonging to a group with a relatively complex and highly developed culture. It is notable, however, that the vocabulary of any group, however simple its culture, appears to be indefinitely expansible. As new cultural items are invented or borrowed, the vocabulary increases or changes to meet the new requirements imposed upon it.

Finally, all languages possess a definite and clear-cut system of grammar. Grammar may briefly be defined as the meaningful arrangement of sounds or combinations of sounds to produce words, phrases, and sentences. Well-defined rules governing such arrangements are found in all languages, whether they are spoken by the pre-literate Pygmies of the Congo forest or the culturally advanced groups of modern Europe.

The basic similarities mean, of course, that language has so long been a human possession as to have developed to about the same level among peoples the world over. There remain today no traces of an earlier and cruder stage of linguistic development.

The Origin of Language

Spoken languages obviously leave no trace in the ancient deposits which mark the history of man's cultures. Written records of human languages began only a few thousand years ago; before that time no human group possessed the technique of writing. It is evident, then, that we have no direct evidence as to the origin of language or of the long period of history that elapsed between its beginnings and the first written records. The problem of the origin of language will never therefore be solved in the sense that we shall know directly the circumstances under which language arose or be able to trace in terms of specific historical events the course of its development.

Many theories have been advanced as to the origin of language. Most of these, however, are based on two central hypotheses: the interjectional and the sound imitative or onomatopoeic theory of the origin of language.

Interjectional theories maintain, in general, that interjections or involuntary cries, because these are a good deal alike in all modern tongues, form the earliest stratum of words used by man. All other forms, it follows, must have been derived from these in one or other manner. Sound imitative theories look to words like *bow wow, meow, choo choo* or *ding dong*, and similar attempts by men to imitate animal cries and noises as marking the beginnings of language. From such imitations of sounds encountered in his environment, man formed the hundreds of languages we now find spoken.

Both hypotheses fail to solve our problem, however, largely because they fail to account for true linguistic forms. Neither involuntary cries nor sound imitative words are as such true linguistic forms. An involuntary cry is really part of an individual's response to strong stimuli. The involuntary ejaculation of surprise is not the same as the conventional word written *Oh!* because the former represents part of the response itself and does not, like the conventional *Oh!*, symbolize the response of surprise. True linguistic symbols, such as words, are all conventional and arbitrary, and their meanings must be learned by speakers. No one learns an involuntary cry; a baby may cry out long before it learns to speak.

Sound imitative words must similarly not be confused with attempts to reproduce sounds characteristic of man's environment. A word like *ding dong*, for example, is a conventionalized representation of the sound of a bell, not necessarily self-evident to anyone except a speaker of English who has learned to associate the sound *ding dong* with the ringing of bells. To understand how languages came into being we must know how man came to establish his arbitrary or conventional habits of associating speech sounds with experience. This is not explained by the sound imitative hypothesis which points out merely that men sometimes name things and actions by the noises they make and that on occasion such names become truly a part of language.

It follows, then, that a useful theory of linguistic origins must be based on a more careful analysis and study of modern tongues. Such studies, as we have suggested, reveal that the elements of speech, such as words, phrases, and sentences, are arbitrary symbols. By this we mean symbols which are themselves no part of the reality or experience symbolized. Thus, for example, the particular succession of sounds which make up the word *horse* have no necessary relation to the class of animals symbolized by it. There is, in short, nothing horselike about the word *horse;* it is simply that speakers of English have learned to associate the sounds written *horse* with a given class of animal, just as they have learned to associate the forms *dog* and *cat* with wholly different groups of animals.

The fact that linguistic symbols are nearly all arbitrary in nature emphasizes the social aspect of language. Languages are always associated with groups of individuals; they never belong exclusively to a single individual. An individual acquires his language from the group with which he lives. If he deviates widely in speech from other members of the group, he runs the risk of being misunderstood or of not being understood at all. *Horse* is not just a word peculiar to an individual speaker of English, it is a word used and understood in much the same way by all English-speaking peoples.

Languages function in human societies primarily as a means of communication and cooperation. By means of language an individual is able not only to re-create his own personal experiences and so share them with others, but he is also able to co-ordinate his labors with those of others. A group of men can thus work together in a task too heavy or too complex to be undertaken by any one of them singly. To exemplify this point, let us imagine that a man, hunting alone, manages to kill an animal too large for him to handle. He leaves the dead animal and returns to his encampment or village. There he tells the others what he has done and secures their assistance. They return to his kill with him and assist him to skin the game, cut up the meat and carry it back to camp. During the whole of this procedure, one individual may take charge, indicating in words the task each is to perform, so that the separate acts of each man will assist rather than obstruct the total performance.

Contrast the action we have just described with a similar

incident among, let us say, a pack of wolves. Here, too, we have a social group albeit one composed of animals who lack language. When one of the wolves makes a kill alone, he will eat as much as he can; he will not be concerned or able to inform the pack of his feat. But should the other wolves come upon him as he makes the kill or while he is eating the carcass, they will certainly join him uninvited. Each wolf will get as much as he can and if there is not enough to go around, the weaker wolves will get none at all. The actions of the wolves in disposing of the meat will be separate and individual, with no coordination or cooperation whatsoever.

It is probable that the ancient animals from whom man evolved lived in groups very similar to those of present-day animals. Their behavior was only in a small degree coordinated. Each worked for himself alone, with the exception that the very young had to be cared for by an adult. On occasion, however, necessity must have enforced some degree of cooperation and coordinated effort. Man's primitive ancestor was not a formidable animal in comparison with many others who shared his environment. He must often have had to defend himself against stronger predatory animals and he probably discovered very early that such defense was more effective if undertaken in cooperation with his fellows. When such cooperative enterprises increased in frequency, the habit pattern built up may easily have led to cooperation under other circumstances, such as, for example, the hunting of large animals for food. Even wolves hunt together and, while so doing, correlate their efforts, at least to some degree.

The development of cooperative labor did not alone bring about language, however. Many insect groups are effectively cooperative without language. But cooperation among insects is evidently on a different basis than among men. Unlike the social insects men are not born to a given role in their social groups. Men must learn to adapt their behavior to the roles provided by the society, and language provides a vital tool to this kind of learning.

How and in what way man's animal ancestors came to employ language as an aid in cooperative labor we shall never know. We may safely assume, however, that man's primitive ancestor could and did make noises and perhaps the noises which accompanied the tasks undertaken together came slowly to symbolize the several actions and ends involved in such tasks. In any case, it appears to be fairly certain that language arose as a result of men learning to work together toward a common end. For whatever reasons, man's primitive ancestors were obliged to acquire such learning, and so they, alone of the animals, stumbled upon the tool, language, which more than any other makes cooperative and coordinated activity effective.

The Structure of Language

Languages, like many other cultural phenomena, cannot be observed or studied directly. Just as we can describe a method of making baskets only by observing the actions of individuals who are weaving them, so can we describe a language only by observing the speech behavior of those who use the language.

Individual acts of speech are called utterances. These are complete in themselves and consist of a flow of speech sounds uninterrupted by the speech of another individual. Some utterances may be quite short, like *Oh!, Come!, Who?*, or *John.* Others are longer: *John runs, I see a man,* or *The man we saw yesterday is dead.* Still others may be very long; examples of these are found in speeches, lectures, or sermons. A first step in studying a language is then to collect utterances, as many as possible, from native speakers of the language.

Once this has been done, it soon becomes obvious that utterances differ not only in length but also in structure. Some of them consist of a single unit which cannot be interrupted without considerable change in meaning. If, for example, we say *John runs?*, it is evident that the forms *John* and *runs* are interdependent. To stop after we have said *John* is like playing an unresolved chord on the piano; the listener awaits impatiently the completion of the utterance. We can of course say *John? Runs?* but here we create a new meaning, quite different from that of *John runs?*

Utterances consisting of a single unit are called constructions and the interdependent parts of this unit are said to be united grammatically to one another. An utterance like *John?*

Runs?, on the other hand, is made up of two units which are not held together grammatically but only follow one another without interruption.

Grammarians express the difference we have illustrated by comparing *John runs?* with *John? Runs?* by saying that *John runs?* consists of one sentence while *John? Runs?* is two sentences. A sentence, then, is an utterance the parts of which are united grammatically into a construction and which is not itself a part of some larger construction. All utterances, it is clear, must contain at least one sentence.

Sentences, like utterances, vary in length and complexity. Thus, all of the following are sentences, though from first to last they increase both in length and complexity. *John, John runs, Poor John runs fast, Poor John runs very fast, Poor John, the boy next door, is decidedly the best runner of the group.* These examples reveal that sentences may be divided into still smaller units called phrases and words. A word may be defined as the smallest portion of a sentence which can be pronounced alone and still retain meaning. All of the forms written separately in the examples cited above are words, since all of them, pronounced alone, have meaning to a speaker of English. Phrases consist of two or more words, not a sentence, which compose a construction. It is obvious that some combinations may function sometimes as sentences and at other times as phrases. Thus, the combination *Poor John,* taken alone, is a sentence, but as part of *Poor John runs fast,* it functions as a phrase.

All sentences, it is clear, must possess at least one word. Longer sentences may contain two or more phrases, but the limits of sentence length depend so much upon individual or social preferences as to defy accurate definition.

The total stock of words possessed by a language is called its vocabulary or dictionary. Languages differ as to the size of their vocabularies. In general the size of a vocabulary is directly related to the culture of a speech community. If the culture is complex, as among most English-speaking peoples, the vocabulary may be very large and contain numerous highly technical subdivisions. In a simple and relatively uniform culture, such as that of the Polar Eskimo, the vocabulary will be correspondingly smaller and contain fewer technical aspects. It should not be assumed, however, that so-called primitive peoples have very small vocabularies. We frequently hear, for example, of very primitive folk whose languages possess at most only a few hundred words. This is obvious nonsense for even the simplest culture requires a far greater number of words merely to enumerate the many objects and acts dealt with in the course of everyday occupations.

When we examine the vocabulary of a language and compare the words it contains with one another we soon discover that words, like sentences and utterances, also vary in size and complexity. Take for example English pairs like *dog, dogs; work, worker; black, blackish; combine, recombine; do, undo. Dogs* is obviously derived from *dog* by the addition of -*s, worker* from *work* by adding -*er, blackish* from *black* by adding -*ish, recombine* from *combine by adding re-,* and *undo* from *do* by adding *un-.* Each of the added elements conveys meanings: -*s* denotes the plural, -*er* means "one who," -*ish* means "something like" (that is, a blackish object is one which is colored something like one which is black), *re-* means "to do something again" (in this case, to combine again), and *un-* conveys a negative or opposite meaning (to undo a knot is the opposite or negative of "doing" or tying a knot.) These added elements are not words, however, because they are never spoken alone but always in combination with some other form (either a whole word or part of a word.) Some words may contain more than one such element, each adding a measure of meaning to the completed word. Thus, the word *ungentlemanly* is formed by adding *un-* (not) to *gentlemanly. Gentlemanly,* in turn, consists of *gentleman* plus the ending -*ly,* meaning "in such and such a way or manner." Finally, *gentleman* is itself composed of *gentle* plus *man* though the meaning of the combination is no longer the same as the sum of the meanings of its two constituent parts.

Words and parts of words like *dog, –s, work, –er, combine, re-, black, -ish, do,* and *un-* are called simple linguistic forms or morphemes. Some morphemes, like *dog* and *work,* may be pronounced alone; these are called free morphemes. Others, like -*ish* and *un-,* are never pronounced alone and are therefore called bound morphemes. Combinations containing more than one morpheme, such as *dogs* or *worker,* are complex linguistic forms. Complex linguistic forms also include phrases, sentences, and utterances, however. Words having more than one morpheme are usually described as derived words or derivations.

Languages differ greatly in word structure. In some of them, Chinese is a good example, most words have but one morpheme; derivations are extremely rare. In others, like English, there may be many single morpheme words plus a large number of words having two or three morphemes and a smaller number having more than three morphemes. Languages like Navaho or Eskimo are found at the opposite extreme in so far as word structure is concerned, for here we may find large numbers of so-called polysynthetic words possessing as many as eight or ten or even more morphemes.

When morphemes are combined to form words and when words are combined into phrases and sentences, these combinations always follow definite rules of arrangement. Some morphemes, like *re-* and *un-* always precede the forms with which they are combined and so are called prefixes. Others, like *-er* and *-s,* follow the elements to which they are attached; these are suffixes. Rules of arrangement having to do with the structure of words in a language make up its morphology, one branch of grammar, which we may define as the meaningful arrangement of linguistic forms. The second branch of grammar is called syntax and has to do with the meaningful arrangement of words to form phrases and sentences.

Languages differ widely in grammar. In English sentences of the type *he runs,* for example, the verb *runs* has an ending *-s* because the pronoun is singular and third person. With pronouns like *I, you, we,* and *they,* we use *run,* not *runs.* Similarly, we say *a man runs* but *men run.* Grammarians express this rule of grammar by saying that third person forms of present tense verbs must agree in number with the pronoun or noun which precedes them. If the noun or pronoun is singular, the verb is also (as in *he runs, a man runs*), but when the noun or pronoun is plural, so also is the verb *(they run, men run).*

In German, however, the matter of grammatical agreement

between pronoun and verb in the present tense is more complicated. Here, very often, we find a different verb form for every pronoun as in *ich laufe* "I run," *du läufst* "you run," *er läuft* "he runs," and *wir laufen* "we run."

Similar differences occur in English and German nouns. In English, the definite article *the* is used before almost any noun, as in *the man, the woman,* and *the maiden.* The German definite article, however, is different in each of these cases: *der Mann* "the (masculine gender) man," *die Frau* "the (feminine gender) woman," and *das Mädchen* "the (neuter gender) maiden."

A final step in understanding linguistic structure is to compare morphemes with one another. Such comparison reveals that morphemes are composed of distinctive sounds called phonemes. Thus in English it is obvious that the morphemes *cat* and *pat* are alike except for the initial phoneme, that *cat* and *cot* differ only in their medical phonemes, and that *cat* and *cap* are distinguished by their final phonemes. *Cat,* then is composed of three phonemes and any change in any one of them will change *cat* to some other English morpheme or to an Englishlike nonsense word (for example *cet*).

The same thing is true of all other languages, that is, in all languages morphemes are built up of one or more phonemes. Languages vary greatly, however, in the complexity of their morphemes and in the kinds of phonemes they may employ. In some languages, morphemes may be very simple, in others the average morpheme may include a relatively large number of phonemes. Similarly, the kinds of phonemes employed, even in languages closely related, may be quite different in pronunciation. Thus the German phoneme written *ch* (as in *buch* "book," or *lachen* "to laugh") is quite unknown in English; our closest sound is *h,* a very weak imitation of the harsher German *ch.*

The number of phonemes employed in a language is usually quite small, rarely exceeding thirty. These are of course used over and over again to produce a great variety of morphemes. The following English morphemes illustrate this point; the eighteen morphemes listed employ only six phonemes; *man, map, mat, mass, nan, pan, tam, sam, pat, pap, gnat* (pronounced *nat*), *sap, tap, sat, nap, pass, tan, tat.*

It may be noted, however, that not all the possible combinations of the six phonemes are actually employed in English. Thus combinations like *san, tas,* and *nam* have no meaning in English; they are Englishlike nonsense words. Other combinations, like *psa, pnt, nmt,* or *psn,* however, are not at all like English words; indeed, all of them involve habits of pronunciation so different from those employed by a speaker of English that he would regard the forms as wholly unpronounceable.

It is clear, then, that the phonemes of a language must be combined according to definite rules. Each language has such rules of combination which are observed strictly by those who speak the language as a mother tongue, and which may differ markedly from the rules characteristic of other languages.

Linguistic Change

From what has been said about linguistic structure we might easily get the idea that the habits of speech characteristic of a given community always remain the same. This is not true, however. All languages are in reality undergoing constant change. We may demonstrate this in two ways: by studying the history of a single language or by comparing and classifying the many languages now spoken.

The history of a language can only be studied directly if the community which speaks it has possessed writing for a considerable period of time. The first written records in English, for example, appear about A.D. 900 and continue in a more or less unbroken stream to the present day. Examination of these records reveals that from A.D. 900 to the present, a period of little more than 1000 years, English has changed radically in pronunciation, grammar, and vocabulary.

This change may be illustrated by comparing the word *acre* with two of its earlier forms, *acer* and *aecer. Acer* belongs to the Middle English period (about 1100-1500) while *aecer* is an Old English or Anglo-Saxon word (900-1100). The principal phonetic difference between *acre, acer,* and *aecer* is the pronunciation of the initial vowel. In

Middle English *acer,* the vowel *a* was pronounced somewhat as the *o* of *sot* while Old English *ae* has a pronunciation similar to that of the *a* in *man.*

The three words also differ in grammar and meaning. Old English *acer* belongs to a category called 'strong nouns' and had several distinctive case forms, much like the strong nouns of modern German. These are distributed as follows:

	SINGULAR	PLURAL
Nominative	aecer	aeceras
Dative	aecere	aecerum
Genitive	aeceres	aecera

During the Middle English period the noun endings became more and more alike until today modern English *acre* has but one major variant, the plural *acres.*

Old English *aecer* referred primarily to a cultivated field; thus, in the Anglo-Saxon Bible, the passage describing Jesus and his disciples going on the Sabbath into a field of ripened wheat uses the form *aeceras* to mean a field on which a crop is growing. Later the term was also used to mean a measure of land. The Middle English *acer* came gradually to mean a field small enough to be plowed by a man with a yoke of oxen in a single day. Later in the Middle English period the term was a more accurate measure of land size though its application was still restricted to cultivated or cultivatable land. *Acre* now has a still more precise meaning (160 square rods or 1/640 of a square mile) and though it is most often used as a unit of measure for land it may apply to cultivated farm lands, wild land (such as forests or mountain areas), or to the land occupied by a city (as in the phrase, "acres of houses, factories, and other habitations").

Since, however, only a few languages have been written for a considerable period it is not always possible to demonstrate linguistic change directly. In such cases we must resort to indirect evidences of change. These are found in the fact that all modern speech communities exhibit geographical differences in pronunciation, grammar, and vocabulary. English, for example, is not the same everywhere that it is spoken. The English of England has a number of major dialects as we go from one part of the island to another and all of them differ from the English spoken in Canada, the United States, Australia, and South Africa. In the United States, too, English is not everywhere the same; differences in pronunciation and vocabulary are found between the English spoken in New York and that of New England, the south, the midwest, and the far west. This can only mean that English has changed and furthermore that change has taken different directions in different regions of the English-speaking world. What was once one more or less uniform language has divided into a large number of mutually distinct dialects.

The Classification of Languages

The discovery that languages change led to a method of classifying languages. English, as we have seen, does not really refer to only one language but to a whole group of languages or dialects broadly alike but differing in many details of pronunciation, grammar, and vocabulary. Linguists express this by saying that the modern English languages are descendants of a single common ancestral English and so belong to a single "family" of languages. Each of the modern idioms is the ancestral English plus those changes in pronunciation, grammar, and vocabulary peculiar to the area in which it is spoken. Actually, of course, this statement is not precisely accurate historically for we know that the older forms of English were also dialectically divided. Some of the modern dialects may have developed from one dialect of the early period, others from quite a different one.

The modern dialects of English do not of course differ very greatly from one another. Much more marked differences are found between English, German, Dutch, Swedish, Danish, and Norwegian. Most of these are mutually unintelligible; that is, a native speaker of English cannot without special instruction, either speak or understand the other languages. Despite this, however, it is evident that these languages do have many features in common; they are not so markedly different as, for example, Chinese is from English. To illustrate this let us compare the words from one to ten in English, German, and Swedish by putting these in parallel columns as follows:

ENGLISH	GERMAN	SWEDISH
one	ein	en
two	zwei	två
three	drei	tre
four	vier	fyra
five	fünf	fem
six	sechs	sex
seven	sieben	sju
eight	acht	åtta
nine	neun	nio
ten	zehn	tio

Here, it is evident, there are both differences and similarities. The differences are often marked but in only a few cases are the words unrecognizably different. Many other examples would reveal that these differences and similarities pervade the entire vocabularies of the three languages. The similarities are indeed so marked and so frequent that they cannot be due wholly to chance nor to mutual borrowings. Indeed, the latter possibility is largely ruled out by the fact that the three languages have for centuries been spoken in quite separate areas.

It follows, then, that these languages resemble each other because, like the separate dialects of English, they are descendants of a common earlier tongue. We have no record of this early ancestral language; as far back as our records go, the three languages are recognizably distinct. But, on the basis of the numerous and far-reaching similarities which today exist between these languages we can and do class them together as members of the same linguistic stock or family.

A linguistic stock, then, is a group of modern and ancient tongues between which there exist a large number of similarities and systematic differences in pronunciation, grammar, and vocabulary, too great to be explained by chance or borrowing. The member languages of such a stock are said to be derived from a single ancestral form, usually called the prototype language of the group. Thus, the languages of the Germanic stock, such as English, German, Dutch, Swedish, Norwegian, Danish, and a number of less important idioms, are modern descendants of a theoretical or assumed language called Proto-Germanic. We have no records of Proto-Germanic, for our written records do not go back far enough in time.

In a few rare instances, however, we may verify an historical classification of this type. Thus, for example, we note that French, Spanish, Italian, Roumanian, and a number of other languages exhibit the same kind of similarities and systematic differences found in the Germanic group. They are for that reason classed as members of the Romance stock and are said to be derived from a language called Proto-Romanic.

But here we have historical records which confirm, in part at least, the inferences drawn from our comparison of the modern languages. These reveal that Latin, once spoken only in the city of Rome and its environs, was spread throughout much of southern and western Europe by the developing Roman Empire. When first established, these outlying colonies spoke much the same language ·as Rome. Each of the colonies and Rome, however, modified their Latin in the course of time, and since they were more or less isolated from one another these changes were largely independent of each other. As time went on, the changes became progressively greater until today the modern Romance tongues are not only different from Latin but also differ markedly from each other. Such resemblances as still exist between the Romance languages are due to the fact that all of them are connected by a continuous tradition to Latin. Spanish, Italian, French, Portuguese, Roumanian, and the other Romance languages are, then, modern versions of Latin, each characteristic of the population of a particular region in Europe.

How Languages Change

When we compare the several stages in the history of a given language we may note not only that the language changes in pronunciation, grammar, and vocabulary but also that changes take place in accordance with three major processes. Some of the words of modern English, for example, are direct descendants of Old English words having the same or similar meanings. Thus, modern English *cow, house, mouse,* and *louse* are directly derived by change of vowel from Old English *cū, hūs, mūs,* and *lūs,* where the vowel *ū* had approximately the sound of the vowel of *soothe.* Similarly, *why, bride, mice,* and *fire* come from Old English *hwȳ, brȳd, mȳs,* and *fȳr* (*ȳ* pronounced as in German *grün* "green" or French *rue* "street"), while *stone, boat, bone,* and *go* are derived from Old English *stān, bāt, bān,* and *gān* (*ā* pronounced somewhat as in *calm*). A goodly portion of our modern English vocabulary, then, existed in Old English as well, the modern forms as we have seen differing from those of the early period in pronunciation, grammar, and meaning.

We also find, however, that Old English possessed a number of forms no longer used in modern English, forms which have been replaced by modern words of different origin. Similarly, there are large numbers of words which have been added to the English vocabulary since the Old English period, words which had no counterparts at all in the earlier language. Words of this type illustrate the two remaining processes of change: analogic change and borrowing.

Analogic change takes place when the speakers of a language create new words by combining older materials on the pattern of already existing forms. In Old English, for example, the plural of *cū* "cow" was *cȳ.* As we have see, Old English *cȳ,* had it persisted to modern times, would have given some such form as **kye,* a word we mark with an asterisk to denote that it does not actually exist. But while we do not use **kye* as the plural of *cow,* we have a form *cows* which has this meaning. *Cows* is made up of two elements; *cow-* from Old English *cū* and *-s* from Old English *-as* (compare Old English *stán* "stone"; *stán-as* "stone-s"). The combination **cū-as* never existed in Old English; it was created much later on the analogy of *stone, stones; book, books;* and other similar singular-plural alternates. In brief, *cows,* though it is made up of two linguistic elements (*cow* and *-s*) which go back to Old English, is a new creation made by combining two forms not hitherto joined. Modern English has lost *cȳ* but has added *cows*.

Analogic forms are very numerous and mark every stage in the history of language. Also numerous in English and in other languages are words taken over by one speech community from another; so-called borrowed forms. Take note, for example, of the following Biblical passage in Old English, its literal translation, and its form in modern English.

Se Haeland for on reste-daeg ofer aeceras; sothlice his leorning-chihtas hyngrede . . .

The/Healing one/fared/on/rest-day/other/(the) acres;/ soothly/his/learning-knights/hungered/ . . .

Jesus went on the Sabbath through the corn; and his disciples were a hungered . . .

Note in particular the Old English words *Haeland, reste-daeg,* and *leorning-chihtas,* replaced in the modern English text by *Jesus, Sabbath* and *disciples. Haeland* is derived from *haelan* "to make well, to make whole" by adding *-end* to the stem *hael-. Hael-* is today found in the phrase *hale and hearty* (*hale* in the sense of healthy is no longer freely used) and in the word *heal* and its derivatives. The ending *-end,* which in Old English made the noun "the healing one" from the verb *haelan* "to heal, make whole," no longer is used in modern English. It survives unrecognized, however, in such words as *fiend* and *friend* from Old English *feond* "one who hates" and *freond* "one who loves." *Haeland* too has been lost and replaced, this Biblical sense at least, by the proper name *Jesus.*

Reste-daeg is of course an obvious compound, the elements of which still exist in modern English. But the compound does not; we may say *day of rest,* but we oftener use *Sabbath,* borrowed ultimately from the Hebrew *Shabbath,* or *Sunday* from quite a different Old English word *sunnan-daeg* "sun's day." Similarly, *leorning-chihtas* "learning-knights" has been replaced by *disciples,* borrowed from the Old French *disciple,* ultimately from Latin *discipulus.* Here are exemplified three instances in which Old English words have been replaced in modern English by words borrowed from other languages. In addition, of course, there are a large number of modern English borrowings for things, sections, and concepts which were not expressed in Old English. Professor Jespersen, an authority on the English language, estimates that nearly two-thirds of our modern English vocabulary is made up of words borrowed from the Scandinavian languages, French, Latin, Greek, and other sources.

Phonetic Correspondences

The method we have described for the classification of languages is called by linguists the comparative method. It results, as we have seen, in a division of the world's languages into historically distinct groups, called linguistic stocks or families. Within any stock there are certain words common to most or all of the languages of that stock and these words are presumed to have existed in the prototype languages as well. Thus, for example, we find that French *coeur* (earlier *cor* and *cuer*) "heart" is paralleled in the Romance stock by such forms as Italian *cuore*, Provençal *cor*, Spanish *corazon* (from Old Spanish *cuer*), and Portuguese *coração* (from Old Portuguese *cor*). From these similarities we may infer that Proto-Romanic had a word pronounced something like *cor* which also meant "heart," an inference which is borne out when we actually find in Latin the form *cor* "heart."

When the words common to most or all the languages of a given stock are examined we find that their similarities and systematic differences in sound can be summarized in a series of descriptive statements called phonetic correspondences. Such statements deal with sounds or phonemes rather than words. Properly constructed, a statement of phonetic correspondences between two or more languages will concisely describe all the phonemic differences and identities that exist between them.

A good example of a phonetic correspondence, and one which also illustrates how such descriptive statements are formulated, is found when we compare the Germanic languages with Latin and Greek and their modern descendants. The oldest known Germanic language, Gothic, had, among others, the consonants *f*, as in *fadar* "father," *þ* (pronounced as the *th* of thick), as in *þreis* "three," and *h*, as *haírto* "heart." These correspond to Latin *p*, as in *pater* "father," *t*, as in *tres* "three," and *k*, as in *cor* "heart." Initially, then, we may proceed on the hypothesis that Latin *p*, *t*, and *k* (written *c*) correspond always to Gothic *f*, *þ*, and *h*, respectively.

This hypothesis is not entirely valid, however. First, we discover that Gothic *speiwan* "spew" corresponds to Latin *spuere*. Gothic *gasts* "guest" to Latin *hostis* "enemy," and Gothic *fisks* "fish" to Latin *piscis*. Here it is evident that a Gothic *p*, *t*, and *k* correspond to Latin *p*, *t*, and *k*. Further examples of a like nature disclose that whenever Latin *p*, *t*, and *k* are preceded by an *s* (as in *spuere, hostis,* and *piscis*) the corresponding sounds in Gothic are not *f*, *þ*, and *h* but *p*, *t*, and *k*.

Were we to develop this rule still further, other exceptional instances might be found until ultimately our statement of correspondences could be so formed as to cover all or nearly all of the forms in which the sounds in question occur.

Phonetic correspondences, properly stated, give the ultimate proof of relationship between languages of the same stock or family. For such relationship is never to be demonstrated by random similarities; any two languages, related or not, will reveal some unsystematic resemblances. It is only when two or more languages can be connected by regular sound correspondences, demonstrably linking forms in terms of systematic identities and divergencies in sound feature, that we may legitimately conclude that they have a common historical origin.

Why Languages Change

Many reasons have been advanced to account for linguistic change. Most of these, however, scarcely bear repetition, for they are in general based upon incomplete or premature analysis. Indeed it may well be said that linguists even today know too little of linguistic change to be able to account for it.

One reason why we know so little about the actual circumstances under which languages change is that we have so far been concerned primarily with the results of change and not enough with the functional relation between language and other aspects of man's cultures. Languages are obviously and clearly related to cultures through vocabulary; as a culture increases in complexity so does the vocabulary of the language which is associated with it. English, which is associated with a highly complex series of cultures, has a far larger and more complicated vocabulary today than it had in the Old English period, when the culture of its speakers was considerably simpler than it is today. Furthermore, we can show that English changed more rapidly during the Middle and modern English period than in the Old English period. Very possibly, then, the series of extremely rapid changes which marked the shift from Old English to modern English were, directly and indirectly, associated with the accompanying shift from the relatively simple rural and isolated culture of the speakers of Old English to the highly industrialized world culture of the speakers of modern English.

It is also significant that some European languages have changed much less than English. An outstanding example is found in Lithuanian, which has changed so little that it today retains scores of older traits which have long since disappeared from English. The significance of this lies in the fact that Lithuania has also been less affected by cultural changes than the English-speaking regions of the world. It has remained very largely a rural and isolated region, participating much less in modern world cultures than the English-speaking areas.

These facts suggest that linguistic change is part and parcel of cultural change taken as a whole. The difficulty in demonstrating this hypothesis lies in the nature of language itself. For though there is an obvious relation between vocabulary and culture, the precise effect of vocabulary changes upon the sounds and grammatical processes of language is far from being clear. Is it true, for example, that large and rapidly accumulating additions to the vocabulary of a language actually results in sound changes and changes in grammatical structure? And if this is so, precisely how are such results brought about? We do not possess the data with

which to answer these questions and until we can acquire
such data it would appear that the factors responsible for
linguistic change must remain unknown.

*The rules of conduct which a society is prepared to defend
with sufficient determination—with physical coercion if
necessary—may be defined as its body of laws. Law is thus an
intrinsic part of cultural anthropology; any rounded study of
a society must include the rules and regulations which govern
it. A statement by the famous American jurist Oliver Wendell
Holmes, Jr., quoted by Hoebel, emphasizes the relationship.
"If your subject is law, the roads are plain to anthropology,"
says Holmes. ". . . it is perfectly proper to regard and study
the law as a great anthropological document. The study pursued for such ends becomes science in the strictest sense." The
archaeologist describing the ancient civilization of Babylonia
finds invaluable source material in the Code of Hammurabi.
The laws formulated by Solon were as important a part of
Athenian civilization as the great tragedies. Without knowledge of Canon Law, a thorough understanding of the Catholic
Church is impossible. The Common Law, the Code of
Napoleon, the Constitution of the United States have been
essential elements in the development of Western cultures.*

*Civilized societies are not alone in their recognition of the
importance of law. The bushman of Australia or the Eskimo
of Greenland may have no rigidity formulated code; they are
unable to write it down or preserve it accurately. Nevertheless,
the code exists. It is recognized by the community as a whole
and individuals are forced to abide by it. As in more complex societies, the law changes to fit the changing needs of the
social structure. Despite the difficulty in defining law which
Hoebel discusses, it is possible to set up certain standards to
which primitive law as well as the majestic edifices of Western
society conform. Hoebel explains what these standards are.
He also describes how they are applied by primitive societies
on a number of levels of cultural development. Hoebel's book
The Law of Primitive Man and such studies as Law-ways of the
Primitive Eskimos and The Political Organization and Law-*

ways of the Comanche Indians are an indication of his qualifications to discuss the growth of law, its cultural background, and its trends, as a society becomes increasingly complex.

LAW AND THE SOCIAL ORDER

E. ADAMSON HOEBEL

TO SEEK a definition of law is to set forth upon a quest for the Holy Grail. Anyone who has made the search will readily sympathize with the lament of Max Radin, "Those of us who have learned humility have given over the attempt to define law." However, if there is a science of law, there must be a determinable body of phenomena for it to study. We must have some idea of what constitutes law.

Law is obviously a complex of human behavior. The problem is: What kinds of behavior? What sets off legal behavior from that which is nonlegal or other than legal? What is it that makes law law?

It is not legislation, despite contrary notions of typical code-trained European lawyers. Most primitive law is not legislated, and modern sociological jurisprudence and legal realism from Holmes down have made it perfectly clear that much of modern law is not legislated either. English jurisprudence has long since given assent to this point of view, as witness the remarks by Salmond:

But all law, however made, is recognized and administered by the Courts, and no rules are recognized by the Courts which are not rules of law. It is therefore to the Courts and not to the Legislature that we must go in order to ascertain the true nature of Law.

The now classic formulation of this concept of the nature of law is Cardozo's statement that law is "a principle or rule of conduct so established as to justify a prediction with

reasonable certainty that it will be enforced by the courts if
its authority is challenged."

This behavioristic concept of law gives the anthropologist
a handle he can grasp, but it is still not enough. For if we
think of courts in our traditional manner, i.e., a formal
sitting of professional judges, with bailiffs, clerks, and
advocates, we must conclude: no courts, no law. This is what
bothered Max Radin, who well understood the anthropologist's problem, and perhaps led him to assert,

> But there is an infallible test for recognizing whether
> an imagined course of conduct is lawful or unlawful. This
> infallible test, in our system, is to submit the question to
> the judgment of a court. In other systems exactly the same
> test will be used, but it is often difficult to recognize the
> court. None the less, although difficult, it can be done
> in almost every system at any time.

Max Radin is right. But what sort of courts did he have in
mind? Some courts are difficult to identify. Anthropologically,
they may be regularly constituted tribal courts such as the
tribal council of an American Indian pueblo sitting in judicial
capacity, or a court of the West African Ashanti, constituted
of the chief, his council of elders, and his henchmen.

That type of primitive court is not hard to recognize. Any
member of the American Bar Association would readily see
it for what it is. But a more obscure type of court may be
found in the Cheyenne Indian military fraternity. Consider
the case of Wolf Lies Down, whose horse was "borrowed"
by a friend in the absence of the owner. When the friend
did not return from the warpath with the horse, Wolf Lies
Down put the matter before his fraternity, the Elk Soldiers.
"Now I want to know what to do," he said, "I want you to
tell me the right thing." The fraternity chiefs sent a mes-
senger to bring the friend in from the camp of a remote
band. The friend gave an adequate and acceptable explanation of his conduct and offered handsome restitution to
the complainant in addition to making him his blood
brother. Then said the chiefs, "Now we have settled this
thing." But they went on, half as a legislature, "Now we shall
make a new rule. There shall be no more borrowing of

horses without asking. If any man takes another's goods without asking, we will go over and get them back for him. More than that, if the taker tries to keep them, we will give him a whipping." Can anyone deny that the Elk Soldiers were in effect sitting as a court for the entire tribe? The test is first, one of responsibility. That they knew. It is second, one of effective authority. That they achieved. It is third, one of method. Unhampered by a system of formal precedent that required them to judge according to the past, they *recognized* that the rule according to which they were settling this case was *new*, and so announced it.

Among the Yurok Indians of California, as typical of a less specifically organized people, the court was less definite, but it was nevertheless there. An aggrieved Yurok who felt he had a legitimate claim engaged the services of two non-relatives from a community other than his own. The defendant did likewise. These persons were called *crossers*, because they crossed back and forth between the litigants. The litigants did not face each other in the dispute. After hearing all that each side offered in evidence and argument the crossers rendered a judgment on the facts. If the judgment was for the plaintiff, they rendered a decision for damages according to a well-established scale that was known to all. For their footwork and efforts each received a piece of shell currency called a *moccasin*. Here again we have a court.

On an even more primitive level, if an aggrieved party or his kinsmen must institute and carry through the prosecution without the intervention of a third party, there will still be a court, if the proceedings follow the lines of recognized and established order. There will be then at least the compulsion of recognized legal procedure, although the ultimate court may be the bar of public opinion. When vigorous public opinion recognizes and accepts the procedure of the plaintiff as correct and the settlement or punishment meted out as sound, and the wrongdoer in consequence accedes to the settlement because he feels he must yield, then the plaintiff and his supporting public opinion constitute a rudimentary sort of court, and the procedure is inescapably legal.

Consider the Eskimo dealing with recidivist homicide.

Killing on a single occasion merely leads to feud, inasmuch as the avenger enjoys no recognized privilege of imposing the death penalty on the murderer or his kinsman with immunity against a counterkilling. A feud, of course, is an absence of law, since blood revenge is more a sociological law than a legal one. But to kill someone on a second occasion makes the culprit a public enemy in the Eskimo view. It then becomes incumbent upon some public-spirited man of initiative to interview all the adult males of the community to determine whether they agree that he should be executed. If unanimous consent is given, he then undertakes to execute the criminal, and no revenge may be taken on him by the murderer's relatives. Cases show that no revenge is taken. A community court has spoken. Such are the kinds of courts Max Radin had in mind.

Although courts in this sense exist in most primitive societies, insistence on the concept of courts is not really necessary for the determination of law. The really fundamental *sine qua non* of law in any society is the legitimate use of physical coercion. The law has teeth, and teeth that can bite, although they need not be bared, for as Holmes put it, "The foundation of jurisdiction is physical power, although in civilized times it is not necessary to maintain that power throughout proceedings properly begun."

But force in law has a special meaning. Force means coercion, which in its absolute form is physical compulsion. There are, of course, as many forms of coercion as there are forms of power, and only certain methods and forms are legal. Coercion by gangsters is not legal. Even physical coercion by a parent is not legal, if it is extreme in form. The essentials of legal coercion are general acceptance of the application of physical power, in threat or in fact, by a privileged party, for a legitimate cause, in a legitimate way, and at a legitimate time. This distinguishes the sanction of law from other social rules.

The privilege of applying force constitutes the official element in law. He who is generally or specifically recognized as rightly exerting the element of physical coercion is a fragment of social authority. It is not necessary that he be an official with legal office or a constable's badge. In any primitive society the so-called "private prosecutor" of a private injury is implicitly a public official *pro tempore, pro eo solo delicto*.

Regularity is what law in the legal sense has in common with law in the scientific sense. Regularity, it must be warned, does not mean absolute certainty. There can be no true certainty where human beings enter. Yet there is much regularity, for all society is based on it. In law, the doctrine of precedent is not the unique possession of the Anglo-American common-law jurist. Primitive law also builds on precedents, for new decisions rest on old rules of law or norms of custom, and new decisions tend to supply the foundation for future action.

Hence we may say that *force, official authority,* and *regularity* are the elements that modern jurisprudence teaches us we must seek when we wish to differentiate law from mere custom or morals in whatever society we may consider.

Thus we may form a working definition of law that fits primitive as well as civilized law in the following terms: *a law is a social norm the infraction of which is sanctioned in threat or in fact by the application of physical force by a party possessing the socially recognized privilege of so acting.*

Recognition of the privilege of applying the sanctions prevents revenge reactions by the offender or his kin. Where this does not exist there is no legal law. Thus the so-called "law of blood revenge" unrestrained by social limitations is no law at all but is merely a social norm. When the killing of a murderer by his victim's kinsmen leads to a counter-killing, and on and on, we have the reign of feud, not of law. Feud is internecine warfare. It is a form of anarchy, not order. Such is the present law of nations, which measured against the background of the world society is amazingly similar to private law on the primitive level.

Primitive law is predominantly private law. The concept of community of interests is not easily recognized by men on the more primitive levels of life. For them kinship is more real than society. The family and the clan are often preferred as the security group. Thus, offenses are more often seen and treated as injuries primarily to individuals and the kin group rather than as crimes against the society as an entity.

The Eskimos serve well as an example of law on the lowest levels of cultural development. The small Eskimo local group rarely numbers more than 100 heads. Its organization is based on the bilateral family, beyond which there is nothing. There is no lineage, no clan, no clubs of either men or women, and no government. Each group has its headman, he who is "tacitly, half-unconsciously recognized as first among equals," he who is variously called *ihumatak,* "he who thinks (for others)," *anaiyuhok,* "the one to whom all listen," or *pimain,* "he who knows everything best." The headman leads, but he does not govern. He lends direction to his people's activity, but he does not direct. No Eskimo will give an order to another; therefore the headman exercises no legal or judicial authority.

Many acts that we consider heinous are accepted as necessary by the Eskimos. Thus certain forms of homicide are socially justified and legally privileged. Infanticide, invalidicide, suicide, and senilicide fall in this category. They are all responses to the basic principle that only those may survive who are able, or potentially able, to contribute to the subsistence economy of the community. Life is precarious in the Arctic.

There can be few legal offenses against property among the Eskimos, since there is no property in land, and free borrowing of goods makes stealing pointless.

Eskimo law grows out of the aggressive status struggle that bedevils the men. The society is wholly democratic, but prestige rivalry among the men is strong. Status is attainable by superior hunting skill and by stealing the wives of other men. The better the reputation of a man, the more likely he is to have his wife stolen. The reason behind wife stealing is not primarily sexual. An Eskimo can enjoy sex without running the risks involved in home breaking. The motive lies in an attempt to outrank the man whose wife he takes, if he can get away with it.

Wife stealing is not a crime, but most litigation arises from it. The challenge results either in murder or wager of song, wrestling, or buffeting. Rasmussen found that all the adult males in a Musk Ox Eskimo group had been involved in murder, either as principals or as accessories; "the motive was invariably some quarrel about a woman." The fact that Eskimo husbands will lend their wives does not mean that they are free of sex jealousy. If a man lends his wife, he enjoys the prestige of a giver of gifts. But if another man assumes sexual rights without permission, that is adultery and an assault on the husband's ego that cannot go unchallenged. Murder must be avenged, sooner or later. And since it is usual Eskimo custom for the killer to marry his victim's widow and to adopt his children, a man may raise the boy who will slay him when he comes of age.

The alternative to killing an aggressor (and thus becoming involved in feud) is to challenge him to a juridical song contest. In the manner of Provençal troubadours of the thirteenth century, the two litigants scurrilously abuse each other with songs composed for the occasion.

Now I shall split off words—little sharp words
Like the splinters which I hack off with my ax.
A song from ancient times—a breath of the ancestors
A song of longing—for my wife.
An impudent, black-skinned oaf has stolen her,
Has tried to belittle her.
A miserable wretch who loves human flesh.
A cannibal from famine days.

Like amateur night at the local theater, he who receives the most applause wins. Thus is the case settled without reference to the right or wrong of the case. But what is more important, the dispute is laid to rest.

Recidivist homicide, excessive sorcery (which is *de facto* recidivist homicide), and chronic lying are crimes punishable by death under the procedure described earlier in this chapter. Such is the nature of rudimentary law in the Eskimo anarchy.

Comanche Indian law-ways represent a somewhat higher development on the same general plane as Eskimo law.

The Comanches had chiefs, both civil and military. The band was larger than the Eskimo local group, and the Comanches had considerable property, especially in horses.

They shared with the Eskimos a fierce drive toward male dominance and competitive rivalry among males for status by means of wife stealing. To this they also added the road of military glory. The Comanches recognized nine common legal offenses against the individual, viz., adultery, wife absconding, violation of levirate privileges, homicide, killing a favorite horse, sorcery, causing another person to commit suicide (a form of homicide), failure to fulfill a contract, and theft.

Homicide called for the killing of the offender by the aggrieved kin of the dead man. This was a true legal penalty inasmuch as custom prevented the kin of the man so executed from retaliating.

Adultery and wife absconding were handled variously, but in every case the aggrieved person was forced by public opinion to act. He could, and often did, proceed directly against the erring wife, killing her, cutting off her nose, or otherwise mutilating her hapless body. This was a husband's legal privilege. Or, if he preferred, he could collect damages from the male offender. This would be done by a direct demand. Whether he got what he first went after or not depended on how courageous the defendant was. If the aggrieved husband, on his part, was not strong enough or fearless enough, he could call in his friends or kinsmen to prosecute for him. But then "the lawyers got the a' of it." Or, lacking kin and friends, he could call upon any brave warrior to prosecute for him. Great braves were willing, for prestige reasons, to do this without any material recompense whatever.

The Comanches recognized no clear-cut types of criminal offenses. There are a couple of cases, half-legendary, of obnoxious sorcerers who were lynched, which indicates that excessive sorcery was a crime. Unlike most Plain tribes, the Comanches did not consider violation of the rules of the communal buffalo hunt to be a clearly defined crime.

The Ifugaos represent yet another interesting example of law on the primitive level of organization. These mountain-dwelling head-hunters of Luzon possess no government worthy of being called such. Over 100,000 tribesmen live scattered throughout the deep valleys that crease their rugged homeland. Although there are clusters of houses in the more favorable spots, they have not even formed true villages, nor do they have a clan organization. But the bilateral group of kinsmen is tightly knit. In the course of centuries, the Ifugaos have carved the steep walls of their mountains into stupendous rice terraces fed by intricate irrigation systems. Their paddies are privately owned and protected by a complex body of substantive law. Ifugaos are capitalists who have many legal rules controlling credit and debt. In addition, they are litigious in the extreme, for each man is sensitive about his "face" and quick to take offense. Their list of possible legal wrongs is long indeed.

How do they handle a legal case? A man with a grievance or a claim tries first to exact a satisfactory settlement from the opposite party. Failing this, he must go to a *monkalun*, a man of the highest social class, who has a reputation as a man of affairs and a number of enemy heads to his credit. The *monkalun* hears his story. Next he accosts the defendant with the charges. The defendant in turn pleads his cause. Meanwhile, both plaintiff and defendant are marshaling their fighting relatives—just in case. The *monkalun* shuttles back and forth between the two parties, wheedling, arguing, threatening, cajoling—attempting to induce them to give ground so that they may meet on terms acceptable to each. Customary law makes the penalties and obligations of both parties quite explicit for every conceivable offense. But first there must be agreement on the exact nature and degree of the offense. Claim must be balanced against counterclaim. Each side weighs the fighting strength and inclination of the other. But at long last, if the patience of the *monkalun* and the litigants endures, a settlement is reached and damages are paid (if it is an assault case) or the debt is satisfied (if it is an economic dispute). But if no settlement satisfactory to each disputant is reached, the *monkalun* finally withdraws from the case. Then the plaintiff or his kinsmen undertake to kill the defendant—or any convenient kinsman of his.

Feud is forthcoming. The creaking legal machinery has broken down.

The *monkalun* represents the public interest by his intervention. Yet he is only incipiently a public officer. He makes no decision and enforces no judgment, but he provides the means through his good offices of bringing disputants to a resolution of their conflict. All Ifugao legal offenses are wrongs to be prosecuted by the aggrieved individual. There are no recognized crimes against society at large.

The Cheyenne Indians represent a more mature and sophisticated development of law on the middle level of primitive culture. The state was well organized. It had a large tribal council of civil chiefs with a ten-year tenure of office. There were no clans, but military societies flourished.

Adultery was a private wrong, but most rare. Wife absconding was not culturally countenanced and gave little cause for trouble. Prestige drives in Cheyenne life had been effectively socialized or turned against the outside world. A man made his aggressive record against enemies, not against fellow tribesmen.

Homicide was a sin and a crime. As a sin it corrupted the viscera of the killer, which "rotted within him," so that he gave off a putrid odor. His stench was obnoxious to the buffaloes, who shunned the Cheyennes, so that starvation threatened. What is more, murder still pollutes the four sacred Medicine Arrows that are the tribal fetish. Blood gets on the feathers. And while blood is on the Arrows, bad luck dogs the tribe. To purify the Arrows and clear the air, two things must be done. In the old days, the great tribal council sat in judgment. The murderer was exiled. Then an impressive ceremony of purifying the Arrows was performed before the whole tribe—with the exception of murderers and their families.

Such a system makes blood revenge, feud, and capital punishment impossible. The Cheyennes in their own way had found the means to suppress internal disruption without recourse to autocracy.

Violation of the rules of the annual communal buffalo hunt was summarily punished by the military society in charge of the occasion. The culprit's weapons were destroyed and his horse beaten. But if he showed contrition, the very men who punished him bestowed free gifts upon him to set him once more on the road to right living. The Cheyennes understood that the purpose of punishment is to correct and reform.

Finally, the Ashanti of West Africa may be cited as a primitive people well on the road toward civilized law by the middle of the last century. Today they are part of the new nation of Ghana.

The Ashanti are a powerful nation with a constitutional monarchy. Clan feuding has been checked and all private law brought within the potential jurisdiction of the royal criminal courts. Any private dispute ordinarily settled between the household heads of the two disputants can be thrown into royal hands by the simple device of one of the quarreling persons swearing an oath on the Great Forbidden Name of a god that the other is guilty of an offense against him. In rebuttal his adversary swears on the same forbidden name that he did not commit the wrong. One or the other is guilty of a false oath—perjury. This act is a capital crime for which the liar must lose his head.

Whoever hears the swearing must arrest the two, for every citizen is the king's agent in such an event. He leads them to a log kept for the purpose and chains them to it, after which he trots off to the king's bailiff with the news. A day for the trial is set. When hauled before the king and his council of elders, each litigant tells his story. The stories are repeated verbtaim by the king's speaker, and each affirms the accuracy of the repetition. So is the issue joined. Now one or the other of the prisoners before the bar names a witness. He is brought forth to swear a deadly conditional curse that what he shall say is the truth of the matter. In this the Ashanti place implicit faith, for the whole trial hinges on what is now said. On the testimony of the single witness, one party is freed and the other condemned to be beheaded —unless the king in deference to the needs of his treasury allows the luckless one "to buy his head," i.e., pay a fine.

Aside from this crude but remarkable device for extending the king's peace, there is also a great body of criminal regulations, every one of which is punishable by death. These range from homicide—"only the king may wield the knife"—to carrying a chicken on top of a load. Even suicide is a capital offense. It constitutes a usurpation of the king's exclusive right to kill. The corpse of the suicide is hauled into court, tried, and decapitated. As a more practical gesture, his properties are also confiscated on behalf of the king.

Ashanti criminal law overreached the mark in much the same way as the law of eighteenth-century England with its two hundred capital crimes. It is significant as an example of the way that monarchy becomes the means of expressing the social interest in the maintenance of order by replacement of private law by criminal. This is a genuine social advance over the chaos of societies that allow feuding.

Modern jurisprudence has much to tell the anthropologist about leads for the study of the formation of law through the processes of litigation. Sociological jurisprudence points up the fact that breach and disputes in conflicts of claims are the most constant source of the law. "Breach," says Seagle, "is the mother of law as necessity is the mother of invention." On the authority of Holmes we have it that "a law embodies beliefs that have triumphed in the battle of ideas and then translated themselves into action," and in the same vein Pound has written, "The law is an attempt to reconcile, to harmonize, to compromise . . . overlapping or conflicting interests." Law exists in order to channel behavior so that conflicts of interest do not come to overt clash. It comes into existence to clear up the muddle when interests do clash. New decisions are ideally so shaped as to determine which interests best accord with the accepted standards of what is good for the society. Of course, it is unfortunately true that tyrants, usurpers, and pettifoggers can and do pervert the ends of law to their own designs without regard to social interests or prevailing standards of what is right.

As a canon of realistic law it may be said, and this is particularly important for anthropologists, that unless a dispute arises to test the principles of law in the crucible of litigation, there can be no certainty as to the precise rule of

law for a particular situation, no matter what is said as to
what will or should be done. A law that is never broken may
be nothing more than an omnipotent custom, for one will
never know more than this until it is tested in a legal action.

The role of the claimant is the most important single factor
in the development of law in primitive societies. Numerous
writers have commented upon the relative absence of legislative enactment by primitive government. Lowie, who is distinguished among American anthropologists for his unique
contributions to the study of legal phenomena, has offered a
general statement that is fairly typical of the prevailing
opinion: ". . . it should be noted that the legislative function
in most primitive communities seems strangely curtailed
when compared with that exercised in the more complex
civilizations." Salmond parallels this with the statement that
"the function of the State in its earlier conception is to *en-
force* the law, not to *make* it." Lowie continues, "All the
exigencies of normal social intercourse are covered by customary law, and the business of such governmental machinery as exists is rather to exact obedience to traditional
usage than to create new precedents."

Now this would be true for wholly static societies, but, as
Lowie would be among the first to acknowledge, no society
is wholly static. New exigencies always arise. One thing
permanent about human society is its impermanence. Especially when strange cultures come into contact do new
materials, new ways of behaving, and new ideas enter into
the cultural picture.

These new elements are not usually adopted simultaneously by all members of the society. The inevitable consequence is that when some members get new goods and new
ideas, they have new interests for which the old lines of the
culture have made no provision. Their use of their new
acquisitions almost certainly comes into conflict with the old
standards held by others. New custom and new law must
then be generated.

However or by whomsoever the judgment may be rendered in any dispute, it is the claimant and the defendant
who lay the grounds of the claim and counterclaim or denial.
If one or the other does it skillfully, soundly, and wisely, the

basis of decision is likely to be found in his statement of his claim. No matter how selfish the motivation of a disputant may be, unless he be a fool indeed, he poses his claim against the background of "right" social principles, general rightness, and the well-being of the entire social group. How else can he gain enduring social acceptance of his position? Naturally, also, the more skillfully he argues his case in terms of the consonance of his claim with the well-established principles of social order, the greater the probability that he will shape the law as he wishes it to be determined.

Any lawsuit or criminal trial involves at least two questions. Is the alleged offense an illegal act? If so, is the defendant guilty of the offense? The first is a question of law. The second is a question of fact. If the first can be brought to a negative answer, then there is no need to seek an answer to the second. The case must be dropped.

Assuming there is a legal rule covering the alleged act, how are the facts then determined?

On the lower levels of legal development the question of evidence is not of great importance. In a small community not much behavior is secret. As a Shoshone once commented to the author, "They just wait around. Sooner or later the facts will come out." In Comanche trials the question of guilt or innocence was rarely raised. The usual point of argument was only the extent of damages.

Judges or prosecutors with skill in cross-examination or detectives with mastery of the techniques of scientific investigation are not of the primitive world. Extortion of confessions by third-degree methods occurs in a few tribes, as in the case of the Comanche husband who could choke his wife or hold her over a fire until she named her lover. But more commonly the primitive man, when he cannot get at the facts by direct means, has recourse to the supernatural.

Divination is the most common device. An Eskimo seer ties a thong around the head of a reclining person, or a bundled coat, or even the diviner's own foot. When the proper spirit has entered the object, the questions may be put. As it is hard or easy to lift, the answer is "yes" or "no."

Conditional curse enters into trial procedure among almost all peoples. It is the assertion that always includes or implies the clause, "if what I say is not true, *then* may the supernatural destroy me." "You [Sun] saw me. May the one who lies die before winter."

Even our own courts do not rely wholly upon our laws against perjury, since every witness must first swear a conditional curse—"So help me God." ("May God smite me, if I lie!") Or is it, since the laws of criminal perjury are more recent than the conditional curse, that the courts do not have full faith in the efficacy of the curse?

Ordeal is peculiarly rare in the New World, which was to the good fortune of the Indians, to say the least. But most of the hideous forms known to medieval Europe were practiced with variations throughout Asia, Indonesia, and Africa. The ordeal by hot iron, with which Ibsen opens his historical play *The Pretenders,* had its counterpart in Ifugao. Various Philippine tribes used the old technique of tying up the two litigants and throwing them in a river. He who rose to the surface first was guilty. Ordeal by poison is popular in Africa. In Ashanti the defendant to a trial may drink a poison brew. If he vomits, he is innocent. If he does not vomit, he dies. And that is proof enough for any man.

Each society is confronted by the imperative of selection in the formation of its culture. Human behavior must be narrowed down from its full range of potential variety to a moderately limited body of norms. Expectancies of probable behavior must be maintained so that people can manage their lives with a high degree of certainty that their own activities will achieve anticipated responses and results from their fellow men. Culture sets such patterns. Selectivity in the building of cultures is done in accordance with a number of basic postulates, existential and normative. Social control is exercised to guide the learning process; it rewards success in adaptation to the norms and expectancies. It penalizes failure in adaptation and deviation from the norms and expectancies. Law is an aspect of social control. It is one of the major devices used by society to penalize behavior that varies too much from certain selected norms.

Substantive law identifies the norms that are to be sanctioned by legal action. *Procedural* or *adjective law* consists of the legal designation of the persons who may rightly punish a breach of substantive law as well as how and under what circumstances.

In most instances, substantive law undertakes to translate basic cultural postulates into social action by decision as to what particular behavior in a given instance may best be interpreted as conforming to the basic assumptions underlying the culture. Law implements the imperative of selection by saying implicitly, "In this society this is permitted and that is not." Law is, therefore, a major instrument in the shaping and maintenance of cultures.

Law in culture performs four fundamental functions essential to the maintenance of society:

1. The first to define relationships among the members of a society, to assert what activities are permitted and what are ruled out, so as to maintain at least minimal integration between the activities of individuals and groups within the society.

2. The second is derived from the necessity of taming naked force and directing force to the maintenance of order. It is the allocation of authority and the determination of who may exercise physical coercion as a socially recognized privilege-right, along with the selection of the most effective forms of physical sanction in order to achieve the social ends which law serves.

3. The third is the disposition of trouble cases as they arise so that social harmony may be re-established.

4. The fourth is to redefine relations between individuals and groups as the conditions of life change.

Any society may manage these functions with more or less skill; its legal system may function with sure effectiveness, achieving justice and order with a minimum of bungling and harshness; or it may be crassly brutal, clumsy and stiff in the joints, with order the product of tyranny and justice a fugitive in the land.

It is a seeming paradox, on first thought, that the more civilized a society becomes the greater is the need for law, and the greater the law becomes. But it is no paradox if the functions of law are kept in mind. Simple societies have little need of law, and on the earliest levels of human culture there were probably no legal institutions. In such rude contemporary groups as the Shoshones, Eskimos, Andaman Islanders, and African Bushmen there is little of what we would call law. Almost all relations in the tribe are face-to-face and intimate. The demands imposed by culture are relatively few; child training is direct and comprehensive. Ridicule is keenly felt, for there is no escape in anonymity. Tabu and the fear of supernatural sanctions cover a large area of behavior. Special interests are few, for there is little accumulated wealth. Conflict arises mostly in interpersonal relations. Hence, homicide and adultery are the most common legal focuses. Sorcery as a form of homicide always looms large as an illegal possibility, but among the simpler peoples sorcery, which uses supernatural techniques, is usually met with supernatural countermeasures rather than with legal action.

Among the higher hunters, the pastoralists, and the ruder gardening peoples, the size of the group and the increased complexity of the culture make possible greater divergence of interests between the members of the tribe. Conflict of interests grows and the need for legal devices for settlement and control of the internal clash of interests begins to be felt. Private law emerges and spreads. It exerts a restraining influence but, like the clan, it has inherent limitations that prevent it from completely satisfying the need it must meet. As no man is competent to judge his own cause, procedure under private law leads too often not to a just settlement but to internecine fighting. A society that is to advance beyond the limited horizons of lower savagery must master the feudistic tendencies of kin-group organization. And every society that has survived for us to study has some set procedures for avoiding feud or for bringing it to a halt if once it gets under way.

As the scope of commonality expands, as community of interest reaches out beyond the kindred and clan, beyond the local group and tribe, men gradually create the means to check internecine strife within the bounds of the larger society through the expansion of the scope of law.

Experience in the development of other branches of culture is also accompanied with experience in the manipulation of the social-control phases of culture. Instruments and devices of government are created. To a greater and greater extent private law is replaced by public law. The state and its agencies corrode away the family and its legal powers. "Through all its course, the development of society," wrote Maine, "has been distinguished by the gradual dissolution of family dependency and the growth of individual obligation in its place."

The following article pursues one of the interesting byways in the study of law and the social order. It offers evidence in support of the doctrine that law is neither logic nor morality but an expression of the will of society. Born at Paterson, New Jersey, in 1844, William Graham Sumner studied at Yale, Göttingen, and Oxford, and became a tutor at Yale in 1866. He took orders in the Protestant Episcopal Church and was for a time a minister at the Calvary Church in New York. He became professor of political and social science at Yale in 1872, where he was a popular teacher and lecturer. He died in 1910. His most famous work, in which he presented an enormous mass of data on the workings of society, is entitled Folkways. *It was published in 1907 and is considered a classic. The present selection is a chapter from the book. If written today, it might well include descriptions of the treatment of Negroes in Mississippi or of Jews in Nazi Germany.*

THE MORES CAN MAKE ANYTHING RIGHT

WILLIAM GRAHAM SUMNER

AT EVERY TURN we find new evidence that the mores can make anything right. What they do is that they cover a usage in dress, language, behavior, manners, etc., with the mantle of current custom, and give it regulation and limits within which it becomes unquestionable. The limit is generally a limit of toleration. Literature, pictures, exhibitions, celebrations, and festivals are controlled by some undefined, and probably undefinable, standard of decency and propriety, which sets a limit of toleration on the appeals to fun, sensuality, and various prejudices. In regard to all social customs, the mores sanction them by defining them and giving them form. Such regulated customs are etiquette. The regulation by the mores always gives order and form, and thus surrounds life with limits within which we may and beyond which we may not pursue our interests (e.g., property and marriage). Horseplay and practical jokes have been tolerated, at various times and places, at weddings. They require good-natured toleration, but soon run to excess and may become unendurable. The mores set the limits or define the disapproval. The wedding journey was invented to escape the "jokes." The rice and old shoes will soon be tabooed. The mores fluctuate in their prescriptions. If the limits are too narrow, there is an overflow into vice and abuse, as was proved by seventeenth-century puritanism in England. If the limit is too remote, there is no discipline, and the regulation fails of its purpose. Then a corruption of manners ensues. In the cases now to be given we shall see the power of the mores to give validity to various customs. The cases are all such that we may see in them sanction and currency given to things which seem to us contrary to simple and self-evident rules of right; that is, they are contrary to the views now inculcated in us by our own mores as axiomatic and beyond the need of proof.

Medieval punishment for criminals, leaving out of account heretics and witches, bore witness to the grossness, obscenity, inhumanity, and ferocity of the mores. There was no revolt against them in anyone's mind. They were judged right, wise, and necessary, by full public opinion. They were not on the outer boundary of the mores, but in the core of them. Schultz says that the romancers have not exaggerated the horrors of medieval dungeons. Many of them still remain and are shown to horrified tourists. There was no arrangement for having them cleaned by anybody, so that in time they were sure to become horribly dangerous to health. They were small, dark, damp, cold, and infested by vermin, rats, snakes, etc. Several dungeons in the Bastille were so constructed that the prisoners could neither sit, stand, nor lie, in comfort. Fiendish ingenuity was expended on the invention of refinements of suffering, and executions offered public exhibitions in which the worst vices in the mores of the time were fed and strengthened. Many punishments were not only cruel, but obscene, the cruelty and obscenity being destitute of moral or civil motive and only serving to gratify malignant passion. A case is mentioned of a law in which it was provided that if a criminal had no property, his wife should be violated by a public official as a penalty. In the later Middle Ages, after torture was introduced into civil proceedings, ingenuity and "artistic skill" were manifested in inventing instruments of torture. A case is given of extravagant cruelty and tyranny on the part of a man of rank towards a cook who had displeased him. It was impossible to obtain protection or redress. The standpoint of the age was that a man of rank must be allowed full discretion in dealing with a cook. In many cases details were added to punishments, which were intended to reach the affections, mental states, faiths, etc., of the accused, and add mental agony to physical pain. "Use and wont" exercised their influence on people who saw or heard of these acts of the authorities until cruelties and horrors became commonplace and familiar, and the lust of cruelty was a characteristic of the age.

The prisons of England, in Queen Anne's time, were sinks of misery, disease, cruelty, and extortion, from which debtors suffered most, on account of their poverty. Women contributed to the total loathsomeness and suffered from it. The Marshalsea prison was "an infected pest house all the year long." There were customs by which jailers and chaplains extorted fees from the miserable prisoners. In the country the prisons were worse than in London. Pictures are said to exist in which debtor prisoners are shown catching mice for food, dying of starvation and malaria, covered with boils and blains, assaulted by jailers, imprisoned in underground dungeons, living with hogs, with clogs on their legs, tortured with thumbscrews, etc. "Nobody ever seems to have bothered their heads about it. It was not their business." In 1702 the House of Commons ordered a bill to be brought in for regulating the king's bench and fleet prisons, "but nobody took sufficient interest in it, and it never became an act." If the grade and kind of humanity which the case required did not exist in the mores of the time, there would be no response. It was on the humanitarian wave of the latter half of the century that Howard succeeded in bringing about a reform. The prisons in the American colonies were of the same kind as those in the old country. The Tories, in the revolution, suffered most from their badness. It is not known that personal abuse was perpetrated in them.

Political factions and religious sects have always far surpassed the criminal law in the ferocity of their penalties against each other. Neither the offenses nor the penalties are defined in advance. Great persons, after winning positions of power, used all their resources to crush old rivals or opponents (Clement V, John XXII) and to exult over the suffering they could inflict. In the case of Wullenweber, at Lubeck, burgesses of cities manifested the same ferocity in faction fights. The history of city after city contains similar episodes. At Ghent, in 1530, the handicraftsmen got the upper hand for a time and used it like savages. All parties fought out social antagonisms without reserve on the doctrine: To the victors the spoils; to the vanquished the woe! If two parties got into a controversy about such a question as whether Christ and his apostles lived by beggary, they understood that the victorious party in the controversy would burn the defeated party. That was the rule of the game and they went into it on that understanding.

In all these matters the mores of the time set the notions of what was right, or those limits within which conduct must always be kept. No one blamed the conduct or general grounds of wrong and excess, or of broad social inexpediency. The mores of the time were absolutely imperative as to some matters (e.g., duties of church ritual), but did not give any guidance as to the matters here mentioned. In fact, the mores prevented any unfavorable criticism of those matters or any independent judgment about them.

One of the most extraordinary instances of what the mores can do to legitimize a custom which, when rationally judged, seems inconsistent with the most elementary requirements of the sex taboo, is bundling. In Latin Europe generally, especially amongst the upper classes, it is not allowed that a young man and a young woman shall be alone together even by day, and the freer usage in England, and still more in the United States, is regarded as improper and contrary to good manners. In the latter countries two young people, if alone together, do not think of transgressing the rules of propriety as set by custom in the society. Such was the case also with night visits. Although the custom was free, and although better taste and judgment have abolished it, yet it was *defined* and regulated, and was never a proof of licentious manners. It is found amongst uncivilized people, but is hardly to be regarded as a survival in higher civilization. Christians, in the third and fourth centuries, practiced it, even without the limiting conditions which were set in the Middle Ages. Having determined to renounce sex, as an evil, they sought to test themselves by extreme temptation. It was a test or proof of the power of moral rule over natural impulse. "It was a widely spread custom in both the east and the west of the Roman empire to live with virgins. Distinguished persons, including one of the greatest bishops of the empire, who was also one of the greatest theologians, joined in the custom. Public opinion in the church judged them lightly, although unfavorably." In the Middle Ages several sects who renounced marriage introduced tests of great temptation. Individuals also, believing that they were carrying on the war between "the flesh" and "the spirit" subjected themselves to similar tests. These are not properly cases in the mores, but they illustrate the intervention of sectarian doctrines or views to traverse the efforts to satisfy interests, and so to disturb the mores.

Two cases are to be distinguished: (1) night visits as a mode of wooing; (2) extreme intimacy between two persons who are under the sex taboo (one or both being married, or one or both vowed to celibacy), and who nevertheless observe the taboo.

The custom in the second form became common in the

woman cult of the twelfth century and it spread all over Europe. As the vassal attended his lord to his bedchamber, so the knight his lady. The woman cult was an aggregation of poses and pretenses to enact a comedy of love, but not to satisfy erotic passion. The custom spread to the peasant classes in later centuries, and it extended to the Netherlands, Scandinavia, Switzerland, England, Scotland, and Wales, but it took rather the first form in the lower classes and in the process of time. In building houses in Holland the windows were built conveniently for this custom. The custom was called *queesten*. Parents encouraged it. A girl who had no *queester* was not esteemed. Rarely did any harm occur. If so, the man was mobbed and wounded or killed. The custom can be traced in North Holland down to the eighteenth century. This was the customary mode of wooing in the low countries and Scandinavia. In spite of the disapproval of both civil and ecclesiastical authorities, the custom continued just as round dances continue now, in spite of the disapproval of many parents, because a girl who should refuse to conform to current usage would be left out of the social movement. The lover was always one who would be accepted as a husband. If he exceeded the limits set by custom he was very hardly dealt with by the people of the village. The custom is reported from the Schwarzwald as late as 1780. It was there the regular method of wooing for classes who had to work all day. The lover was required to enter by the dormer window. Even still the custom is said to exist amongst the peasants of Germany, but it is restricted to one night in the month or in the year. Krasinski describes kissing games customary amongst the Unitarians of the Ukraine. He says that they are a Greek custom and he connects them with bundling.

Amongst peasants there was little opportunity for the young people to become acquainted. When the cold season came they could not woo out of doors. The young women could not be protected by careful rules which would prevent wooing. They had to take risks and to take care of themselves. Poverty was the explanation of this custom in all civilized countries, although there was always in it an element of frolic and fun.

All the emigrants to North America were familiar with the custom. In the seventeenth century, in the colonies, the houses were small, poorly warmed, and inconvenient, allowing little privacy. No doubt this is the reason why the custom took new life in the colonies. Burnaby says that it was the custom amongst the lower classes of Massachusetts that a pair who contemplated marriage spent the night together in bed partly dressed. If they did not like each other they might not marry, unless the woman became pregnant. The custom was called "tarrying." It was due to poverty again. Modern inhabitants of tenement houses are constrained in their customs by the same limitation, and the effect is seen in their folkways. The custom of bundling had a wide range of variety. Two people sitting side by side might cover themselves with the same robe, or lie on the bed together for warmth. Peters defended the custom, which, he said, "prevails amongst all classes to the great honor of the country, its religion, and ladies." The older women resented the attempts of the ministers to preach against the custom. Sofas were introduced as an alternative. The country people thought the sofa less proper. In the middle of the eighteenth century the decline in social manners, which was attributed to the wars, caused the custom to produce more evil results. Also the greater wealth, larger houses, and better social arrangements changed the conditions and there was less need for the custom. It fell under social disapproval and was thrown out of the folkways. Stiles says that "it died hard" after the revolution. In 1788 a ballad in an almanac brought the custom into popular ridicule. Stiles quotes the case of Seger *vs.* Slingerland, in which the judge, in a case of seduction, held that parents who allowed bundling, although it was the custom, could not recover.

A witness before the Royal Commission on the Marriage Laws, 1868, testified that night visiting was still common amongst the laboring classes in some parts of Scotland. "They have no other means of intercourse." It was against custom for a lover to visit his sweetheart by day. As to the parents, "Their daughters must have husbands and there is no other way of courting." This statement sums up the reasons for this custom which, not being a public custom, must have varied very much according to the character of individuals who used it. Attempts were always made to control it by sanctions in public opinion.

Perhaps the most incredible case to illustrate the power of the mores to extend toleration and sanction to an evil thing remains to be mentioned—the lupanars which were supported by the medieval cities. Athenaeus says that Solon caused female slaves to be bought by the city and exposed in order to save other women from assaults on their virtue. In later times prostitution was accepted as inevitable, but it was not organized by the city. Salvianus (fifth century, A.D.) represents the brothels as tolerated by the Roman law in order to prevent adultery. Lupanars continued to exist from Roman times until the Middle Ages. Those in southern Europe were recruited from the female pilgrims from the north who set out for Rome or Palestine and whose means failed them. It is another social phenomenon due to poverty and to a specious argument of protection to women in a good position. This argument came down by tradition with the institution. The city council of Nuremberg stated, as a reason for establishing a lupanar, that the church allowed harlots in order to prevent greater evils. Never until the nineteenth century was it in the mores of any society to feel that the sacrifice of the moral welfare of one human being to the happiness of another was a thing which civil institutions could not tolerate. It could not enter into the minds of men of the fifteenth century that harlots, serfs, and other miserable classes had personal rights which were outraged by the customs and institutions of that time.

Witch persecutions are another case of the extent to which familiarity with the customs prevents any rational judgment of phenomena of experience and observation. How was it possible that men did not see the baseness and folly of their acts? The answer is that the ideas of demonism were a part of the mental outfit of the period. The laws were traditions from generations which had drawn deductions from the doctrines of demonism and had applied them in criminal practice. The legal procedure was familiar and corresponded to the horror of crimes and criminals, of which witchcraft and witches were the worst. The mores formed a moral and civil atmosphere through which everything was seen, and rational judgment was made impossible. It cannot be doubted that, at any time, all ethical judgments are made through the atmosphere of the mores of the time. It is they which tell us what is right. It is only by high mental discipline that we can be trained to rise above that atmosphere and form rational judgments on current cases. This mental independence and ethical power are the highest products of education. They are also perilous. Our worst cranks are those who get the independence and power, but cannot stand alone and form correct judgments outside of the mores of the time and place. It must be remembered that the mores sometimes becloud the judgment, but they more often guide it.

In the following article, Ruth Benedict discusses the various techniques and forms of religion, as well as the concept of the supernatural and the theory of its two manifestations: as an attribute of objects, and as will and intention. As Dr. Benedict has pointed out, the emphases of primitive religion may be contrasted in somewhat the same manner that she uses to contrast primitive societies as a whole in Patterns of Culture. Among certain Siberian tribes, for example, the practice of religion is through divination. The shaman, a man or woman gifted with supernatural powers, consults the spirits while in a state of trance or hysteria and conveys their wishes to the community. The Zuñi Indians of the Southwestern United States have no such individualistic approach. Religion is the concern of the entire society, highly formalized, characterized by elaborate ceremonies whose rules are endlessly detailed. The religion of the Indians of the plains is based on the personal spiritual experiences of individual members of the tribe. In a young man entering manhood these experiences are induced by solitary reveries, fasting and often self-torture. He thus obtains a spiritual patron who guards him in all his experiences, particularly in war. With the Dobuans of Melanesia, magical techniques, whether in agriculture or fishing, sex or family relations, birth or death, predominate. There is a spell for the handling of all events in the lives of the islanders.

Dr. Benedict discusses certain "recurring aspects of the religious complex . . . ceremonialism, the use of borderline psychological states, and the ethical sanction." Each of these has nonreligious significance as well. She also points out that the concept of good or evil, and of a good and omnipotent god, while they are essential elements of Christianity, play no part in many primitive religions. The supreme creator may be a trickster, a fool, or a knave. The idea is by no means foreign to Western thought: "As flies to wanton boys, are we to the gods," says Shakespeare.

Ruth Benedict was born in New York City in 1887. She graduated from Vassar in 1909 but it was not until her mid-thirties, through the influence of Franz Boas, that she became interested in anthropology. She received her Ph. D. in anthropology at Columbia University in 1923 and became successively a lecturer, an assistant professor, an associate professor and in 1948 a full professor on the Columbia faculty. She was the author of Patterns of Culture; Race: Science and Politics, and The Chrysanthemum and the Sword: Patterns of Japanese Culture. She died in 1948 after a distinguished career.

RELIGION

RUTH BENEDICT

THERE IS a fundamental difficulty in the problem of religion that is not present in the study of other cultural traits. All other social institutions rise from known bases in animal life, and our problem is to relate them to their point of departure among the natural endowments and note the very different forms they have assumed among different peoples. The social organizations of the world, however diverse, are built on the physical facts of sex, infancy, and the interdependence of individuals living in groups. Economic complexities are varying organizations of the quest for food and shelter and of man's need for stability in material things. However small the original starting points may bulk in the final traits, they are nevertheless of prime importance in their interpretation and integrate our studies of the institutions that have been built around them.

With religion this is not true. We cannot see the basis of religion in animal life, and it is by no means obvious upon which of the specifically human endowments it is built up. All studies of religion reflect the chaotic disagreement of its students on this point. The most diverse origins of religion have been proposed. Herbert Spencer regarded the fundamental datum of religion as respect for the elder generations of one's family, and derived all its manifestations from an original ancestor worship. Tylor believed that dreams and visions furnished the experiences from which man organized the concept of his own soul as separate from his body; this concept man then extended to the whole material universe, arriving at animism or the belief in spirits. This belief, in Tylor's formulation, was the inescapable minimum and least common denominator of all religions. Durkheim, on the other hand, believed that religion was the outcome of crowd excitement. Over against the unexciting daily routine which he regarded as typically pursued by the individual in solitude or in small groups, he saw in group ritual, especially that connected with totemism, the original basis on which all religion has been elaborated. Religion therefore, he says, is ultimately nothing more than society. J. W. Hauer has derived religion from mystic experience, which, he argues, is a permanent endowment of a certain proportion of the individuals of any community, and this experience communicates itself with such overwhelming authority that it outranks other experiences and seeks expression through dogma and through rite.

There are innumerable other theories of the origins of religion. One of the most familiar is that popular version which derives religion from fear, and to which Petronius gave the classic expression. It is somewhat the fashion now to derive it from the dissatisfactions of life, and a modified version of Durkheim's social theory of religion is gaining ground, according to which the religious life is the social life at those points at which it is felt most intensely.

According to our emphasis upon one or other of these "origins" of religion we shall regard very different aspects as important or as negligible. The mere fact of their diversity and contradiction is proof of our bewilderment about the essential bases of religion. In no case are any of these origins related to the total complex in the way, for instance, that the physiologically determined food quest is related to economic arrangements.

Methodically it is evident that we need to keep closer to the concrete material of primitive religions, and until we are surer of our ground concern ourselves with their religious categories rather than our own. Fortunately for our purpose, once we turn from theoretical discussions of religion to the concrete data from all parts of the world, there is an amazing unanimity. No observer of even the most alien culture has ever failed to recognize certain aspects of its life as religious and to set them down as such. It is only the closet philosopher afterward who denies religion to the Australians because they have no belief in an all-powerful god; the man in the field never confuses the nature of a nonreligious Crow Indian age-society ceremony with the religious character of their sun dance rites.

The striking fact about this plain distinction between the religious and the nonreligious in actual ethnographic recording is that it needs so little recasting in its transfer from one society to another. No matter into how exotic a society the traveler has wandered, he still finds the distinction made and in comparatively familiar terms. And it is universal. There is no monograph in existence that does not group a certain class of facts as religion, and there are no records of travelers, provided they are full enough to warrant such a judgment, that do not indicate this category.

This category, moreover, is commonly made explicit in language. There are several terms that have been widely used in discussions of religion. Three of these, in three different American Indian languages, are *manitou, orenda,* and *wakan,* and they have all the same general range. They are all terms for supernatural power.

Not all people have the same range of meanings in their analogous terms. Distinctions are made along various lines. Especially can a distinction be made dividing personal from impersonal, a distinction that is not made in terms like *wakanda* and *manitou*. The Melanesian term *mana* is definitely a term for impersonal power. Objects are regarded as having *mana* in varying degrees, and this *mana* makes them religiously important. But *mana* is not a term that designates supernatural beings.

The fundamental concept that is represented by these native terms is the existence of wonderful power, a voltage with which the universe is believed to be charged. This voltage is present in the whole world in so far as it is considered supernatural, whether it is regarded as animate or inanimate. A stick or a stone is *wakan* and is used as an amulet; a place, and is used as a sacred grove; a formula, and by faithful repetition it will accomplish what is inaccessible to the techniques of everyday routine. Or it may be persons of particular attainments or in particular circumstances that are *wakan:* a seer who can foretell events or bring about wonderful cures, a warrior who has killed an enemy, a menstruating woman, the dead. Different civilizations regard as *wakan* different objects or aspects of life, sometimes in narrowly limited designated objects, sometimes very unsystematically, almost pantheistically. They are at one only in the universal recognition of the existence of this wonderful power. Always, moreover, the manipulation of this wonderful power, and the beliefs that grow out of it, are religion. They are elaborated by specifically religious techniques.

We have tended in our civilization to keep the phraseology of religion and to discard the ideas that, throughout the history of religion, have been associated with it, and this makes it particularly difficult for us to be explicit about the basic attitude on which religion has been built. We have definitely discarded the picture of the universe as operating on two parallel and contrasted sets of causations, but this has been the fundamental premise of religions. Primitive peoples recognized a matter-of-fact universe that obeyed definite causal relations, where work could be checked against achievement, and trial and error were possible. They built good boats and knew the rules for building them; they cooked wholesome food, or knew the rules for making it wholesome. On the other hand, they recognized also more wonderful causations, the techniques of which were not checked against natural laws and the inalienable properties of the objects they dealt with, but which were solely concerned with manipulating a special potency that had its own rules quite distinct from these matter-of-fact ones of craft and industry. This is often quite clearly phrased by primitive people. An Omaha, pressed to put into words some aspect of his religion, drew his hand contemptuously over the typewriter and camera that were on the table and said witheringly, "But we are not talking of *these things.*" And quite rightly. The distinction they make between the workaday techniques and supernatural ones is a fundamental one. *Wakan* and *manitou* are in the baldest translation simply "the wonderful," and the human imagination has elaborated in religion a really "wonderful" world, freeing itself from the limitations of natural law and material causation.

This supernaturalism among primitive peoples has two different formulations, and they both are extensions of the knowledge man had gained in dealing realistically with the universe. On the one hand, in so far as he extended his concepts and experience of inanimate objects and made these a basis of supernaturalism, he saw this supernatural quality as an attribute of objects just as color and weight are attributes of objects. There was just the same reason that a stone should have supernatural power as one of its qualities as there was that it should have hardness. It did not imply the personification of the stone in one case or the other. On the other hand, in so far as man extended his knowledge of himself and his fellows as the basis of his religious notions, the supernatural was a function of the fact that the external world was person just as he was himself. The tree or the storm felt love or resentment toward the seeker just as he himself did toward other men or other men toward him, and it had the power to act upon its feeling just as men had.

These two religious formulations have had different consequences in the development of religion. The whole train of ideas that is set up is different according as the imputed power is patterned after analogies with color and weight and other properties of objects, or after analogies with will and intention in the human world. These two beliefs have been distinguished as animatism, or the belief in *mana;* and animism, or the belief in spirits. There have been efforts to relate them chronologically and by logical sequences. There is no need to argue the one or the other; methodologically such attempts at single origins are unnecessary and grow out of our human desire to make the argument as trim and neat as possible. Logically it is quite conceivable that supernaturalism should have followed two analogies instead of one, and that neither should have priority over the other. In both the analogies, man seized upon a major aspect of the external world and projected it; these gave him two patterns well-known in his experience, both of which his imagination seized upon and elaborated in its creation of the supernatural world. In the process of this elaboration the two patterns intersected each other in innumerable ways, and there is a middle ground in which distinction between the two concepts is unnecessary. Nevertheless at the extremes of the gamut the two poles are always apparent, and without a recognition of them much of religious practice is unintelligible.

Before we discuss the techniques of religion that are associated with these concepts that form the core of religion, it will help to define our problem if we point out what religion is *not*. There are certain aspects of the religions of our own cultural background that we tend to make fundamental also in the history of religions, whereas they are local developments of our particular culture area or fortunate by-products of a complex civilization.

In the first place religion is not to be identified with the pursuit of ideal ends. It is so natural to us to associate with religion the desire to live more virtuously and to interpret the transitory in terms of the eternal that we introduce unnecessary complications even when we are concerning ourselves with religion in our own civilization. But to select this particular development of the higher ethical religions as the thread which holds together the history of religions and explains that of primitive people is to misconceive that history.

Spirituality and the virtues are two social values which were discovered in the process of social life. They may well constitute the value of religion in man's history just as the pearl constitutes the value of the oyster. Nevertheless the making of the pearl is a by-product in the life of the oyster, and it does not give a clue to the evolution of the oyster.

Religion was used. Its function was to accomplish something, and it was first and foremost a technique for success. It was as material, in that sense, as the agriculture or the hunting which it furthered. Anything that came within the range of an individual's wishes, without regard to its ideality, was sought in religion. The prayers are for definite desired objects:

> Let me kill a Pawnee. See, I have cut off strips of my skin; have pity upon me. Give me a scalp.

Or the Indian lifts up a buffalo chip from his medicine bundle and says:

> Hello, Old Man. I am poor. Look at me and give me good things. Let me live to be old, let me capture horses, let me take a gun, let me count coup. Like a chief, asking help of no one, may I make a good living, may I always have plenty.

He cuts off a joint of his finger and says:

> Old Woman Grandson, I give you this. Give me good pay for it.

The theory that a wonderful power is present in the external world as simply as hardness is present in the stone or greenness in the grass is found to some degree among every people of the world. It may in any society be dwarfed in comparison with a great development of the alternative theory of animism, the personalizing of the universe. But even in such a society there may be amulets of specially shaped or colored stone, for example, that have no connection with the predominantly animistic reading of the universe. They are *per se* powerful, not, as spirits are, contingently so. If they have the rough shape of an animal, they are carried in the belt on the hunt and their magic power will give success in the killing of that animal. If they have instead the shape of a fruit, they are laid at the root of the tree and it bears a rich harvest in its season. No spirit is entreated, no rapport needs to be achieved with the power used; the power that is imputed to these amulets is as axiomatic as any other attribute of the same object.

Logically enough, the kind of magic power that is imputed to objects in this way is most often suggested by some analogy with its other material attributes. Not only does its shape suggest the use to which it shall be put as an amulet for the hunt or for fertility, but its outstanding qualities as an object may be transferred bodily to the magic realm. In order to secure long life for themselves, the Eskimo sew to their clothing bits of the hearth stone, which has proved its enduring qualities by resisting the fire. Similarly, to make a boy a great hunter, they sew on the talons of the hawk, the greatest hunter of the Arctic. To give him the fox's cunning they attach a bit of the fox's dung. In parts of Melanesia where every magic procedure must have its potency given it by the magic "specific" that is the esoteric secret of every magician, these specifics are chosen because of similar analogies. A twin berry is the specific of the curse that will cause a woman to have twins, and the leaves of a lush-growing water plant are a well-known garden specific.

Formulaic spells are one of the frequently recurring expressions of this attribute theory of supernatural power. If the proper words are said, the spell has power *per se*, just as an herb has curing virtues. In the everyday world, if a dam is built the water will rise; in the supernatural world, formulas in this case act in a matter-of-fact fashion as dams do in the matter-of-fact world. It is only necessary to know the formula. Techniques develop luxuriantly in the soil of this idea, and have had great consequences in the history of religious practices.

The alternative theory of the supernatural is based not on man's experience with things and their attributes, but on his recognition of power in himself and in his fellows; power is attributed to the external world after the analogy with human will power.

Animism is a confusion between two of our most carefully separated categories, the animate and the inanimate. Tylor and Spencer, who first examined animistic beliefs in their relation to religion, found animism bewildering and well-nigh incredible. They were exponents of nineteenth-century ra- of the human processes. This ascription of being to the ex- tionalism, and were accustomed to rely upon the rationality ternal world, and the behavior that this occasioned in re- ligious practice, were from their point of view gratuitous and irrational.

Tylor derived animism from those experiences which give man the notion of the separable human soul. These are primarily dreams, but also shadow, reflection on the water, etc. Once primitive man had arrived at the hypothesis of his own soul, he transferred the notion first to other humans and then to the inanimate world. It was a belief, according to Tylor, based on a logical chain of reasoning. Modern psychology is less given to tracing the origins of fundamental human attitudes to logical chains of reasoning. We are more inclined to see the concept as secondary and the total reaction to the situation as primary.

It is important to realize that this division of the world into animate and inanimate, with accompanying appropriate behaviors for each, is a sophisticated one that is alien to folk custom even among ourselves and has to be learned by each generation of our children. Modern child psychology is full of examples of the personalization of the inanimate world. The child endows a moving object with the will and intention a human being has. He strikes the door that has slammed upon him to pay it back for the injury. These are expressions of an attitude that has not yet made our fixed distinction into animate and inanimate, but brings the whole of experience under one rubric, treating the entire external world according to the pattern that has been acquired in dealings with human individuals.

Throughout man's history it has been the mechanistic theory of the universe that he has found fantastic, not the animistic one. He is equipped with a consciousness of his own purposes and motivations, but no stretch of the imagination is sufficient to give him a conception of the workings of inanimate life. His experience of his own inner life he uses to picture to himself those other sequences of which he has no such knowledge. Instead of admitting his ignorance of the reasons for the succession of rain and drought, he sees in it rain gods blessing their chosen people—or, at the least, rain falling on the fields of the just. He uses the motivations he is familiar with in himself to explain the world that would otherwise remain a puzzle to him. He domesticates the world and makes it intelligible. He sees in the external world the playing out of a human drama actuated by moral significance; that is, he sees it humanly directed toward rewarding those who have performed their required obligations and denying those who have failed in them. He is no longer in a blind and mechanistic universe. This wishful thinking, which is embodied in the religions of the world, and is worked out conceptually in mythology and theology and behavioristically in the religious techniques of petition and rapport, ranks with the great creations of the human mind.

Just as the theory of the supernatural swings between two poles, one of which is magic power as an impersonal attribute of objects and acts and the other the will power of a personalized universe, so also religious techniques cover a gamut one extreme of which is mechanistic manipulation of impersonal magic power, and the other personal relations with the supernatural.

Magic is mechanical procedure, the compulsion of the supernatural according to traditional rules of thumb. It is, in the realm of the supernatural, the technique of science in the realm of the natural. As Frazer has pointed out, magic is primitive man's science. As opposed to other techniques of the magico-religious realm, it operates with cause and effect sequences. It does not involve submission, petition, conciliation, consecration. If a man knows the rules and follows them in detail, the effect is secured. The danger lies all in faulty knowledge, involuntary missteps, oversights on the part of the practitioner. From his point of view, and according to his view of the universe, which does not separate natural from supernatural, he is following inexorable law. He is, in Frazer's word, the primitive scientist.

The distinction between magic and science, nevertheless, is as obvious as the procedure they have in common. Science has no place for supernaturalism, whereas it is the sole concern of magic. The distinction in any given procedure is always clear. If the object is to secure a good harvest, in so far as primitive man is scientific he prepares the ground, buries the seed at the proper depth, keeps it weeded, and frightens away insect, bird, and animal pests. But he employs also stones shaped like the desired fruit, and these are considered to have *mana* to increase the harvest. This is making use of supernatural power by sympathetic magic. Or, when the taro has come up, the magicians go through the field breaking off its lower leaves, because full-grown taro sheds such leaves, and this magical procedure therefore ensures its arrival at that stage. These acts are as mechanistic as the scientific procedure, but they employ a completely different cause and effect sequence.

The alternative religious technique is that which grows out of animistic beliefs. If the universe is person in its motivations and purposes, behavior toward it must be the familiar behavior men have found useful in their relations to their fellows. Love, punishment, reverence, command, are all tried and tested means of attaining ends in dealing with persons, and they are indicated therefore in dealings with the personalized universe.

One of the types of behavior that are used toward the supernatural by virtue of its known availability toward persons is reverence, or awe as it is usually called in religious connections. Awe has been singled out by some writers as the comprehensive religious attitude, that attitude which sets off religion from other human traits. Awe, however, is only one among many attitudes characteristic of religious behavior. Cajolery and bribery and false pretense are common means of influencing the supernatural, and are especially characteristic of regions of Melanesia. The Kai of New Guinea "swindle ghosts as they do men," and the near-by Tami deceive the spirit in the grossest fashion, "outwitting it like an arrant blockhead," and giving as offerings the shabbiest things they

can find. Reprisals and vehement expressions of anger also
are relied upon in dealing with the supernatural. The Tsim-
shian of the Canadian Pacific coast, when they suffer great
misfortune, vent their anger against heaven without inhibi-
tion. Scolding is one of the recognized means of dealing with
the recalcitrant supernatural. "They raise their eyes and
hands in savage anger to heaven, and stamp their feet on the
ground. They reiterate, 'You are a great slave.' It is their
greatest term of reproach." The Manus of the Bismarck Archipelago keeps in his house as a tutelary a skull of a recent ancestor, and expects from its aid good fortune in all his undertakings. If he is not satisfied, he consults an oracle or a diviner to find out for what the tutelary has punished him, and
will immediately make restitution. If his business does not
prosper thereafter or if the illness is not alleviated, he is justly angry at his tutelary and threatens that he will throw him
out of the house, "to be washed by all rains, scorched by all
suns," to be homeless and forgotten. "You will then be made
to understand! You will have no house to rest in; you will be
cast out and you will be miserable a long time before you become a crab or a jellyfish."

On the other hand the accepted attitude toward the supernatural may be that of courteous hospitality. If human
beings are the more likely to be gracious after they have been
happily entertained, how much more might this not be true
in the case of the gods. Among the Langalanga of Northern
Mala, of the Solomon Islands of Melanesia, the dead are the
recognized supernaturals and are represented by their skulls,
which are kept in a house prepared for them. When the Langalanga play the panpipes for dancing in the village, they
bring the skulls out of their house and range them in an hon-
ored audience, saying, "Now you may watch the dance."
They gather the leaves of fragrant herbs with which the
women are accustomed to perfume themselves, and stuff
these up the noses of skulls. They desire that they shall enjoy
the most hospitable entertainment that they know how to
provide. The same attitude is found also in the Southwest
pueblo of Zuñi. There too the dead are the supernaturals.
They dance continuously in the sacred lake, but they prefer
to return to dance in Zuñi. Therefore impersonation in the

masked dances provides them with the opportunity to in-
dulge themselves. They come and are entertained by participation in a dance, the favorite pastime of the people. It is the
most pleasing hospitality that the Pueblos know how to give
either to humans or to the supernaturals.

There is probably no customary behavior toward one's fellows that is not to be found somewhere as a religious technique, even acts that belong to specific situations in human
life such as birth and courtship. In the Malay peninsula the
rice at planting is given all the ceremonies of childbirth and
cradled by the wife of the planter; the tree whose sap is
sought is appealed to as a mother: "O mother, often before
you have given me the breast, yet still I thirst. I ask four pot-
fuls more." Or before the tree is cut it is wedded with all the
appropriate human ceremony and taken as bride by the
woodsman. In these cases it is the appropriate behavior of the
mother and the child and the bridegroom that has set the
pattern for behavior toward the supernatural.

Every form of religious behavior runs the gamut between
the two techniques we have discussed: a technique patterned on behavior toward things, and a technique patterned
on behavior toward persons.

Speech that is intended to achieve supernatural ends is at
the one extreme the prayer of the saint whose only object is
to place himself in the most intimate communion with the
god, and at the other the recital of magical formulas. The
prayer of intimate personal dependence upon the god is
found even among primitive people, and a great many offerings to the supernatural are accompanied by prayers which
detail the efforts of petitioners to please and gratify the supernatural. The Winnebago of the region of the Great Lakes
pray to the Thunderbird: "Oh grandfather, Thunderbird,
here I stand with tobacco in my hand. Grant us what you
granted our grandfathers! Accept our humble offering of tobacco. We are sending you buckskins from which you can
make moccasins, feathers from which you can make a head-
dress; we are preparing a meal for you from the meat of an
animal who is like ourselves. And not I alone, but all the
members of my clan and all the members of the other clans
present here, beseech you to accept our gifts. We have pre-

pared ourselves fitly, and I and all my kinsmen sit here humble in heart, a sight to awaken pity, so that we can receive your blessing and live a good life."

Speech to the supernatural may also be magical forms of words which achieve their end automatically, and this may be in a given society the accepted way of dealing with the supernatural. In parts of Melanesia it is strictly denied that gardens can grow without the use of the magic fertility formulas, and this even in the face of missionaries' gardens which have flourished in certain islands for many years. In northern California there is a strong development of compulsive formulas of this sort which detail incidents in the travels of the animals who figure in the myths of this area. They are used as magic. If recited word-perfect, an incident in Coyote's successful encounter with Wolf and the healing of his wounds will cure bullet wounds after a battle. Every dangerous occasion of life is provided with these incidents from mythology which are used in this magical fashion.

Divination, or control by foreknowledge, is similarly of two contrasted types. Divination among many primitive peoples is accomplished by persons who are possessed by the supernatural spirit. The god himself speaks through them as through the Greek oracle at Delphi. This is a common practice in Africa, in Polynesia, and in Siberia. The priest divines only by himself uttering the words of the supernatural person.

At the opposite pole is divination from the entrails and the scapulae of animals. In order to ascertain the future in this way one requires a technical training in the significance of spots on the liver or the configuration of lines on a scapula. The result is entirely without reference to having placated a god or having achieved any other form of communication with him.

Sacrifice, or control by gift, is at the one extreme a bought-and-paid-for trafficking with a supernatural that cannot choose but accept the arrangement offered it; if the payment is given, the aid must be forthcoming. Sacrifice on the other hand may be one of the means of pleasing the god, and all possible human attitudes toward a gift are found in various religions. The Plains Indians regarded self-inflicted torture as the most important sacrifice to the supernaturals, and they offered it in order to gain their pity. Such sacrifice on the Plains was one of the most important ways of establishing a personal relation with the supernatural. In Melanesia, on the other hand, it is more common to regard objects given to the supernatural as in themselves compulsive, and as having no bearing upon establishing personal relations. The objects are given as an integral part of magical procedure—so many betel nuts or so many skulls, along with a magic formula, to make the canoe seaworthy or the wind propitious.

Taboo, or the control by abstention, is a constantly recurring aspect of man's dealings with supernatural power. Because the supernatural is power, it is dangerous. A whole religion may be devoted to the ritual punctiliousness by means of which this danger is surmounted. The dangerousness of the supernatural to which taboo is the response may be conceived as automatic and an attribute, or as a human quality, and taboo will have a different character in the two cases.

At their most mechanical, taboos are exemplified by the *tapu* charms of Samoa and parts of Melanesia or the *tie-tie* of West Africa, which capitalize the dangerousness of the supernatural. These charms are taboos placed on private property and evidenced by a mark or a dangle placed on the object. Property sanctions in these regions are thus given over to the supernatural. The Fan in West Africa trust all their property to the operation of the supernatural taboo of the *tie-tie*, even a wealth of ebony or ivory tusks left far out in the bush. If anyone desired the ebony he would hold it policy to kill the human owner before breaking the ban. Only after he had thus nullified the supernatural power the owner had affixed to his property would he make off with the ebony. The West Africans have a proverb, "One charm does the work of twenty slaves."

But taboo can be on the other hand a punctilio patterned after that observed toward powerful persons. It may be a removing of one's hat or one's shoes or one's blanket when one enters the presence of the supernatural just as one shows these marks of respect to any person of power and prestige. In Polynesia, in the treatment of chiefs, punctilio is carried to the point where by virtue of their great sacredness and dangerousness chiefs may not feed themselves or be touched by anyone, but are fed on long prongs which are manipulated carefully so that they will not touch the sacred teeth. The chiefs can do no work, nor go out of the confinement of the chieftain's house. The supernatural power which fills them makes them too sacred, too dangerous for participation in ordinary life, and sets them apart by elaborate taboos. Sacred places, sacred objects, the defiling, and the dead have usually been surrounded by taboo. A medicine bundle or fetish has always its rules of punctilio consequent upon its not being an object to handle lightly.

Taboo may be, in its most extreme use as an element in a relationship with a personal supernatural, the asceticism of the saint. The higher ethical religions have elaborated formal restrictions and proscribed indulgences not for their magic efficiency but for the sake of ruling out "the world." Primitive peoples also have retreats and sacred personages, and the taboos associated with them are sometimes thought of as setting them off in a peculiar dedication to the supernatural. Such taboos are characteristic of the American Indian vision quest and of the Siberian shaman, and are very differently conceived from the *tapu* of Polynesia.

Taboo is one of those subjects under which a great deal of miscellaneous material can be grouped; it has in consequence been given great prominence in discussions of religion. This is due very largely to the fact that taboo is by definition all that is forbidden; that is, it is the negative aspect of everything. It is a category of prohibitions. Taboos and prohibitions are fundamental in religions, but the category loses its significance when it is separated from the positive aspects of which it is the negative. For this reason taboo is best regarded not as a primary aspect of the religious complex but as a ubiquitous form of religious behavior, that form which takes into account the dangerous aspect of supernatural power and surrounds it with punctilious observance.

Material objects when they are treated as supernatural are either amulets if they are the seat of supernatural power in its guise as an attribute of things, or fetishes in its animistic guise. Amulets by definition possess supernatural power in the same fashion and by the same token that they possess color or any other attribute. They work automatically, as fire does, or pressure, and are not prayed to or personified.

The term "fetish" is that used in Africa where the material object is handled on the opposite theory. The fetish is given gifts and talked to, and reviled if necessary. It is regarded as being strongest in its youth, and after use it is laid aside to recuperate its powers as a man rests after a campaign. It may or may not be conceptually regarded as person, but the behavior toward it is behavior between persons, not that of a person toward an inanimate object as in the case of amulets. Most West Africans treat not only medicine bundles but all material objects in this fashion. The native about to set out for a hunt sits about for days talking to his spear, rubbing it, and telling it how much he has given it and how great his reliance is upon it. He addresses it in terms of friendship as he does all objects he wishes to use.

The guardian spirit of the North American Indian was a personal tutelary with which he alone had dealings. This relationship was strictly according to the pattern of human relationships between a benefactor and his protégé. In order to obtain the tutelary in the first place, the youth had to go out alone fasting, concentrate on the blessing he desired, and often torture himself in order to make himself more pitiable to the spirits. At last he entered into complete rapport with the supernatural and his tutelary appeared to him. All his life thereafter he could ask for help from his spirit, but in return he had to give a place of honor in the tipi to the bundle which he kept as a sacred memento, feed it at every meal, observe punctilio in regard to it, and open and incense it at due seasons. If his tutelary was displeased with him at any time, the power was no longer available. All his prayers to it were a statement of the human relationships between them. At the same time the tutelary spirit might assume obligations and become the "servant" of the person who had acquired him.

The attitude toward the individual supernatural in witchcraft often contrasts strongly with this. The supernatural slave was obtained by a legalistic contract, and compulsion was the technique that was relied upon. This slave technique is, of course, one that has been notoriously used toward human beings, but it is that of dealing with persons as things and it is for that reason that it is repulsive to present-day ethics. Witchcraft, like many primitive magic practices, carried it into the supernatural realm. You had only to rub the lamp and the djinn came. You had only to obtain the name of the demon and he was at your service.

These two techniques for handling the supernatural—at the one extreme compulsion and at the other rapport—occur in all types of religious behavior. It is clear that they are always alternative methods for dealing with the supernatural, and that neither gives any indication of being derivative from the other. They are two poles between which religious behavior ranges, each pole representing one of the two major human experiences outside of the religious realm: on the one hand man's experience with things, and on the other his experience with persons.

IV. Some Primitive Cultures

IV. Some Primitive Cultures

The articles which make up this final section offer glimpses
of a number of unusual cultures, some extremely primitive,
others on the borderline of sophisticated civilization, from the
arctic to the equator. They have been chosen for the intrinsic
interest of their subject matter and because they illustrate some
of the ideas and opinions expressed in previous sections. They
represent only a tiny fraction of the material that has been
collected by the cultural anthropologist. Yet they indicate how
much fascinating information can be uncovered by careful
observation in communities which too frequently have been
dismissed as being unworthy of study.

The following selection is taken from a volume entitled
Primitive Man and His Ways in which an eminent Danish
anthropologist gives "an outline of six characteristic cultures
from widely different parts of the world as they have developed,
adapted to their environment." The culture here discussed
has survived in one of the more inhospitable sections of the
earth, under constant pressure from stronger and more successful neighbors. The manner in which it has succeeded in
doing so offers comparisons and contrasts with other rude
cultures faced by similar problems.

The author was born at Copenhagen in 1893 and received
his Ph.D. at the University of that city. He has made ethnological studies of the natives of Greenland and Alaska, as well
as of the Philippines and the Solomon Islands. He is a member
of the Royal Danish Academy of Letters and Sciences and
is Keeper of the Ethnographical Department of the National
Museum at Copenhagen.

THE LAPPS

KAJ BIRKET-SMITH

MOST TRAVELERS to the north of Scandinavia remember their encounter with the Lapps as a colorful experience of something far off and strange. To the local peasants the Lapps, as they pass by with their enormous herds of reindeer, are something of a thorn in the flesh. To jurists and statesmen their seasonal wanderings and their long-standing contempt of state boundaries and international problems have proved a trial of professional skill and diplomacy. To scientists they are a mystery—the only purely European Arctic people and the first of any Arctic peoples to be known. Their way of life is as completely adjusted to Arctic conditions as that of the Eskimo—though in a completely different way. And in many respects they and their origins remain a mystery to this day.

The first reference to the Lapps, then described as Finns (*Fenni*), is in the year A.D. 98, when Trajan became Roman Emperor. The reference is in Tacitus, who writes:

> They live like savages in a state of frightful poverty. They have no weapons, no horses, no houses even. For food they have wild herbs, for clothes animal skins, for a bed the earth. They put all their faith in their arrows which, in the absence of iron, are tipped with bone.

Finns is the old Norse name for the Lapps and has been preserved in Norway down to our own times. The word Lapps, or rather Lapland, does not occur before about A.D. 1200, when Saxo Grammaticus writes of *utraque Lappia*, i.e., the regions on either side of the Gulf of Bothnia.

The popular impression of the Lapps as a largely nomadic people will not stand close examination. Of the 32,600-odd

souls nowadays reckoned as Lapps, by far the majority—
about 20,000—live in Norway, and of them only a small
minority are nomadic reindeer herdsmen. By far the greater
number of settled fishermen and sealers on the Arctic coast.
In Sweden the Lapps are far fewer, in all scarcely 9,000, and
again less than a third of them are nomads. In Finland the
Lapps are fewer still—about 2,500—and in the Soviet Union
1,800.

Few in numbers though the population is, it is scattered
over an enormous area, from North Cape as far south as the
Rørås district in Norway and down to northern Dalecarlia in
Sweden, and from the Atlantic coast to the eastern point of
the Kola Peninsula. The Lapps are in a majority only in the
northern districts, i.e., in the counties of Finnmark and
Troms in Norway, in Norrbotten and Västerbotten in Swed-
en, and in Utsjoki and Enontekiö, the narrow arm of Finland
which stretches in between Norway and Sweden.

Who precisely are the Lapps? To which race do they in
fact belong? The old idea that they are purely and simply
"Mongols" is no longer acceptable. But where these small,
lean people with their swarthy, wrinkled skin, curious
screwed-up faces and pointed chins really belong is still one
of the unsolved mysteries of physical anthropology. In some
respects they do not even constitute a racial unit. In spite of
all their similarities and the inevitable admixture of Scandinavian and Finnish blood which has taken place down the
centuries, there remains a not inconsiderable difference between the eastern and western Lapps, a difference which is
reflected in their language and also to an extent in their culture.

True, they are all brachycephalic—but in the former the
skull is low and the distribution of blood groups corresponds
to that found in eastern Europe. In the Scandinavian Lapps
we find a high cranium, and the distribution of blood groups
corresponds to that usual in western Europe. There is no
doubt that in the eastern Lapps there is a racial strain which
is also found in the Samoyeds east of the White Sea. But
some anthropologists believe them to be also akin to remote
European racial elements. In the Valdai Hills south of Lake
Ladoga bones of a Stone Age people have been found which

are reminiscent of the Lapps, and even in Poland traces of Lapplike elements are said to occur.

The language provides fewer difficulties—seemingly. No one has any doubt that it is related to Finnish and thus belongs to the big Finno-Ugrian group which, with Samoyed, constitutes the Uralian linguistic stock. Even though present-day Lappish and Finnish appear to differ widely, they are not so far apart that they could not have sounded almost identical 2,000 years ago.

But the Finns are so different physically from the Lapps that the difference in the two races cannot possibly have been brought about in such a brief space of time. The only reasonable explanation seems to be that one of the two races must have changed its language.

Romantic archaeological researchers of a hundred years ago saw the Lapps as the aboriginal population of Scandinavia. Curiously enough, this idea had been received by modern science, though in a different way. In 1925 the Norwegian archaeologist Anders Nummedal began a series of excavations which lasted many years and which completely upset all the beliefs which had hitherto been held about the oldest human settlements on the Arctic coast. One site after another was found on the coast of Finnmark, containing curious crude stone artifacts which were in many ways reminiscent of the primitive tools left behind by Ice Age people farther south.

We now have a pretty fair knowledge of the old Finnmark or Komsa culture, the area of which stretches from Alta Fjord to the north coast of Kola. At one time the region must have been inhabited by a hunting people who scraped a living together by fishing and hunting on land and sea in much the same way as the people of Greenland do. The similarity with the Greenlanders goes further, for at the time when the Komsa culture was at its height, the mountains of the interior were largely buried under the remains of the great Ice Age glaciers and an icy sea lapped the bare coasts. Though it cannot be proved, it is possible that the Komsa people are the distant ancestors of the western Lapps.

Opinions as to the origin of this culture are still divided. Some seek its links eastward across the Kola Peninsula—

either right across the way to Siberia, or failing that to Russia and Poland. One archaeologist considers the related and largely contemporaneous Fosna culture between Trondheim and Bergen to be an offshoot of the Komsa culture.

In contrast to this, Johannes Brondsted maintains that it is the Komsa culture which is derived from the Fosna culture, and that its roots are to be found in the Holstein and Danish Ahrensburg and Lyngby culture from about 10,000 B.C.[1]

Later Stone Age and Bronze Age finds on the Arctic coast are few and not very informative. Not until the Iron Age do any clear lines emerge. The question as to who were the bearers of the oldest cultures is still open. What is certain, however, is that the graves from Nesseby in Varanger and Olennii Ostrov on the Kola Peninsula—where stone was still being used—as well as the finds belonging to a later period at Kjelmøy in Varanger, are all Lappish. The date of the excavations at Kjelmøy is put at A.D. 400–500, thus corresponding to the beginning of the late Danish Iron Age. They provide evidence of a typical fishing and sealing culture with implements of bone, antler, and iron together with comb pottery which has some affinities to Russian and Siberian types.

So much for habitation on the coast. Things look different when we inquire into the distribution of Lapps inland. The later Stone Age in Finland and northern Scandinavia, which so far as northern Norway is concerned starts about 2300 B.C., is characterized by slate tools, and pottery similar to that found at Kjelmøy. These are in fact the westernmost evidence of a circumpolar hunting culture. In Norway it extends as far south as Romsdal, and traces of it can be followed right across to northeastern North America. To what extent its presence in Scandinavia is due wholly or in part to the Lapps cannot be determined with absolute certainty. But the idea is not impossible.

It is perhaps worth mentioning in this connection that some of the place names on the Møre coast between Trondheim and Molde are said to be survivals of an old Lapp set-

1.   The idea, advanced by Wiklund, that the Komsa culture goes back to the last interglacial period has, however, never gained acceptance among archaeologists.

tlement, and that a peculiar form of heavy, edge-ground stone implement, the Rovaniemi ax of northern Scandinavia, and certain bronze axes in Finland, are attributed to the Lapps. Evidence that bronze was known in early times appears from the fact that, in contrast to the names of other metals, the term for bronze is pure Lappish. Finds of skis from circa 2000 B.C. are also regarded as evidence that the Lapps must have been present in northern Sweden as early as the late Stone Age.

Gustaf Hallström, on the other hand, and Wiklund too, maintain that the Lapps did not make their push from the Arctic coast before the middle of the last millennium prior to the Christian era. And why just then? Because, it is said, of the climate. In the milder climate which prevailed all over Scandinavia throughout the later Stone and Bronze Ages, the southern type of deciduous forest extended to the far north of Finland and the Scandinavian peninsula, and wild reindeer would hardly have flourished in such conditions. And so long as reindeer breeding was unknown, only wild reindeer could have formed the basis of the Lapps' existence.

Then at the beginning of the Iron Age a deterioration of the climate took place. The summers became colder and damper. The spruce made its way across Finland and Sweden from the east, and in its wake came the reindeer. The "Fimbul winter" descended on the country.

It was a heavy blow to the agricultural Bronze Age inhabitants of the region. Extreme poverty characterizes Finnish finds of the period. But to the ancestors of the Lapps the change meant that they moved south into the interior of the country where reindeer hunting attracted them. If, on the other hand, the later Stone Age finds are Lappish, of which there is much evidence, then the deterioration of the climate must at most have caused a renewed push southward.

However that may be, sometime during the Iron Age reindeer breeding must have been introduced, and it certainly came from the east. So far, the earliest traces of domesticated reindeer are in the form of a pair of small wooden figures which were the result of archaeological excavations in the Minusinsk region in southern Siberia some years ago. This find dates from the first or second century A.D. Some centuries later, circa 500, tame reindeer are mentioned in a Chinese source. Moreover, it is certain that reindeer breeding was known in Scandinavia in the second half of the ninth century, for at that time Ottar, "who of all Norsemen lived farthest north," owned many reindeer which were presumably tended by Lapp herdsmen. But the southern or woodland Lapps in particular remained essentially huntsmen and fishermen right to the close of the Middle Ages, and even after then their reindeer herds were always small in comparison with those of the mountain Lapps.

We shall not delve into the subject of reindeer domestication here. Suffice to say that it seems to have proceeded at two tempi. The older form was certainly the direct result of the method of hunting, individual reindeer being used as decoys. Gradually they were also used as draft animals for sleighs, in the same way as dogs had long been used. But it was not until much later, under the influence of horse and cattle breeding from the south, that reindeer came to be used as riding and milking animals. This last development evidently came about independently in two widely separated areas —eastern Siberia and Scandinavia. It is significant that Lapp words for such things as milking, etc., evince a long-standing connection with the Scandinavians and that—in contrast to the Siberian Soyot and Tungus—the Lapps never ride on reindeer. Even today there is a considerable difference in the way the reindeer is used by different groups of Lapps. Right down to our own time neither the Russian nor the Finnish Lapps milk their reindeer.

The common basis of reindeer breeding is thus an ancient hunting and fishing culture, and a description of the economic life of the Lapps might most suitably begin by elaborating that.

The Lapps were sustained by hunting wild reindeer, and the methods used were broadly those found throughout the northern coniferous zone, both in Siberia and North America. Right up to the fateful decline in the stock of wild reindeer during the last centuries, hunting survived as a living Stone Age relic, even though iron had come into use for arrow- and spearheads and, later, firearms had been adopted.

The autumn and early winter, when the reindeer were still fat from their plentiful summer food and their skins were most suitable for clothes, was the time of the big collective hunts.

Lines of converging fences, miles in length, still bear witness to the way in which entire herds were driven toward a lake, where the huntsmen lay waiting in boats to turn the lake into a veritable blood bath as the poor beasts tried to swim away. Sometimes the fences ended in a precipice which the animals fell over—sometimes in an enclosure where they became easy prey. Or there were large systems of pitfalls, sometimes with a sharp stone or a spear in the bottom. In the forests snares were hung from trees around the enclosure, or a kind of crossbow was set up which would shoot an arrow into an animal which moved it.

In the rutting season decoy animals were employed—a reindeer cow was tethered in the forest and decoyed wild bulls into close shooting distance. Or a snare was attached to the antlers of a tame reindeer bull so that a wild bull became hopelessly entangled if it engaged in a fight with its rival. In the winter and spring, when the country was covered in deep snow and the reindeer, in spite of their broad hooves, sank through its frozen top surface, the Lapps followed them on skis and shot them with bows and arrows.

One single Lapp bow has been preserved for us. It is slightly longer than a man, and, like the Siberian bows, is made of two strips of birch and spruce glued together. The arrows had heads of reindeer antler or iron and were carried in a skin quiver on the back.

In the forests, elk were also much-prized game. They live in herds only in the winter, and even then never in such numbers as the reindeer. Great collective hunts were thus an impossibility. Many kinds of furry animals were also hunted: beaver, otter, fox, marten, etc. But there are grounds for thinking that this developed to any degree only after fur traders and tax collectors had begun to make an impact on Lapp economy. Evidence that the Lapps knew how to exploit their resources is, however, provided by the big sixth- or seventh-century hoard discovered at Laksefjord, which contained gold and silver objects worth some £ 2,500.

More recently the larger beasts of prey were hunted mainly to protect the reindeer herds from them. The only exception was the bear. This provides another example of an ancient circumpolar culture link. From Lapland to Labrador the bear was considered as being in a class apart. It possessed sacred powers and had to be treated with respect. So the Lapps never spoke of it in ordinary terms. Instead they used words of Norse origin to describe the parts of its body: *fuotte* for foot, *nasek* for nose. Evidently bears could not understand foreign languages! Even the normal term for bear, *bierdna,* was a taboo word (primitive Norse: *bernu*).

But the bear had itself made it clear that it had no objection to being killed provided the proper ritual was observed. The principal method of bear hunting practices by the Lapps was to drive it out of its lair at the onset of winter. Having received due notice of the hunt, the men of the camp made off in solemn procession with their heavy bear spears, the man who discovered the lair going first. He carried a staff fitted with a brass ring—brass possessed magical powers.

When the bear had been killed they struck it with twigs and sang the first part of a hymn in its praise. At one time the meat was cooked and eaten on the spot, but later the carcass was carried back to the camp. But for a whole year afterward no woman was allowed to ride behind the reindeer which had brought it home.

The huntsmen sang all the way back to camp, and as soon as they were within earshot the women made ready to receive it. Dressed in their best clothes they stood in the tents with their backs to the entrance, for the carcass was never allowed to pass through it. In their hands they held a brass ring, and when the men crept in under the tent cover at the back of the tent the women greeted them with songs, peered at them through the brass rings and sprinkled them with the blood-red juice of chewed alder bark, thereby neutralizing the dangerous power of the bear which had been transferred to the huntsmen.

The meat had to be eaten up in a single day with special ceremony. But only certain parts were permitted to the women who, not even daring to touch it with their hands, raised it to their mouth with a stick. During the meal all those present gave expression to their joy by antiphonal singing and by smearing themselves and the tent poles with blood. The bones of the bear had on no account to be broken. They were carefully collected, and to the accompaniment of an incantation, were buried with the snout and tail, a bark vessel of alder juice being placed in front of the snout. The skin was stretched between two trees and then, with eyes blindfolded, the women shot arrows at it, for the husband of the woman who first hit it would kill the next bear. Many other ritual details could be mentioned. Let it merely be added that for three days and nights the hunters had to keep away from their wives. After that they had to run around the fire three times while the women threw ashes on them and sang the concluding verses of the bear song. It was only then that they were sufficiently cleansed to resume normal life.

To the coast Lapps the wealth of sea mammals—the smaller whales, walruses, seals of various kinds, particularly the spotted seal, the gray seal and the saddleback—was of great importance. Among the Kjelmøy treasure are several harpoon heads of reindeer antler, some of them barbed for getting a secure hold on the quarry, others had toggle heads that turned in the wound once the animal had been hit. Seals were also caught in nets or they were killed on shore with a club. Another method of catching is mentioned in Finnmark and the Gulf of Bothnia: when the tide was out a log with strong hooks attached to it was buried in a sand bank where seals had a habit of gathering at high water. Thus they got caught on the hooks.

As already mentioned, reindeer breeding started as an adjunct to the hunting of wild reindeer and several features in the care of domesticated reindeer today still survive from that time, while other less widespread features resulted from the influence of neighboring people. A feature common to all reindeer breeders, both nomadic and seminomadic, is the lassoing of animals—a practice which in fact is nothing but throwing a snare. There is indeed a Lapp tradition that wild reindeer also were caught in this way. The practice of luring reindeer with urine which they like to lick on account of its salt content also probably derives from hunting, and so does enticing them with a smoke fire which keeps the mosquitoes and gadflies at bay. The round pens into which the mountain Lapps drive the reindeer herds in order to sort them out according to their different owners also had their origin with the Lapp hunters. They are made of horizontal untrimmed tree boles and have long converging arms like the enclosures used for deer hunting.

So much for the heritage of hunting. Other old and common features of reindeer breeding proper are earmarking and the castration of draft animals and those intended for slaughter. The usual method of castration, which was preferably carried out just before the rutting season, was for one man to seize the reindeer by the antlers and turn it over on its left side, whereupon another bit its spermatic cords with his teeth and then crushed its sexual glands with his fingers. Castration by knife is probably a more recent method and belongs to the so-called "extensive' method of reindeer breeding practiced by the mountain Lapps—of which more later—and has spread southward with it during the course of the last hundred years.

Slaughtering is carried out by plunging a knife into the beast's heart or neck. This is evidently an old method of slaughtering and has been superseded among some Siberian peoples by strangling.

Reindeer traction, as already mentioned, followed the pattern of dog traction. Evidence of this is the fact that in its original form the harness is clearly derived from the dog harness and is quite different from horse and oxen harnesses. It consists of no more than a loop of skin which is put round the reindeer's neck and then goes down between its front legs where the trace is fastened so that it continues between the hind legs. A broad back girth more or less richly decorated kept the harness in place. It is only recently that this primitive type has been supplanted in many places by a pair of hames. The reins consist of either a single thong or of several strips twisted together and fastened to a noose around the reindeer's forehead.

Various features of the Lapps' reindeer breeding cannot have formed part of their original nomadic life, however, but must be Scandinavian loans. Among these are the use of herd dogs, the pack saddle and—above all—milking and the making of milk products. A pack saddle similar to the one used by the Lapps still occurs on Norse ground in the Faroes. It consists of two thin, curved boards connected above by an ingenious joint ending in a pair of short horns on which the load could be hung and tied together beneath the reindeer's body. Household goods are packed in a kind of oval pannier with sides of wooden chip bent and tied together and a bottom of osier. Around the upper edge of the sides are eyes through which the contents can be lashed.

Milking, which as already mentioned, is not practiced by Finnish and Russian Lapps, is carried out once or twice a day during the summer. A reindeer cow yields less than a quarter of a pint of milk daily—but it has the fat content of cream. To prevent the calves from drinking the milk, the cows' udders are smeared with reindeer manure, or the calves are fitted with a kind of bit to prevent them from sucking. Milking is usually done by women. In the left hand they hold a round, scoop-shaped milk cup hollowed out of birch. Milk that is not drunk immediately, or used for porridge or gruel, is employed in various ways: it is turned sour with the aid of the leaves of common or mountain sorrel; or it is made into dried milk by being poured into a bladder which has fine holes at the bottom so that the whey runs out; or it is churned into butter or made into cheese with the help of rennet. For this, round forms of wood or coiled basketry are used, many of them ornamented so that the finished cheese is attractively decorated in relief. Then it is dried on a slatted shelf in the tent, and afterward the cheeses are drawn in pairs by string to dry them still more. Sometimes they are smoked over the fire.

The methods of reindeer breeding employed by the Lapps varied, of course, according to local conditions and the historical background. This will be sufficiently obvious from the following description of their life during the course of a year.

From the flat and monotonous coast of the Kola Peninsula the country rises westward to the low, fjord-indented mountains of Finnmark. Although the entire country is well inside the Arctic Circle, the climate only borders on the arctic, thanks to the warming effect of the Gulf Stream, which keeps the sea free of ice throughout the winter. Poor drainage and a minimum degree of evaporation in the cool summers result in the northern part of Kola being covered with tundra, bog moss and cotton grass, and it is some way into the interior before woods of low birches and stunted conifers begin to appear.

Many of the present-day coast Lapps, particularly those in Nordland and southern Troms, are descended from former mountain nomads who have lost their reindeer herds, but the nucleus is certainly descended from ancient stock. This particularly applies to the so-called Skolt Lapps in parts of South Varanger and what was once Finnish Petsamo.[2]

The Skolt Lapps are best described as seminomads. Hunting and fishing have always been their principal means of existence. Their reindeer are few in number, and only in more recent times have they begun to keep a few sheep. The hunting ground, the *sijt*, is therefore still the basis of their society. The important thing about the *sijt* is not the geographical concept, not the earth as such, but the right to exploit its stock of game and fish. A number of families are connected with each area, and nowadays the families are not necessarily related. Originally the *sijt* seems to have been exogamous and the kinship system regulated mutual relationships between its members. The heads of the separate households constituted a council which had supreme authority. It was responsible for the distribution of fishing and hunting rights and the return they yielded. The *sijt* members had collective rights in the common fishing grounds in the sea and in the large rivers, and all of them took part in the collective wild reindeer hunts and shared the spoils. Rights in salmon fishing in the lakes were, however, distributed among the families, although with the approval of the council they usually descended from father to son. The same applied to the bear and beaver hunting grounds.

If a member of another *sijt* violated the hunting rights, the matter was not dealt with by the council of the *sijt* whose rights had been violated. Instead, the council complained to

2. When Petsamo became Russian in 1944 after the war between Finland and the Soviet Union, the Skolt Lapps were moved to the Lake Enare district.

the lawbreaker's own council, which then took the matter in hand.

These are the conditions under which the Skolt Lapps' year runs through a constantly recurring cycle, with their habitation shifting according to the season. In the summer, when the sun remains above the horizon for two months on end, they stay by the open sea and fish. Meanwhile the reindeer herds are left to wander at will over the coastal mountains. When the autumn storms make the coast uncomfortable and the night dew softens the reindeer moss in the forests of the hinterland, they move on to the fish spawning grounds in the lakes and rivers. This being the rutting season, the reindeer tend to collect in large herds, and watching over them is therefore comparatively easy. This is also the time when the big collective hunts of wild reindeer take place— or rather, used to take place.

At the end of November the long winter night begins, and the time has come to make for the winter camps, where the deep snow forces the inhabitants to stay quietly indoors and work, while their reindeer remain nearby. Only when the light gradually starts to return once more and the snow is still firm do they start serious hunting once more. Then, before the snow has melted and the ice on the rivers has broken up, they make for their spring grounds up the fjord, where the reindeer calve and there are plenty of opportunities for profitable salmon fishing. And so the year ends by their making once more for the summer ground by the sea.

As already mentioned, the Lapps have disappeared from Finland except in the far north, and of those remaining on Finnish soil a number are descended from Norwegian Lapps who immigrated in the eighteenth century, while others, of Swedish descent, were incorporated into Finland by the Peace Treaty of 1809. Even at that time the original Finnish Lapps, apart from the Skolts, were confined to the region of Lake Enare, whereas formerly they had been distributed over practically the whole of the country. The surface, an old peneplain of pre-Cambrian rocks, gradually falls in level from the north and east down toward the Gulf of Finland and the Gulf of Bothnia. It was furrowed by the ice of bygone ages and later partially covered by moraine gravel, sand eskers, and deposits from the sea. There are thousands of lakes, rivers, and an abundance of pine and spruce forest. On the hills the forests give way to heath and barren land, while stagnant water has turned extensive tracts of the highlands into moorland; no less than a third of the country is bog and marsh.

Like the coast Lapps, the Finnish forest Lapps lead a semi-nomadic existence, with the emphasis on hunting and fishing. Not much is known about the southern groups, which have long since disappeared. But it is possible to piece together a more or less satisfactory picture of the early existence of the northern Finnish Lapps.

They were peculiar in using domesticated reindeer exclusively as draft animals, beasts of burden and decoys, so that they never became numerous, and in leaving them to themselves for much of the year. As with the Skolts, the *sijt* was the basis of society. In the summer, i.e., from the middle of June to the end of July, the reindeer were allowed to roam the forests or the islands in the lakes while their owners fished. Then some of them were brought back for use at the big autumn hunts which lasted until some time in November. During the course of November the rest of the reindeer were caught so that they could take part in the journey to the winter camp where the old people, the women and children, remained until it was time for everyone to move off to the summer fishing grounds. In December and January the men were employed in catching beaver, etc., and in February some of them went to market while others hunted. In the spring the collective wild reindeer hunts took place, and at the end of April the domesticated deer were let loose once more, after which thoughts turned again to the summer move.

The life of the Swedish and Norwegian inland Lapps is considerably different from that of the Finnish Lapps, partly because reindeer milking leads to far more intensive reindeer breeding by the forest Lapps and partly because the mountain Lapps own such enormous herds that they are almost completely dependent on them and must therefore be regarded as true nomads—in the more restricted sense of the term.

The pine forests provided the forest Lapps with a home throughout the year. The same old system of division into

hunting grounds and hunting fellowships exists with them—
as it also does with the mountain Lapps—under the name of
siida. The *siida* comprises a group of families who move
within the same area. The herds belonging to the forest
Lapps seldom contain more than a few hundred beasts—
often fewer—and their wanderings are much more restricted
than those of the mountain Lapps.

The mountain Lapps have aimed at self-sufficiency in their
economy to a far greater extent or at any rate for far longer
than the forest Lapps have done. As an eighteenth-century
Swedish author, writing of the mountain Lapps' reindeer, put
it:

> To the Lapps they are their fields and meadows, their
> horses and cows. From their reindeer they get all that we
> get from the land and the sea, from India and the Levant.

The herds can number many thousand. But the remarkable
thing is that this form of life, so generally regarded as typical,
scarcely goes back further than the sixteenth century, and
came into existence only after the introduction of firearms
had more or less exterminated wild reindeer. It is thus an intensified form of the original Lapp culture, brought about by
the pressure of Scandinavian civilization, and thus in a way
a counterpart of what happened to the Plains Indians. In a
similar way a change in their basic activity radically changed
the social organization. The old idea of joint ownership in
the reindeer herds by the *siida* gave way to ownership by
individual families, and this in turn led to revised ideas on
the concept of reindeer stealing. Furthermore, fully developed nomadism led to a big Lapp advance southward across
the uninhabited mountain plateaus. Incidentally, the principal ways in which the habits of the mountain Lapps differ
from those of the Scandinavian forest Lapps are in the long
treks of the former and in the difference between their spring
and autumn grounds on the one hand and the summer
grounds on the other.

Shortly before the calving season a move is made to the
birch forests of the foothills. At this season trekking has to
be done by night, when the surface of the snow is frozen,

while resting is done by day. About a month and a half is spent at the spring grounds until calving is over and before the plagues of insects and the sun have begun to get too overpowering. Then a move is made to the summer grounds. The most northerly mountain Lapps, in Karesuando and Jukkasjärvi, who have no mountain plateaus available, make their way right down to the Norwegian Coast, where during the summer the reindeer herds can roam the islands and the shut-in valleys in comparative freedom. The more southerly Lapps, on the other hand, make for the mountains and for the pastures above the timber line, where they mark their calves and start milking. Milking is carried out daily in a special pen or in a natural enclosure. So long as the herds are tended in the high mountains there is no need for animals belonging to different owners to be kept apart. In the autumn, after the move down into the birch forests where there are plenty of fungi for them to eat, the reindeer are let loose for the rutting season, which starts at the end of September. A few weeks later, when this is over, the herds are rounded up once more and the big autumn sorting takes place. Meanwhile milking continues and slaughtering is carried out to provide for the following spring. Finally there is the trek into the pine forests, where reindeer moss and beard lichen provide the herds with winter food. Here they stay until it is once more spring.

Means of transport are obviously of prime importance to a people who move about as much as the Lapps do. In the deep winter snow skis are indispensable both to men and women. On rough ground the Lapps are probably unsurpassed as skiers. To help them they have a single stave, with a ring at the bottom to prevent it from sinking into the snow and a narrow shovel at the top which the reindeer herdsman uses to discover what sort of grazing exists beneath the snow. Sometimes he throws a lasso around a reindeer's neck and gets pulled along at a breakneck speed.

In snow reindeer are otherwise mostly used for hauling sleighs. Never more than one reindeer is harnessed to a sleigh —no matter whether it is carrying people or goods. This contrasts with the Samoyeds, who harness several together.

In snowless terrain the reindeer serve as beasts of burden

with pack saddles. An infant having to make the journey is entrusted to an especially reliable animal. It is carefully wrapped in skins and lies in a sort of cradle which is hung onto the saddle. The last reindeer in the procession haul the tent posts, which are tied into two bundles, one on each side of the animal.

To cross waterways the Lapps sometimes make shift with a raft of dry spruce or pine logs. But the Lapps are in fact no mean boat-builders, especially at the coast or near fast-flowing rivers. Their oldest craft was quite certainly of skin, of a type which seems to have been widespread throughout the Arctic. Not only are there quite credible traditions about them, but from Trondheim to the White Sea there are numerous rock engravings which can hardly be construed as anything but pictures of skin boats. And the way the Kola Lapps still sew their plank boats together with sinews is certainly a last survival from them.

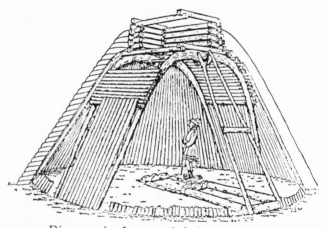

Diagram of a Lapp earth lodge (after Manker).

Everything that the mountain Lapps possessed gradually came to be adapted to facilitate removal, the habitation (*kåhte, goatte*) included. The seminomadic coast and forest Lapps on the other hand spent part of the year in permanent houses. In Finnmark as late as close on the year 1900 it was possible to come across old-fashioned earth lodges which were the original winter habitation of the coast Lapps. The frame consisted of four curved posts facing each other in pairs so that they formed arches. These arches were connected at the top by a ridge pole and farther down the sides by a pair of braces. The lower part of the walls consisted of logs placed close together, which leaned against the braces. The upper part was either of similar construction or consisted of logs placed horizontally. Outside, the whole building was clad first with birch bark and then with sods. In the middle of the house was an open hearth and in the roof above was a smoke hole, which could be closed by means of either a wooden shutter or a pane of bladder skin. No other window existed.

The permanent dwellings of the southern forest Lapps are quite different from those of the coast Lapps. The ground plan is quadrangular or (more rarely) hexagonal. It has a low wall of horizontal logs, and above them rises a high pyramid roof consisting of two layers of upright boards with birch bark between them. In former times they were possibly covered with sods.

There are also various basic types of tent. One of them is exceedingly simple and of a type which is found all over the Arctic, i.e., a conical tent with a frame consisting of three posts forked at the top which are interlocked and which support a number of loosely stacked poles. Over these the tent cover is spread. This was originally of birch bark in the summer and of reindeer skin in the winter; nowadays these have been replaced by ordinary canvas and heavy homespun respectively. This conical tent requires long and comparatively straight posts, so its real home is in the forests and well-wooded valleys, though it does in fact occur all over Lapland, at least as a temporary habitation for reindeer herdsmen and hunters.

Storehouses of various kinds are erected on regularly frequented camping grounds. Things not required for immediate use are put on staging at man's height out of reach of the dogs, whereas supplies of meat are hidden away from wolverines and other animals in a timber box mounted on a single smooth pole as is done in Siberia. Sometimes the box is erected on two or four posts.

Furniture and equipment are as simple as the actual dwelling. The pots—now of metal—hang above the earth. The space behind is used for eating. In olden times it was sacred and was where such things as the shaman's drum were kept. Places near the back wall are still reckoned the most important. Oh both sides of the hearth are places for sleeping, with a thick layer of spruce or birch twigs below and a reindeer skin above. At night the northern Lapps hang a mosquito net of cotton over the bunk. Household goods are few, as befits a nomadic people, and apart from the cheese forms, cheese shelves and cradle already mentioned, comprise no more than one or more oval wooden chests, some food bowls, wooden dishes, etc. Spoons are carved from reindeer antler in medieval Nordic shape with a broad bowl and a short handle. The father of the family prepares the meat and serves it out—a survival from hunting, but this does not imply that the woman's position is lowly. On the contrary, in household matters she has most say.

Apart from the immediate family members, the household often includes a married daughter and son-in-law, it being customary for a newly married couple to live with the bride's parents. It is no doubt a consequence of this that in matters of inheritance the youngest son takes priority over his elder brothers, for they will usually be married and out of the home before the father's death. Marriage between cross-cousins, i.e. between the children of a brother and sister, are common; and as mentioned before it is possible that originally the *siida* was exogamous.

In olden times clothes were always of skin, preferably of reindeer skin, which is both light and warm—necessary virtues in a blizzard or minus 90° F. of frost. Winter clothes are still made of the same material, though for summer wear they have been replaced long ago by woven cloth. Furs are dried and softened by being rubbed with fat made of boiled reindeer hoofs, bones or fish roe, whereas a dehaired skin needs more elaborate treatment. First it is soaked in water until the hairs loosen. Then it is scraped with an S-shaped iron scraper fastened to the middle of a wooden handle which is held in both hands—a common Siberian type, incidentally. After being scraped it is put in a decoction of bark—birch, willow or alder—alder if the skin is to be dyed red. After renewed drying it is rubbed with fat and finally made pliable by being drawn backward and forward over an iron hoop which is fastened to a tree or to a tent post. Sinews twined on the knee or cheek are used for sewing. Weaving is a Scandinavian or more probably a Finnish loan. The coastal Lapps used to have a real old-fashioned upright loom. Ribbon weaving is widespread. For this a gridlike implement of reindeer antler or bone is used, and the women make such things as belts and shoelaces on it in the most attractive designs.

Clothing is more or less the same for both men and women and in spite of Nordic influences displays an obvious connection with ancient arctic types of clothing. The basic garment is the simple poncho, consisting of a loosely draped skin with a hole for the head. To this day a poncho made out of bear-cub skin is worn above the normal clothing by reindeer herdsmen who have to be out in the extreme cold.

Trousers, which are similar for both sexes, are so short in the body that they do not reach above the hips and are so narrow that slits are necessary at the bottom. But while there is only one basic type of jacket, there are two distinct types of cut in the trousers. Those worn by the southern Lapps seem to have developed from a long pair of gaiters like Indian leggings which are sewn together with a median seam. Those worn by the northern Lapps, on the other hand, have side seams and must be derived from what was once a breech-cloth.

Nowadays all the Lapps are Christian—the Scandinavians Lutheran, the Skolts and Kola Lapps Greek-Catholic. Missions started up in a small way in the Middle Ages, but they only really got going in Scandinavia in the seventeenth and, especially, in the eighteenth centuries. In the beginning the most successful was the Orthodox church, for the Russian popes were considerably more liberal than the zealous Lutherans, and quite a number of Scandinavian Lapps crossed the border in consequence. What most interests us, however, is their original religion—ancient shamanism with its tinge of Asia. Among the Scandinavian Lapps it also contained a well-defined strain of old Norse mythology and to a certain extent even in heathen times included some Christian ideas. Curiously enough it is obviously deeply rooted in hunting life, whereas nomadism has had little influence.

According to ancient Lapp ideas, nature was alive just as man was, and contained forces with which it was essential to be on good terms but over which it was also possible to gain power. Danger from bears could be counterbalanced by the careful observance of the hunting rites and a hunter could make certain of a good bag by magical means by engraving pictures of his quarry on rocks situated in places favorable to hunting. Any number of such Stone Age pictures exist right from the Atlantic coast through Russia to Siberia. Trees too contained a soul. It is said that when the Finnish Lapps prepared to fell a tree, they would first knock on the trunk to waken this soul; then they chopped off the lowest branch to provide a place of refuge for it. Certain lakes, curiously shaped rocks, or a stone in the apparent likeness of an animal or a man—all such *seides* contained sacred power, and sacrifices were made to them so that the reindeer would multiply and other good fortune ensue. Hundreds of such cult sites have been found, together with piles of antlers from sacrificed reindeer and occasionally a roughly carved wooden figure.

Under the earth there was another world of its own—the *saivo* land—and this was an exact counterpart of our world, where the departed lived a life of bliss together with their reindeer herds, for death did not mean an end of existence. There are also references to a kind of Land of the Dead, *Jabmi-Aimo*. What the connection was between this and the *saivo* land is not quite clear, and it was not perhaps entirely clear to the Lapps either. Sufficient to say that the dead were dangerous, and sometimes they inflicted sickness on the living by stealing their souls. Everything to do with the dead had therefore to be dealt with extremely carefully. When a corpse was buried it was enclosed in birch bark or laid in a sleigh or in a simple coffin of a hollowed-out tree trunk. Three days later the reindeer who had hauled the sleigh was sacrificed at the grave, where its meat was eaten

by the deceased's kin and its bones buried. Each year for
three years afterwards a reindeer was sacrificed at the grave.

In addition to the semi-impersonal beings and forces there
were others which had the character of deities proper. Some
of them are also to be found among other Finno-Ugrian
tribes and among the Samoyeds. Others have been adopted
from old Norse mythology and have partly merged with the
older deities. Jubmal, corresponding to the Finnish Jumala,
was considered supreme among the gods by Finnish Lapps,
just as Radien was by the Swedish Lapps. Possibly there is
at bottom some ancient element in this conception of him,
but obviously there has been some Christian influence too.
Beneath him were other deities who controlled the winds,
game, fish and so on. The most important was Tirmes or
Dierbmes, the God of Thunder. In Scandinavia he was
identified with Thor, was in fact called Horagalles, derived
from Thor-Karlen, i.e., the "Thor-Man," and was represented
carrying a hammer in his hand.

Confronted with all these powers, man was small and
feeble, and when dangers threatened it was essential to know
their will. The father of each family had his drum, which he
used in order to find out from which deity he should seek
help on each separate occasion. These drums, of which quite
a large number are still preserved, occur in two forms. One
of them, belonging to the southern Lapps, has a ring-
shaped frame like the usual circumpolar type, the other,
which is northern, has a bowl-shaped bottom. Pictures of
gods, sacrificial animals and the like were painted in the
sacred juice of the alder on the drum skin. Normally the
drum was kept in the sacred space behind the hearth, and
on journeys it was carried in the last sleigh, for no woman
was allowed to cross its path. It was played by a small
hammer of bone and this caused a ring or some other small
brass object which was laid on the skin to move about
among the figures, and from the path it took the will of the
gods was deduced. If this did not suffice, reference was
made to the *noaidde*, the counterpart of the Siberian
shaman. The monotonous sound of the drum so worked on
the *noaidde*'s nerves that finally he was lost in ecstasy. While
he lay unconscious his soul traveled among the *saivo* people

with his spirit helpers, who had either come to him of their
own free will or had been inherited from former colleagues.
In the *saivo* country there were also a number of animals at
his disposal. With his magic reindeer he could fight an
adversary's reindeer and nullify unfriendly intentions. The
Scandinavian peoples greatly feared the Lapps for their
witchcraft, and as early as the thirteenth century in *Historia
Norvegiae* there is a description of one of their shamanistic
seances. Evidence that shamanistic ideas were at the heart of
their religion appears from the fact that they have persisted
under a veneer of Christianity right down to quite recent
times.

Thus a clear picture of Lapp culture emerges—a culture
influenced by local conditions on an ancient circumpolar
foundation. This same foundation is recognizable in the
Eskimo culture, but whereas the path of development there
is toward increasing dependence on the sea, with the Lapps
it has gone in the opposite direction—toward the forests and
from there up into the mountains.

But now a new factor, also based on geography, comes
into play—namely, the proximity of the Lapps to the Scandinavian agricultural and cattle-breeding culture. It was this
factor alone which enabled the Lapps to take the final step
from seminomadism—and contained dependence on hunting
—to the fully developed nomadic life entirely dependent on
the reindeer herd. The impulse to this came only with the
disappearance of wild reindeer. From this followed the need
to abandon all forms of permanent dwelling and the use of
the tent as the only habitation. Other ways in which the
Scandinavian peoples influenced the Lapps—in dress, for
example, in religion, and, by no means least, in language—
have already been demonstrated. The language influence has
been so strong that the extent of the Scandinavian component in the culture has often been exaggerated by linguists.
From the form of the words it evidently goes back to
primitive Norse times, i.e., to A.D. 300–800. From that time
onward cultural influences have steadily continued through
the Viking period and the Middle Ages right down to our
own day, when, in spite of clinging stubbornly to their

language and to some degree also to their peculiar way of life, the Lapps are gradually merging more and more into Scandinavian, and thus into European, society.

There formerly existed a number of tribes, collectively named the Tupinamba, who occupied the lower Amazon and the Brazilian coast from the mouth of the river to Uruguay. During the period following the arrival of the Portuguese, they migrated to Eastern Paraguay, Bolivia, Peru, and the upper reaches of the Amazon, possibly in quest of a land of immortality. They were farmers, fishermen, and warriors, engaging in constant intertribal combat and torturing and eating their captives. The Portuguese invaders were of course their mortal enemies. They are now almost extinct, but a picture of the lives they led is given in an account published in 1557 and written by a young German named Hans Staden whom they captured in 1549 near what is now the city of Santos, Brazil.

Paul Radin quotes from this account in his Indians of South America. Staden had gone to Brazil in the employ of Portuguese colonists. On being captured he was destined by the Tupinamba, in their usual manner, to be eaten at a feast. He protested that he was a German and not a Portuguese, but his pleas were unavailing and he had already been shaved in preparation for roasting when one of his captors became ill. Staden, by a laying on of hands, was given credit for having effected a cure. As a result of this miraculous feat, he was spared to write an account of his adventures, from which the following excerpt is taken. Many contemporary descriptions of tribes in the process of dissolution will have similar historical value for future generations of anthropologists.

THE TUPINAMBA

HANS STADEN

AMERICA IS a large country inhabited by many tribes of savages who speak several different languages, and there are many curious beasts there. It is a pleasant country to look at, the trees are always green, but there is no wood there like our wood, and the savages are naked.

There is a range of mountains which reaches to within three miles of the sea, more or less, and begins to rise in the neighborhood of Boiga de Todolos Sanctus, which was built by the Portuguese who inhabit there. The range of mountains runs beside the sea for about twenty miles, in latitude twenty-nine degrees south of the equinoctial line, and is in places eight miles from the sea-ports. The land on both sides is similar. Many beautiful rivers flow from these mountains, and there is an abundance of wild life in the heights.

A nation of savages lives on the mountains called *Wayganna*, and these savages have no fixed dwellings like the other nations living on either side of the mountains. The Wayganna wage war against the others, and when they capture them they eat them. This practice is also followed by their enemies. The Wayganna are great hunters in the mountains and are very skillful in shooting game with their bows, and have much cunning in the use of slings and traps, wherewith to take the animals. There is an abundance of wild honey in the mountains, which they eat, and they learn the cries of the beasts and the notes of the birds in order to track and shoot them. They make fire like the other savages with two pieces of wood, and roast their meat before eating. They carry their wives and children about with them.

When they set up their camps close to the enemy's country, they surround the huts with hedges, so that they cannot be surprised, and to protect themselves also against wild beasts. They surround the camp with sharp thorns just as with us one lays down foot-hooks, and this they do for fear of their enemies. All night long they burn their fires, but they extinguish them by day, so that none may see the smoke and track them.

They wear their hair long, and allow their fingernails to grow to a great length. They have rattles called *maraka*, like the other savages, which they look upon as their gods, and they have their own dances and drinking ceremonies. They use the teeth of wild beasts as knives and chop with stone wedges, as did also the other savages before they commenced to trade with the ships.

They make constant war upon their enemies, and when they want to capture them they hide behind the dry wood near to the huts, so that when anyone comes to take wood they can fall upon him.

They treat their enemies with great cruelty and receive the same treatment when they are captured. For example, such is their hate that they often cut off an arm or leg from a living prisoner. Others they kill, before they cut them up for eating.

These people have their dwelling close by the sea, in front of the range of mountains of which I have spoken. Their dwellings extend also some sixty miles inland behind the mountains, and a river flows down from the hills to the sea, on the banks of which they also have a settlement called Paraeibe. They have settlements as well for some twenty-eight miles along the sea shore, and on all sides they are encompassed by their enemies. To the north they are bounded by a nation of savages called *Weittaka* who are their enemies. On the south are the *Tuppin Ikin*. On the land side their enemies are called *Karaya*, while the Way-ganna inhabit the mountains, and between these two are the savages called *Markaya*. These tribes harass them greatly and make war also among themselves, and when they capture one of the others they eat him.

They prefer to set up their dwellings in places where they have wood, water, and game and fish close at hand. When they have exhausted one place they move to another, and their manner of settling is this. A chief among them collects a party of forty men and women, as many as he can get, and these are usually friends and relations. They set up their huts, which are about fourteen feet wide and quite 150 feet long, according to the number of those who are to inhabit them. These huts are about twelve feet high and are round at the top and vaulted like a cellar. They roof them closely with the branches of palms to keep out the rain. Inside, the huts are all one: no one has a separate chamber to himself. Each couple, man and wife, has a space in the hut on one side, the space measuring about twelve feet, and on the other side lives another couple, and so the hut is filled, each couple having its own fire. The chief of the huts has his dwelling in the center. The huts have generally three doors, one at each end, and the other in the middle, and the doors are so low that the people have to stoop to get in or out. Few of the villages have more than seven huts. Between the huts is a space where they knock their prisoners on the head.

The savages fortify their huts as follows. They make a stockade of palm trees, which they first split and then set up to a height of about nine feet. This they build so thickly that no arrow can pierce it, but they leave little holes here and there through which they can shoot. Outside this stockade they build another of higher stakes, which they set up close together, but so that the space between them is not sufficient for a man to creep through. Among certain of the savages it is the custom to set up the heads of the men they have eaten on the stockade at the entrance to the huts.

They sleep in things which are called in their language *Inni*. They are made of cotton yarn, and they tie them to two poles above the ground, and at night they burn their fires beside them. They do not willingly go out of their huts at night for any reason without fire, so greatly are they in awe of their devil whom they call *Ingange*, and whom they often see.

Wherever they go, whether in the forest or on the water, they are never without their bows and arrows. When in the forest they are perpetually watching, with eyes raised towards the trees, and when they hear the noise of birds, monkeys, or other animals in the trees they know well how to shoot them, following them unceasingly until they are successful. It seldom happens that a man returns empty-handed from hunting.

In the same way they take the fish by the sea shore. They have keen sight, and as soon as a fish jumps they shoot and seldom miss. When they have hit the fish they jump into the water and swim after it. Some large fish, on feeling the arrow, sink to the bottom, but the savages will dive to a depth of well-nigh six fathoms to get them. They use also small nets which they make out of long pointed leaves called *tockaun,* and when they fish with nets several gather together, each man having his own station where the water is shallow, and they beat the water, driving the fish down into the nets. He who catches the greatest number divides his catch with his fellows.

It happens at times that those who live at a distance from the sea come down to catch fish which they bake until they are hard, after which they pound them into a kind of meal. This meal when dried lasts a long time, and they carry it back with them to their homes and eat it with roots. Otherwise, if they took the baked fish home, it would not keep for long, since they do not salt it. Also the meal goes further than the fish if baked whole.

The women prepare the drinks. They take the mandioca root and boil it in great pots. Afterwards they pour it into other vessels and allow it to cool a little. Then young girls sit round and chew the boiled root in their mouths, and what is chewed they set apart in a special vessel. When the boiled root is all chewed, they place it back again in the pot which they fill with water, mixing the water with the chewed root, after which they heat it again.

They have special pots, half buried in the ground, which they make use of much as we use casks for wine or beer. They pour the liquid into these and close them, and the liquor ferments of itself and becomes strong. After two days they drink it until they are drunken. It is thick, but pleasant to the taste.

Each hut prepares its own drink, and when the whole village desires to make merry, which happens generally about once a month, they go first of all together into one hut and drink there until the drink is finished. Then they go to the round of the other huts, drinking until they have drunk their fill and there is nothing left.

When they drink they gather round the pots and sit, some on the fire-sticks, others on the ground. The drink is served by the women in a very orderly manner. The drinkers sing and dance round the pots, and on the spot where they drink they pass their water.

The drinking lasts all night, the merry-makers continuing to dance between the fires, with shouting and blowing of trumpets, and when they are drunken the noise is terrible; but they quarrel little. They are also generously disposed, and when a man has more food than his fellow he shares it with him.

The men have a bare space on the head with a circle of hair around it like a monk. I asked them frequently from what they took this fashion, and they told me that their forefathers had seen it on a man called Meire Humane, who had worked many miracles among them, and this man is supposed to have been a prophet or one of the Apostles.

I asked them further how they contrived to cut the hair before the ships brought them scissors, and they told me that they used a stone wedge with another instrument underneath and so cut off the hair. The bare space in the middle they make with a scraper of transparent stone which they use frequently for shearing. They have also a thing made of red feathers called *kannittare*, which they bind round the head.

They have a large hole in the lower lip which they make when they are young. They take the children and prick the hole with a sharpened deer's horn. In this they insert a small piece of stone or wood and anoint it with salve, and the hole remains open. Then when the children are fully grown and fit to bear arms they enlarge the hole and insert in it a large green stone. This stone is shaped so that the smaller end is inside the lip and the larger end outside. The result is that their lips hang down with the weight of the stones. They have also at both sides of the mouth, and in either cheek, other small stones. Some of these are of crystal and are narrow and long. They wear also ornaments made from large snail-shells called *Mattepue*. These ornaments are shaped like a half-moon, and they hang them round the neck. They are snow-white and are called Bogesso.

There is no community of goods among them and they know nothing of money. Their treasures are the feathers of birds. He that has many feathers is rich, and he that has a stone in his lip is also counted among the rich.

Each couple has a particular plantation of roots which supplies both man and wife with food.

Their greatest honor is to capture their enemies and to slay them; for such is their custom. And for every foe a man kills he takes a new name. The most famous among them is he that has the most names.

They put their faith in a thing shaped like a pumpkin, the size of a pint pot. It is hollow within, and they put a stick through it and cut a hole in it like a mouth, filling it with small stones so that it rattles. They shake it about when they sing and dance, and call it *tammaraka*, and each man has one of his own.

There are certain wise ones among them called *paygi*, who are looked up to as soothsayers are with us. These men travel every year throughout the whole country, visiting all the huts and saying that a spirit has been with them from afar off, and that this spirit has endued them with power to cause all the rattling tammaraka chosen by them to speak and grow so powerful that they can grant whatever is required of them. Then each man desires that his tammaraka should have this virtue, and a great feast is prepared, with drinking, singing, and prophesying, and many other strange ceremonies. The wise men then ordain a day, and fix upon one of the huts which they cause to be cleared, no woman or child being suffered to remain there, and they direct that each man shall paint his tammaraka red and decorate it with feathers, and come to the place so that this power of speech may be conferred upon them. After this they all go to the hut, and the wise men sit down at the upper end, each one having his own tammaraka on the ground before him. The others place theirs also there, and each one offers a present to the wise men, such as arrows, feathers, and ornaments for the ears. . . . Then he (the paygi) seizes the rattle by the mouth, shaking it and saying: "Now speak and let us hear you: are you within?" Then he speaks a word or two softly so that one cannot know whether it is he that speaks or the rattle: but the people imagine that the rattle is speaking. Nevertheless, it is the wise man that speaks, and so he does with all the rattles one after the other. Each one then thinks that great virtue has entered into his rattle, and the wise men command them to make war and take many enemies, since the spirit in the tammaraka craves for the flesh of prisoners, and so the people set off to war.

After the paygi (or wise men) have changed the rattles into gods, each man takes his rattle away, calling it his beloved son, and building a hut apart in which to place it, setting food before it and praying to it what he desires, just as we pray to the true God. These rattles are their gods, for they know nothing of the true God, the maker of heaven and earth, believing that the earth and the heavens have existed from the beginning of time. Beyond this they know nothing of the creation of the world.

They say that once upon a time there was a great flood which drowned all their ancestors, save those that escaped in canoes or on to the tops of high trees. This I imagine must have been the Deluge.

When I first came into their hands, and they told me about the rattles, I thought there must be a devil's spirit in them, for they said that they spoke often. But when I went to the huts where the wise men sat to make the rattles speak, and saw their tricks, and that everyone had to sit down apart, I went away marvelling at the simplicity of the people and the ease with which they were beguiled.

They go first to a hut and take all the women, one after another, and fumigate them. After this the women have to jump and yell and run about until they become so exhausted that they fall down as if they were dead. Then the soothsayer says: "See now, she is dead; but I will bring her to life again." After the woman has come to herself they say that she is able to foretell future things, and when the men go out to war the women have to prophesy concerning it.

At one time the wife of the king to whom I had been

presented to be killed began to prophesy and told her husband that a spirit had come to her from far away enquiring
concerning me, when I was to be killed, and as to the club
with which I was to be knocked on the head, and where it
was. The king replied that it would not be long and that all
was prepared, only he was afraid I was not a Portuguese,
but a Frenchman. Afterwards I asked the woman why she
desired my death, seeing that I was no enemy, and whether
she was not afraid that my God would punish her? She
replied that I must not be troubled since they were only
strange spirits seeking news of men. They have many ceremonies of this nature.

They eat one another not from hunger, but from great
hate and jealousy, and when they are fighting with each
other one, filled with hate, will call out to his opponent:
"Cursed be you, my meat." "Today will I cut off your head."
"Now am I come to take vengeance on you for the death of
my friends." "This day before sunset your flesh shall be my
roast meat." All this they do from their great hatred.

When they desire to make war in an enemy's country the
chiefs gather together and take counsel how best to achieve
their purpose, all which they make known in the huts, so
that the men may arm themselves. They name the time of
the ripening of a certain fruit as the date of their departure,
for they have not the art to reckon by the day or year. They
also fix their expeditions by the time of the spawning of a
fish called *pratti* in their tongue, and the spawning time they
call *pirakaen*. Then they equip themselves with canoes and
arrows, and lay in stores of dried root-meal. After this they
enquire of the paygi, their wise men, whether they shall
return victorious. These will say "Yes," but will warn the
enquirers to note well their dreams when they dream of
their foes. If many dream that they are roasting their
enemy's flesh, that signifies victory. But if it is their own flesh
which they see in the pot, that is an evil omen and they had
better stay at home. If their dreams are propitious they arm
themselves and prepare much drink in the huts, after which
they dance and drink with their idols, the tammaraka, each
one beseeching his idol to assist him in catching an enemy.
Then they set out, and when they draw near to the enemy's

country, on the night before the attack, the chiefs once more direct their men to remember their dreams.

I accompanied them in one of their expeditions, and on the night before they intended to attack, when we were close to the enemy's country the chief went up and down in the camp, telling the men to note well their dreams that night, and ordering the young men to set off at daybreak to hunt for game and catch fish, which was done, and the food was cooked. Then the chief summoned the other chiefs to his hut and when they were all seated upon the ground in a circle he gave them to eat, after which they all told their dreams, that is, such dreams as were favorable, and then they danced and made merry with the tammaraka. They spy out the enemy's hut at night and attack at dawn.

If they take a prisoner who is badly wounded they kill him at once and carry home the meat roasted. Those that are un-wounded they take back alive and kill them in the huts. They attack with loud yells, stamping on the ground, and blowing blasts upon trumpets made of gourds. They all carry cords bound about their bodies to make fast their prisoners, and adorn themselves with red feathers so that they may distinguish their friends from their foes. They shoot very rapidly and send fire-arrows into the enemy's huts to set them alight. And if they are wounded they have their special herbs with them to heal their wounds.

In a physical environment markedly different from that of the Lapps, there survives a race whose existence has captured the imagination of civilized man. This race, the pygmies of Congolese Africa, has loomed large in legend and literature. The question of whether the pygmies are actually human or subhuman has sometimes been raised. (It has been stated that the Negroes who occupy the same territory recognize four orders of living beings: people, pygmies, chimpanzees, and other animals.) The pygmies, however, are undoubtedly human beings. On occasion, Negroes marry pygmy women and the marriages result in children. While the mothers are considered of an inferior race, the children are treated by the Negroes like others of the tribe.

Anthropologists had long assumed that these primitive peoples live in a kind of symbiotic relationship with their Negro neighbors, based on the exchange of meat, honey, and wild fruits for plantains, ax blades, knives, and the like. The relationship between a specific pygmy family on the one hand and a specific Negro family on the other was thought to be very close, a break in this relationship constituting a sort of divorce accompanied by hard feeling and even warfare. It is Turnbull's thesis that such a relationship does not exist, that the pygmies have deceived observers and that they are truly children of the forest who have found it possible to exist satisfactorily with only a minimum of dependence on more civilized neighbors.

Colin M. Turnbull came to his interest in anthropology by way of the study of language and music. He took a degree at Oxford, studied Hindi and Sanskrit at the University of London and later in India. Returning to England by way of Africa, he was introduced to the pygmy culture by Patrick Putnam, an anthropologist who lived in Africa for many years. He became interested first in pygmy music and then in the culture as a whole. In pursuit of this study he became associated first with the Royal Anthropological Institute and then with the Museum of Natural History in New York, where he is now assistant curator of African ethnology. He is the author of The Forest People, an account of his life among the pygmies.

THE LESSON OF THE PYGMIES

COLIN M. TURNBULL

IN THE WELTER of change and crisis confronting the lives of the peoples of Africa it would seem difficult to work up concern for the fate of the 40,000 Pygmies who inhabit the rain forests in the northeastern corner of the Congo. The very word "pygmy" is a term of derogation. According to early explorers and contemporary anthropologists, the Pygmies have no culture of their own—not even a language. They became submerged, it is said, in the village customs and beliefs of the Bantu and Sudanic herdsmen—cultivators who occupied the periphery of the forest and reduced them to a kind of serfdom some centuries ago. By the testimony of colonial administrators and tourists they are a scurvy lot: thievish, dirty and shrouded with an aura of impish deviltry. Such reports reflect in part the sentiments of the village tribes; in many villages the Pygmies are regarded as not quite people.

To argue that the Pygmies are people—even to show that they maintain to this day the integrity of an ancient culture —will not avert or temper the fate that is in prospect for them. The opening of the rain forests of Central Africa to exploitation threatens to extinguish them as a people. The Pygmies are, in truth, *bamiki nde ndura:* children of the forest. Away from the villages they are hunters and food gatherers. The forest provides them with everything they need, generally in abundance, and enables them to lead an egalitarian, cooperative and leisured existence to which evil, in the sense of interpersonal malevolence, is so foreign that they have no word for it. After centuries of contact with the "more advanced" cultures of the villages and in spite of all appearances, their acculturation to any other mode of life remains almost nil. They have fooled the anthropologists as they have fooled the villagers. For this reason if for no other, the Pygmies deserve the concerned attention of the world outside. Their success should make us pause to reconsider the depth of acculturation that we have taken for granted as existing elsewhere, as industrial civilization has made its inexorable conquest of the earth.

The reason for the prevailing erroneous picture of the Pygmies is now clear. It has hitherto been generally impossible to have access to them except through the offices of the village headman, who would call the local Pygmies in from the forest to be interviewed. To all appearances they lived in some sort of symbiosis, if not serfdom, with the village people, subject to both the secular and the religious authority of the village. The fact that Pygmy boys undergo the village ritual of initiation in a relation of subservience to village boys was cited as evidence of ritual dependence, and it has been held that the Pygmies are economically dependent on the villages for metal and for plantation foods, presumably needed to supplement the meat they hunt in the forest. The few investigators who got away from the villages did not manage to do so without an escort of villagers, acting as porters or guides. Even in the forest the presence of a single villager transforms the context as far as the Pygmies are concerned; therefore all such observations were still basically of Pygmies in the village, not in their natural habitat.

My own initial impression was just as erroneous. By good fortune my contact with the Pygmies circumvented the village and was established from the outset on a basis that identified me with the world of the forest. Seeing them almost exclusively in the context of the forest, I saw a picture diametrically opposed to the one generally drawn. Instead of dependence, I saw at first independence of the village, a complete lack of acculturation—in fact, little contact of any kind. It was only after two additional stays in the Ituri Forest, the home ground of the Congo Pygmies, that I was able to put the two contradictory pictures of their life together and to see the whole. It turned out that neither is wrong; each is right in its particular context. The relation of the Pygmies to the villagers is a stroke of adaptation that has served their survival and even their convenience without apparent compromise of the integrity of their forest-nurtured culture.

The BaMbuti, as the Pygmies of the Ituri Forest are known to themselves and to their neighbors, may be the original inhabitants of the great stretch of rain forest that reaches from the Atlantic coast right across Central Africa to the open grassland country on the far side of the chain of great lakes that divides the Congo from East Africa. Their origin, along with that of Negrito peoples elsewhere in the world, is lost in the prehistoric past. Most Pygmies have unmistakable features other than height (they average less than four and a half feet) that distinguish them from Negroes. They are well-muscled, usually sway-backed and have legs that are short in proportion to their torsos. Their faces, with wide-set eyes and flat, broad noses, have a characteristically alert expression, direct and unafraid, as keen as the attitude of the body, which is always poised to move with speed and agility at a moment's notice. They do not envy their neighbors, who jeer at them for their puny stature; in the enclosure of the forest, where life may depend on the ability to move swiftly and silently, the taller Negroes are as clumsy as elephants. For his part the Pygmy hunter wins his spurs by killing an elephant, which he does by running underneath the animal and piercing its bladder with a succession of quick jabs from a short-shafted spear.

A BaMbuti hunting band may consist of as many as thirty families, more than one hundred men, women and children in all. On the move from one encampment to another they fill the surrounding forest with the sound of shouted chatter, laughter and song. Along with the venting of high spirits, this ensures that lurking leopards and buffaloes will be flushed into the forest well ahead of the band and not be accidentally cornered on the trail. The women, carrying or herding the infants, dart from the trail to gather food, and the men scout the forests for game on the flanks and in the van of the ragged procession. Arriving at the campsite in no particular order, all join in the task of building huts. The men usually cut the saplings to make the frames and sometimes also the giant Phrynium leaves to cover them; the women take charge of the actual building. The saplings are driven securely into the ground around a ten-foot circle, then deftly bent and intertwined to form a lattice dome; on this structure the leaves are hung like shingles, in overlapping tiers. Before nightfall, with the first arrivals helping the stragglers to complete their tasks, the camp is built and the smoke of cooking fires rises into the canopy of the forest. The entire enterprise serves to demonstrate a salient feature of BaMbuti life: everything gets done with no direction and with no apparent organization.

A morning is usually all that is needed to secure the supply for food. The women know just where to look for the wild fruits that grow in abundance in the forest, although they are hidden to outsiders. The women recognize the undistinguished *itaba* vine, which leads to a cache of nutritious, sweet-tasting roots, the kind of weather that brings mushrooms springing to the surface; the exact moment when termites swarm and must be harvested to provide an important delicacy. The men hunt with bows and poison-tipped arrows, with spears for larger game and with nets. The last involves the Pygmy genius for co-operation. Each family makes and maintains its own net, four feet high and many yards long. Together they string the nets across a strategically chosen stretch of ground. The hunters, often joined by the women and older children, beat the forest, driving the game into the nets.

By afternoon they have brought enough food into camp and sometimes a surplus that will enable them to stay in camp the next day. Time is then spent repairing the nets, making new bows and arrows, baskets and other gear and performing various other chores. This still leaves a fair amount of free time, which is spent, apart from eating and sleeping, either in playing with the children and teaching them adult activities or in gathering in impromptu groups for song and dance.

The BaMbuti have developed little talent in the graphic arts beyond the occasional daubing of a bark cloth with red or blue dye, smeared on with a finger or a twig. They do, however, have an intricate musical culture. Their music is essentially vocal and noninstrumental. It displays a relatively complex harmonic sense and a high degree of rhythmic virtuosity. With the harmony anchored in the dominant and therefore all in one chord, the singing is often in canon form, with as many parts as there are singers and with improvisa-tions and elaborations contributed freely by each. A song may have some general meaning, but it may also be totally devoid of words and consist simply of a succession of vowel sounds. The real meaning of the song, its importance and power, is in the sound. In the crisis festival of the *molimo,* the closest approximation to a ritual in the unformalized life of the BaMbuti, the men of the band will sing, night after night, through the night until dawn. The function of the sound now is to "awaken the forest" so that it will learn the plight of its children or hear of their joy in its bounty.

The spirit of cooperation, seen in every activity from hunting to singing, takes the place of formal social organization in the BaMbuti hunting band. There is no headman, and individual authority and individual responsibility are shunned by all. Each member of the band can expect and demand the cooperation of others and must also give it. In essence the bonds that make two brothers hunt together and share their food are not much greater than those that obtain between a member of a band and a visiting Pygmy, even if he is totally unrelated. Any adult male is a father to any child; any woman, a mother. They expect the same help and respect from all children and they owe the same responsibilities toward them.

When the Pygmies encamp for a while near a village, the character of the band and its activities undergo profound and complete transformation. This happens even when a lone villager pays a visit to a Pygmy camp. Not only do such activities as singing and dancing and even hunting change, but so also does the complex of interpersonal relations. The Pygmies then behave toward each other as they would if they were in a village. They are no longer a single, united hunting band, cooperating closely, but an aggregate of individual families, with which there may even be disunity. On periodic visits to the village with which their hunting band is associated, the Pygmies occupy their own semi-permanent campsite between the village and the forest. Each family usually has a particular village family with which it maintains a loose and generally friendly exchange relation. At such times the Pygmies not only supply meat, they may also supply some labor. Their main function, as the villagers see it, is to provide such forest products as meat, honey and the leaves and saplings needed for the construction of village houses. The villagers do not like the forest and go into it as seldom as possible.

It is on these occasions that travelers have seen the Pygmies and decided that they are vassals to the villagers, with no cultural identity of their own. It is true that this is how the BaMbuti appear while they are in the villages, because in this foreign world their own code of behavior does not apply. In the village they behave with a shrewd sense of expediency. It in no way hurts them to foster the villagers' illusion of domination; it even helps to promote favorable economic relations. As far as the BaMbuti are concerned, people who are not of the forest are not people. The mixture of respect, friendship and cunning with which they treat their village neighbors corresponds to the way they treat the animals of the forest: they use them as a source of food and other goods, respecting them as such and treating them with tolerant affection when they are not needed. The Pygmies have a saying that echoes the proverb of the goose and the golden egg, to the effect that they never completely and absolutely eat the villagers, they just eat them.

In the mistaken interpretations of this peculiar relation the fact that the Pygmies seem to have lost their original language is often cited as evidence of their acculturation to the village. Linguists, on the other hand, see nothing surprising in this fact. Small, isolated hunting bands, caught up in the intertribal competition that must have attended the Bantu invasion that began half a millennium ago, could well have lost their own language in a couple of generations. It is by no means certain, however, that the Pygmy language is extinct. Certain words and usages appear to be unique to the Pygmies and do not occur in the languages and dialects of any of the numerous neighboring tribes. What is more, the Pygmies' intonation is so distinctive, no matter which of the languages they are speaking, as to render their speech almost unintelligible to the villager whose language it is supposed to be.

Some authorities maintain that the Pygmies rely on the villagers for food and metal. As for food, my own experience has shown that the BaMbuti hunting bands are perfectly capable of supporting themselves in the forest without any help from outside. The farther away from the villages they are, in fact, the better they find the hunting and gathering. If anything, it is the villagers who depend on the Pygmies, particularly for meat to supplement their protein-deficient diet.

It is more difficult to determine to what extent the BaMbuti are dependent on village metal. A few old men speak of hardening the points of their wooden spears in fire, and children's spears are still made in this way. Except for elephant hunting the spear is mostly a defensive weapon, and the loss of metal spear blades would not be serious. Knife and ax blades are more important; the word *machetti* —for the long, heavy-bladed brush-slashing knife—is well established in the Pygmy vocabulary. There are thorny vines, however, that can serve adequately as scrapers and others that when split give a sharp if temporary cutting edge, like that of split bamboo. When I have pressed the question, it has been stated to me that, in the absence of metal blades, "we would use stones." On the other hand, I have never succeeded in persuading a Pygmy to show me how. The answer to such a request was invariably: "Why should I go to all that trouble when it is so easy to get metal tools from the villagers?"

This is in fact the core of the Pygmies' economic relation with the villagers, and it renders the term "symbiosis" in-applicable. There is nothing they need badly enough to make them dependent on the villagers, although they use many artifacts acquired from them. Metal cooking utensils are a good example: the Pygmies can get along without these comfortably. They use them only for the cooking of village foods that require boiling, such as rice; forest foods call for no such utensils. The BaMbuti will exchange goods with the villagers and even work for them, but only as long as it suits their convenience and no longer. No amount of per-suasion will hold them. If a villager attempts coercion, the Pygmy simply packs up and goes back to the forest, secure in the knowledge that he will not be followed. On the next occasion he will offer his goods in another village. Tribal records are full of disputes in which one villager has accused another of stealing "his" Pygmies.

In the absence of effective economic control the villagers attempt to assert political and religious authority. The vil-lagers themselves are the source of the myth that they "own" the Pygmies in a form of hereditary serfdom. They appoint Pygmy headmen, each responsible for his band to the ap-propriate village headman. Because the bands not only shift territorially but also change as to their inner composition, however, a village headman can no more be sure which Pygmy families comprise "his" band than he can tell at any time where the band has wandered. In his appointed Pygmy headman he has a scapegoat he can blame for failure of the band to fulfill its side of some exchange transaction. But the Pygmy has no wealth with which to pay fines and can rarely be caught for the purpose of enforcing any other restitution.

The villagers nonetheless believe themselves to be the masters. They admit it is a hard battle and point out that the Pygmies are in league with the powerful and tricky spirits of the forest. The fear the villagers have of the forest goes beyond a fear of the animals; it is also a respect based on the knowledge that they are newcomers, if of several hundred years' standing. This respect is even extended to the Pygmies. Some villages make offering to the Pygmies of the first fruit, acknowledging that the Pygmies were there before them and so have certain rights over the land. This offering is also expected to placate the forest spirits. Ultimately, however, the villagers hope to subject the Pygmies to the village spirits and thereby to assume total domination.

In carrying the contest into the realm of the supernatural, the villagers invoke the full armory of witchcraft and sorcery. To the villagers these methods of social control are just as scientific and real as, say, political control through armed force. Moreover, although witchcraft and sorcery generally get their results by psychological pressure, they can sometimes be implemented by physiological poisons. There are strange tales of illness and of death due to sorcery, and no Pygmy wants to be cursed by a villager. On receiving threats of this kind the hunting band takes to the forest, secure in the belief that village magic is no more capable of following them into the forest than are the villagers themselves.

More subtly, the villagers engage the Pygmies in the various important rituals of the village culture. A Pygmy birth, marriage or death, occurring when the hunting band is bivouacked near a village, sets in motion the full village ceremonial appropriate to the occasion. The "owner" of the Pygmy in each case assumes the obligation of providing the child-protecting amulet, of negotiating the exchange of bride wealth or of paying the cost of the obsequies. Such intervention in a Pygmy marriage not only ensures that the union is regularized according to village ritual; it also gives the owners in question indissoluble rights, natural and super-natural, over the new family. The Pygmies willingly submit to the ritual because it means a three-day festival during which they will be fed by the villagers and at the end of which, with luck, they will be able to make off with a por-tion of the bride wealth. On returning to the forest the couple may decide that it was just a flirtation and separate, leaving the villagers to litigate the expense of the transaction and the wedding feast. Although they are economically the losers, the villagers nonetheless believe that by forcing or cajoling the Pygmies through the ritual they have subjected them, at least to some extent, to the control of the village supernatural.

The same considerations on both sides apply to a funeral. The ritual places certain obligations on the family of the de-ceased and lays supernatural sanctions on them; death also involves, almost invariably, allegations of witchcraft or sor-cery. Once again, therefore, the villagers are eager to do what is necessary to bring the Pygmies within the thrall of the local spirit world. And once again the Pygmies are will-ing to cooperate, knowing that the village funerary ritual prescribes a funerary feast. Even though their custom calls for quick and unceremonious disposal of the dead, they are glad to let the villagers do the disposing and even to submit to head-shaving and ritual baths in return for a banquet.

By far the most elaborate ritual by which the villagers hope to bring the Pygmies under control is the initiation of the Pygmy boys into manhood through the ordeal of circum-cision, called *nkumbi.* All village boys between the ages of nine and twelve are subject to this practice, which takes place every three years. Pygmy boys of the appropriate age who happen to be in the vicinity are put through the same ceremony with the village boys. A Pygmy boy is sent first "to clean the knife," as the villagers put it, and then he is followed by a village boy. These two boys are thereafter joined by the blood they shed together in the unbreakable bond of *kare,* or blood brotherhood. Any default, particularly on the part of the Pygmy, will invoke the wrath of the ancestors and bring all manner of curses on the offender. So once more the Pygmies are placed under the control of the village spirits and the putative bonds between the serfs and their owners are reinforced. Some villagers also see this practice as a means of securing for themselves an assured complement of Pygmy serfs to serve them in the afterworld.

As in all the other ritual relations, the BaMbuti have their own independent motivations and rationalization for submitting their sons to the pain and humiliation of *nkumbi*. For one thing, the Pygmy boys acquire the same secular adult status in the village world as their village blood brothers. The Pygmies, moreover, have the advantage of knowing that the bonds they do not consider unbreakable nonetheless tie their newly acquired village brothers; they make use of this knowledge by imposing on their *kare*. Finally, for the adult male relatives of the Pygmy initiates the ceremony means three months or so of continuous feasting at the expense of the villagers.

Once the *nkumbi* is over and the Pygmies have returned to the forest, it becomes clear that the ritual has no relevance to the inner life of the family and the hunting band. The boys who have gone to such trouble to become adults in the village sit on the laps of their mothers, signifying that they know they are really still children. In Pygmy society they will not become adults until they have proved themselves as hunters.

Back in the forest the Pygmies once again become the forest people. Their counter to the villagers' efforts to bring them under domination is to keep the two worlds apart. This strategy finds formal expression in the festival of the *molimo*. The *molimo* songs are never sung when a band is making a visitation to a village or is encamped near it. Out in the forest, during the course of each night's singing, the trail leading off from the camp is ceremonially blocked with branches and leaves, shutting out the profane world beyond.

The relation between the Pygmy and the village cultures thus resolves itself in a standoff. Motivated as it is by economics, the relation is inherently an adversary one. The villagers seek to win the contest by domination; the Pygmies seek to perpetuate it by a kind of indigenous apartheid. Because the relation is one of mutual convenience rather than necessity, it works with reasonable success in the economic realm. The villagers ascribe the success, however, to their spiritual domination; any breakdown they cannot correct they are content to leave to rectification by the supernatural, a formula that works within their own society. The Pygmies hold, on the other hand, that the forest looks after its own, a belief that is borne out by their daily experience. In the nature of the situation, each group is able to think it has succeeded, as indeed in its own eyes it has. The very separateness of the two worlds makes this dual solution possible. But it is a solution that can work only in the present context.

A breakdown began when the Belgians insisted that the villagers plant cotton and produce a food surplus. The villagers then needed the Pygmies even more as a source of manpower. At the same time, with roads being cut through the forest, the movement of game became restricted. If the process had continued, the Pygmies would have found it increasingly difficult to follow their hunting and food-gathering way of life and would indeed have become the economic dependents of the villagers. The present political turmoil in the Congo has given the Pygmies a temporary reprieve.

In some areas, however, the Belgians had decided to preempt the untapped Pygmy labor force for themselves and had already set about "liberating" the Pygmies from the mythical yoke of the villagers, persuading them to set up plantations of their own. The result was disastrous. Used to the constant shade of the forest, to the purity of forest water and to the absence of germ-carrying flies and mosquitoes, the Pygmies quickly succumbed to sunstroke and to various illnesses against which the villagers have some immunity. Worse yet, with the abandoning of hunting and food gathering the entire Pygmy social structure collapsed. Forest values were necessarily left behind in the forest, and there was nothing to take their place but a pathetic and unsuccessful imitation of the new world around them, the world of villagers and of Europeans.

This whole problem was much discussed among the Pygmies just prior to the independence of the Congo. In almost every case they reached the determination that as long as the forest existed they would try to go on living as they had always lived. More than once I was told, with no little insight, that "when the forest dies, we die." So for the Pygmies, in a sense, there is no problem. They have seen enough of the outside world to feel able to make their choice, and their choice is to preserve the sanctity of their own world up to the very end. Being what they are, they will doubtless continue to play a masterful game of hide-and-seek, but they will not easily sacrifice their integrity.

It is for future administrations of the Congo that the problem will be a real one, both moral and practical. Can the vast forest area justifiably be set aside as a reservation for some 40,000 Pygmies? And if the forest is to be exploited, what can one do with its inhabitants, who are physically, temperamentally and socially so unfitted for any other form of life? If the former assessment of the Pygmy-villager relation had been correct and the Pygmies had really been as acculturated as it seemed, the problem would have resolved itself into physiological terms only, serious enough but not insuperable. As it is, seeing that the Pygmies have for several hundred years successfully rejected almost every basic element of the foreign cultures surrounding them, the prospects of adaptation are fraught with hazards.

Traditional values die hard, it would seem, and continue to thrive even when they are considered long since dead and buried. In dealing with any African peoples, I suspect, we are in grave danger if we assume too readily that they are the creatures we like to think we have made them. If the Pygmies are any indication, and if we realize it in time, it may be as well for us and for Africa that they are not.

The controversial question of whether certain races are inherently superior to others has as a corollary a similar problem as to the morals, intelligence, and general ability of so-called mixed breeds resulting from the intermingling of two or more distinct races. The question of just when such intermingling occurs is itself moot. Many apparent differences in racial stocks can be traced to other than genetic factors. Moreover, racial mixtures can be on varying levels of social and economic disparity. Is the inferior status which the individual of mixed ancestry usually occupies the result of inferior natural ability or of environmental pressures? The answer is obviously a concern of both the anthropologist and the biologist. In general, scientific opinion now holds that there is no conclusive evidence stamping the mixed breed as inherently inferior.

In a booklet written for UNESCO, the United Nations Educational, Scientific and Cultural Organization, Harry Shapiro discusses the subject of Racial Mixture. He points out that in the past five hundred years there has been an unprecedented movement of populations through such influences as colonization and slavery. In more recent times, global wars and easier methods of communication have accentuated the speed of the process. There are no accurate figures on mixed breeds, but they certainly number a substantial proportion of the total population. The problems they present are of significance to the cultural anthropologist. In the following selection, one society composed entirely of racially mixed stock is described.

Harry Shapiro was born at Boston in 1902 and received a Ph.D. at Harvard in 1926. He became in turn assistant curator, associate curator, and curator and chairman of the department of anthropology at the American Museum of Natural History. He has also served as professor of anthropology at Columbia University. He is the author of Heritage of the Bounty and Aspects of Culture.

PITCAIRN

HARRY L. SHAPIRO

. . . PREVIOUSLY I had mentioned the manifold variety of the origins and the diverse expressions of race mixture. Perhaps the best known of them all is the small group of

Polynesian-English mixed bloods that live on Pitcairn Island in the South Pacific. Here, on a tiny volcanic island only about two miles long and about half as wide, were resolved the train of events that the famous mutiny of the *Bounty* set in action. This episode, famous in British naval annals, occurred in the year 1789 shortly after H.M.S. *Bounty* had departed from Tahiti where she had been dispatched under the command of Lieutenant William Bligh to collect breadfruit plants. Reports brought back to Europe by Cook and Bougainville described the breadfruit as a remarkable tree capable of supplying a staple article of food with a minimum of effort. British planters in the West Indies, eager to obtain so easy a source of foodstuff for their slaves, had petitioned for the expedition with which Bligh had been entrusted. Now after six successful months in Tahiti, with the ship's hold full of potted trees, the return trip was interrupted by the mutiny of twenty-five of the men out of the crew of forty-four. The mutineers were led by Fletcher Christian, one of Bligh's officers, and a native of the Isle of Man where his family had long been prominent.

The mutineers, seizing the ship, put Bligh and those faithful to him adrift in a small open boat and reset the *Bounty's* course for Tubuai, an island 300 miles south of Tahiti. Here, an abortive attempt was made to establish a settlement, which failed because of the hostility aroused in the natives by the behavior of the mutineers. Returning after this to Tahiti, the mutineers split into two groups: one, consisting of sixteen men, preferred to remain in Tahiti, where a number of them had already established liaisons with native women and had been welcomed into the island homes; the other contained nine men headed by Christian. These men, apparently anticipating a possible punitive expedition once the news of the mutiny reached England, were eager to leave Tahiti, where they could not hope to escape capture, and to find a more remote and perhaps inaccessible island where they might remain undetected. Accordingly they, together with twelve Tahitian women and six Tahitian men, set sail from Tahiti in September 1789, and until 1808 were virtually lost to the world. In the latter year their retreat on Pitcairn, some 2,500 miles southeast of Tahiti, was discovered by Captain Mayhew Folger. During this interval much had happened on the island. All the Tahitian men and all but one of the Englishmen had died—most of them violently, and after only a short sojourn in their new home. In addition, Folger found eight or nine surviving Tahitian women and twenty-five children, offspring of six of the Englishmen and their native wives. None of the Tahitian men had left issue, perhaps because they were murdered too soon after the settlement on the island.

From this handful of children—half-Polynesian, half-English—the little colony increased by leaps and bounds, until fifty years later there were almost 200 inhabitants on the island. By this time, fear of overpopulation and the recurrence of water shortages induced them to request of the British Government the use of Norfolk Island, some 4,000 miles to the west, as a new home. This considerably larger island had recently been abandoned as a penal colony and was temporarily unoccupied. In 1856 the entire colony moved there and set up a new establishment, but subsequently several families returned to their beloved Pitcairn. In 1864 there were forty-five descendants of the mutineers living on Pitcairn, the remainder having gone on to Norfolk. At present there are on both islands about 1,000 descendants of the original colony, not counting those who have married out of the community or settled in New Zealand, Australia and elsewhere.

As an example of race mixture the Pitcairn Islanders are far from typical. But it is the very singularity of the colony that is full of meaning in interpreting race mixture as we commonly see it. Simply as a cross between Polynesians and English they can be matched in many parts of Polynesia where the same kind of mingling has occurred, often with notable results, as in New Zealand. But unlike all other mixtures of this kind in Oceania, and indeed unlike virtually all race mixture wherever it occurs,[1] the Pitcairn Islanders have lived and developed their common life completely separated from the societies from which they were originally de-

---

1.   The only parallel to Pitcairn known to me is Tristan da Cunha, where a community of mixed Negro-Europeans have lived in isolation for well over 100 years.

rived. Now it is an almost universal consequence of race mixture that the mixed bloods live in contact with the parental
groups and in one or the other of the parental societies. This
can, as we have seen, have profound consequences on the
status and position of the mixed group. And since social
status works both ways, affecting those within it by their
own attitude as members of a special class and by the attitude of others toward them, the association of a mixed group
with one of its parental societies can be a decisive influence
on its development. Where mixed bloods form a class suffering legal disability, economic injustice or social prejudice,
they are victims of the attitudes, well- or ill-founded, of the
dominant element in their society. The extent to which these
circumstances affect the behavior and psychological traits of
the members of such a class is difficult to appraise. And it is
equally difficult to assess the degree to which these socially
conditioned characteristics in turn reinforce the attitudes
that encourage them. Many competent students are convinced that they are significant.

It is because of all this that the Pitcairn Islanders' complete separation from and independence of all other societies assume added importance, for here the entire community
was of the same mixed origin, was free from any social
structuring imposed upon it by a larger society and escaped
the influences that prejudice subtly works upon its object.
This, then, is a community where social prejudice, at least,
is not a factor to be considered and where we can study
the consequences of race mixture divorced from the concomitant effects that being a part of a larger group might
impose.

On the other hand, in any consideration of the colony, its
very isolation must be kept in mind, as it must in appraising
any small community remote from the world and cut off
from the intellectual and material stimuli of a larger society.
For the first eighteen years of its existence, the Pitcairn
colony remained unvisited by any ship. The children growing up in the first generation of the community had never
seen anyone not a member of their little family, for the early
colony lived as one extended family with John Adams, the
surviving mutineer, as their *pater familias*. Even after 1808,

when their existence became known, callers were rare and their visits very brief. Not until the 1820s did ships begin to call at Pitcairn to obtain water and fresh foods As American whaling became increasingly active in the Pacific, these visits increased in number, reaching their highest frequency in the 1840s. With the decline of whaling, Pitcairn once more reverted to its former loneliness. These contacts, although important in bringing to the islanders the goods of the outside world for which they had acquired a taste, were brief and had little or no influence on the social structure of the colony.

It would, of course, be futile to attempt to rate Pitcairn against other communities, mixed or otherwise. There are too many variables impossible to standardize that would have to be taken into account. But it is evident to anyone visiting the island that here is a well-organized settlement, conducting its own affairs successfully under a system devised by the islanders themselves. Like people anywhere, of course, they vary, but the visitor is invariably impressed by the pleasant, friendly manners of the islanders, their charm, their hospitality and self-confidence. There is no trace here of a people conscious of inferiority. They are all literate and have from the earliest days maintained a school system by their own ·efforts. Equally notable is the vigor of their Church. Previously adherents of the Church of England, they were converted to Seventh Day Adventism at the end of the last century. The way in which they made this shift in adherence is typical of their wisdom in managing their own affairs. In making the change, the community was faced with a situation that might have been serious in its consequences. The population was divided on the issue of conversion, and, recognizing the danger of a tiny community being split between two rival Churches, decided to put the matter to a vote, with the minority pledged to go along with the expressed wish of the majority. Thus the whole community unanimously adopted Seventh Day Adventism and preserved the religious unity of the colony.

Remarkable in so small a community, especially one cut off from the developments of the outside world, are some of the social institutions which were established on Pitcairn and maintained there ever since. A democratic rule developed early, with all men and women enjoying equal political rights, long before political rights were granted to women in the Western world and indeed before they were even very seriously discussed there. Education was, from the first, recognized as a necessity and, as the local institutions took form, all children were required to attend school until their sixteenth year. The various families on the island were taxed for the maintenance of the school. Teachers were selected from the students and supported by the revenue levied on the people. Here, too, the Pitcairn Islanders were in advance of educational developments in greater centers of civilization.

The culture that emerged on Pitcairn also reflected the mixed origin of the colony and in a rather striking way illustrates the decisive roles that sex and environment may play in creating a new society. The cultural resources available to the new colony were, of course, English and Tahitian. But it is obvious on reflection that not all the content of either of these cultures could or would be drawn upon, since one culture, the English, was accessible only through men who were sailors by occupation, and the other, the Tahitian, was represented by women, who were familiar with the crafts and skills traditionally exercised in Tahiti by their sex. In addition to this, the colony on Pitcairn faced an unfamiliar environment and, in transplanting their traditional ways, both the Tahitian women and the English sailors found themselves without the usual technical equipment needed to practice whatever skills and arts they knew. Even such a basic and necessary object as a nail was not available, not to mention a variety of common tools that could not be fashioned on Pitcairn. Thus we find tapa cloth universally used by the colony in its early days. The making of this bark cloth is traditionally a women's job in Tahiti and could be carried to Pitcairn intact. Similarly, cooking being a woman's concern, the Tahitian technique of an underground oven was standard on Pitcairn. House building, on the contrary, was the result of a complex of influences. The Tahitian style of house would have been unsuitable in the colder climate of Pitcairn, but in any event it probably could not have been built by the women, who in Tahiti leave the framing of a house to the men. The Englishmen, probably only as adept in carpentry as sailors of those days might be expected to be, were handicapped by the lack of essential building materials and of tools. We find them, as a consequence, building houses ingeniously put together, the frame mortised, the walls constructed of roughly hewn planks fitted into slotted uprights, the interiors provided with bunks as in a ship's cabin. The roof, however, was thatched in the Tahitian manner, since roof thatching is prepared in Tahiti by the women, and this was a contribution the Tahitian women on Pitcairn could make to this novel house.

One of the common allegations made about race mixture is that it produces inferior human beings. This belief is stated in various ways that all come to the same thing: mixed bloods combine the worst features of both parental groups.

As far as the Pitcairn Islanders are concerned, I can offer no objective data on their psychological or moral qualities. None, to my knowledge, is available. Certainly there have been many published impressions of these traits of the islanders and most of them are enthusiastic. How far the romantic aura that surrounds these people has seduced their visitors is beyond calculation. In the mid-nineteenth century the typical reaction was delight in finding so moral, upright and virtuous a colony sprung from mutineers, from violence and from murder. Nowadays, being less concerned with religious matters and having on the whole rather different values, the visitor is less impressed by these qualities and is likely to prize other aspects of their character. For my part, I can only report that, allowing for their isolation and for a consequent lack of sophistication, I found the Pitcairn Islanders an intelligent and attractive people. And I was struck by the number of men and women of impressive character possessed of the qualities that make for leadership.

Although biologically rather more of what might be called objective information is accessible, still it can only be used for comparative purposes with caution. Even such standard criteria as physical vigor, longevity or health cannot be properly used for such purposes without reference to diet, climate and various other environmental conditions. Both on Norfolk and Pitcairn Islands the physical condition of the islanders was excellent. In spite of the inbreeding, which has especially characterized Pitcairn, I found no physical deformities or obvious signs of degeneration. On Pitcairn, with a population of 200 (1936), there were no individuals incapable of taking care of themselves, nor any cases of serious mental deficiency. This is an excellent record compared with the frequency of such cases in Europe and the United States, especially in remote, inbred villages. In view of the fact that neither on Pitcairn nor Norfolk is there any resident medical service or even trained nursing aid, the longevity of the population is impressive. In 1924, out of a population of about 600 on Norfolk, there were twenty-four who were over sixty-five years of age, with the oldest reaching ninety-five years. On Pitcairn there were twelve between the ages of sixty-five and eighty-six in a population of 200.

There have been some claims that hybrids are smaller and weaker than their parents. Davenport and Steggerda on the basis of their study of race mixture in Jamaica believe their data demonstrated this conclusion. The Pitcairn and Norfolk evidence is quite the contrary. Indeed, there is evidence here of hybrid vigor comparable to the vigor that can be demonstrated experimentally in a large number of animal and plant crosses. For example, if we take size as a measure of heightened physiological vigor, as is done for maize or cross-bred domestic animals, we find that the average stature of the parental groups is 171.4 cm. for Tahitian males and 170.6 cm. for the mutineers (based on British Admiralty records but possibly a little low, since some of the sailors were not fully mature men). The modern Englishman averages around 172 cm. The F_1, or first generation descendants, averaged 177.8 cm. (minimum 5 ft. 9½ in., maximum 6 ft. ¼ in.). This represents an average increase of over two inches, with the shortest male exceeding the average of his parental groups by a considerable margin. Although this striking increase has not been fully maintained in the present generation, it is still almost an inch above the parental average.

As another index of this vigor, the reproductive rate of the islanders is equally notable. I have already referred to the prodigiously rapid growth of the colony which has produced in 160-odd years well over 1,000 descendants. This may be appreciated from the birth rate by generations. The first generation averaged 7.44 children per mating, the second 9.10, the third 5.39. Since then there has been a further decline. The rate in the second generation is one of the highest on record for any community and reflects an unusual reproductive vigor.

As far as the evidence goes, then, the Pitcairn experiment lends no support for the thesis that race mixture merely leads to degeneration or at best produces a breed inferior to the superior parental race. In fact, we see in this colony some support for heightened vigor, for an extended variation and for a successful issue of the mingling of two diverse strains.

The American Indians have been among the most intensively studied races of the world. American anthropologists have amassed an enormous amount of artifacts and information on Indian family life, religion, art, and warfare. The difficult conditions under which the Indian is forced to exist and the gradual disappearance of Indian culture have become a matter of concern to anthropologists and conservationists. Oliver La Farge was one of the leaders in the struggle to preserve the Indian's rights and identity. Another is John Collier, author of the following selection. He was born at Atlanta, Georgia, in 1884 and became a social worker among the immigrants in 1905. In 1919, he went to California, where he became a director of community organizations. He gradually became interested in the plight of the Indians, and his views came to the attention of Franklin D. Roosevelt, who appointed him United States Commisioner of Indian Affairs, a post he held from 1933 to 1945. He is the author of the highly regarded Indians of the Americas and Patterns and Ceremonials of the Indians of the Southwest. His book On the Gleaming Way is a study of the cultures of the Navajos, Eastern Pueblos, Zuñi, Hopis, and Apaches. From it has been taken this chapter on the Navajos, a personal record as well as a revelation of the problems of a depressed minority in an alien culture.

THE NAVAJOS

JOHN COLLIER

FROM ALBUQUERQUE, Bill Cutter's four-passenger Fairchild roared upward into the low overcast, and pointed westward. Soon, through a cloud rift Laguna pueblo glimmered below, and then to southward Acoma pueblo on its lofty rock. Then the black land of lava flows, and northward in cloud, Mount Taylor. Beyond the Continental Divide we headed west-northwest, and we crossed the Fort Defiance plateau not a hundred feet above the tops of the high pines. How empty, the Navajos' land; one lonely hogan, and no other for miles, here a herd of wild horses, there little flocks of sheep tended by children or women, then cornfields and a little village of hogans, then wasteland red as blood, where no sheep grazed. The Hopi mesas were forty miles to the west; one ray from the low winter sun illumined the First Mesa, and Walpi tiny as a distant pebble heap. At last, circling to reconnoiter, we grounded on a sagebrush-covered mesa top, a hundred feet above the plain. We were a hundred and forty miles deep within the Navajo reservation.

Scrambling down the mesa's side, we found a car waiting, and as twilight drew near, we skidded and plunged along a road whose deep mud was not yet hardened by the night's freeze. Twenty-five miles in two hours, and then pitch-black night had come, with no stars. On the horizon, a fluctuating glow of fires, and the odor of piñon and cedar smoke drifted around us; and a low chant rising and falling, and then we were at our destination, amid wagon wheels and horses and hundreds of Navajo men, women and children. It was the fifth night of a Navajo sing.

It was Chee Dodge who had suggested our visit—Chee, who until the autumn of 1946 remained the Navajo tribal council's chairman, at eighty-seven years, and who died at the beginning of 1947. A sick Navajo man was being healed through the sing, and Chee Dodge believed the occasion a happy one for discussing with the assembled Navajos the tribe-wide problem of the sick land. We did discuss this subject, for hours, by the wind-fanned firelight, English into Navajo, Navajo into English (for the hundreds discussed it), and all the while the chanting rose and fell from within the sick man's hogan.

And we ate mutton and drank coffee, and there was much joking and laughter while the night deepened its cold; there was happiness, although we were talking about the most painful facts and necessities which have held the Navajos in their grip in this generation.

For at a curing sing, all who attend are happy. There has taken place a disharmony, some prevalence of the dark powers which are in the world. The sing restores harmony, goes back to the sources of light, brings the reign of light; and this, not merely for the sick patient, but for all his family and friends, and not only through the medicine man's suggestion and prayer but through the union of happy emotion and confident willing on the part of every man, woman and child who has joined the ceremony. They have joined from many miles away—twenty, thirty, fifty miles. A Navajo sing is communal healing, and the sick patient throws the healing back to all who are assisting him, in a profound process of therapeutic suggestion and self-suggestion which reaches to the obscure, central deeps of the body and the soul.

There are sixty-odd thousand Navajos; theirs is the largest tribe north of Mexico. First going among them, almost anywhere in the twenty-five thousand square miles of their domain, one is impressed with the extreme material parsimony of their existence. A little patch of cornland, usually dry-farmed; twenty or thirty or fifty sheep and goats, four or five small-bodied horses. Sometimes a wagon, more rarely a decrepit car. Silver and turquoise bracelets, rings, buttons, headbands, Navajo-made, and blankets, Navajo-spun, woven and dyed, from home-grown wool; and dwellings, called hogans, windowless, built circular or octagonal of logs or stone, with dirt floors, with a vent for the fire which burns at their center, and a low doorway facing always east. Material poverty, indeed, and poverty which has intensified with the years, even now lifting only a little here and there.

Such is the first impression, but the next one is sharply contrasting. It is that of vibrant human quality, body resiliency and mind resiliency, beauty of old women and young women, beauty of old and young men, poise and confidence in children, *élan* without aggressiveness in all. So poor they are; and fuller knowledge confirms and extends the first impression of material parsimony and even of a situation which realistically is desperate; and they know their situation, too, and do not try to hide it from themselves, yet the note which their life strikes is exuberance and joy, a winging note and a note of the dance and the dancing star.

How can so rich a flower bloom in a soil so rocky and nearly waterless?

Out in that lonely and hard land of supernal beauty, and within their dearth of the world's goods and under the deepening shadow which rests on the Indian future, these Navajo Indians practice a complicated art of living. Through this art, whose uninterrupted use comes down the centuries, although poverty and insecurity go on increasing, the Navajos are not poor or insecure. Thus as one's knowledge of Navajo life increases, a third impression takes form. *The Navajo has created out of his human material a house of wonder.* His intangible culture matches the splendor of his land. In terms of life, not of goods, it is we who are poor, not the Navajo.

Thus the Night Chant tells of the Navajo's house of wonder:

> *House made of dawn,*
> *House made of evening light,*
> *House made of the dark cloud. . . .*
> *Dark cloud is at the house's door,*
> *The trail out of it is dark cloud,*
> *The zigzag lightning stands high upon it. . . .*
> *Happily may I walk.*
> *Happily, with abundant showers, may I walk.*
> *Happily, with abundant plants, may I walk.*
> *Happily, on the trail of pollen, may I walk.*
> *Happily may I walk.*
> *May it be beautiful before me.*

May it be beautiful behind me.
May it be beautiful below me.
May it be beautiful above me.
May it be beautiful all around me.
In beauty it is finished.[1]

The principal repositories and renewers of the Navajo's life art are his ceremonials, most but not all of them healing ceremonials. There are thirty-five major ceremonials, along with numerous variations of the thirty-five. Each requires from two to nine days for its completion, and all involve communal sharing. A full record of any one of them would require a whole book. Possibly the rite of the Blessing Way is the master ceremony of them all, because it deals with and is addressed to the universe. "A rite," explains the Franciscan Father Berard Haile, "whose legends, songs and prayers are chiefly concerned with the creation and placement of the earth and sky, sun and moon, sacred mountains and vegetation, the inner forms of these natural phenomena, the control of the he- and she-rains, dark clouds and mist, the inner forms of the cardinal points, and life phenomena that may be considered the harbingers of blessing and happiness."

Form-giving, harmony-giving, value-giving, power-giving, joy-giving, virtue-giving: the Navajo ceremonials are all of these, but these adjectives are entirely inadequate. The ceremonials are the nourishers and structurers of the Navajo personality, the expanders and ennoblers of the Navajo human relationship, the ancient renewers of Navajo civilization. Intangible as they are, yet their precision and definiteness and permanence equals that of stone or steel; immaterial as they are, yet they are potent to saturate the Navajo body and soul with a humor and dauntlessness and freedom which are all their own. Well may we of the ponderous and hurrying material civilization turn to the Navajos for a reminder that the goods of life are wrought by souls and stored within souls.

It was Changing Woman who gave to the Navajos the Blessing Way. Changing Woman is Wife to the Sun. She is the ever-renewing, ever-regenerating, ever-benign; she is

---

1. Washington Matthews' translation.

Mother Earth's soul. "Seldom," writes Clyde Kluckhohn, "does a family go for six months without having the Blessing Way sung at least once in their hogan."

And what of this hogan, which to the uninitiated white visitor appears as the very concentration of the material poverty or casualness of the Navajo? Here, with a purpose, I shall draw upon another reporter of Navajo life, rather than upon my own memories. But there do come two memories, and one is from Puertocito, a remote, detached outpost of Navajo life in central New Mexico. It is night, in midwinter; a cold wind blows over a white earth under flashing stars. The hogan's diameter is twenty feet; at its center a piñon-wood fire burns. No air stirs within the hogan; the smoke rises straight to the venthole seven feet above the earthen floor.

The medicine man sits at the patient's right; the medicine man's helpers in their ordered places circle the fire. Blankets cover the floor; there are containers of liquid and powdered sacred medicines, and a silent bull-roarer is at hand. A dozen or more friend-participants are seated beyond the medicine man's helpers.

The patient is a white man; the community has contributed this sing, to help him with power in a political struggle in behalf of the tribe. He notes certain facts, before the converging suggestions shepherd him within to the place where power abides. One fact is the extreme cleanliness of the fire-lit hogan and all within it. Another is the sweetness of the herb-scented air. Another is the orderly utilization, for storage, of every beam and cranny of the interior of the structure. The spaciousness of the place, the slow, harmonious movement of all the people in it, the gradualness of the rhythms of the ceremonial, the poised relation of unhurrying life, so quiet while at its zenith of concentration. What meanings have these words from of old, these symbolic objects from of old, the patient cannot know; but he can feel how they structure a potent, confident flow of good will and good hope. Only within a hogan can a ceremonial healing rite be performed; the hogan, the Navajo's home, is his temple too.

The other memory is of summertime, and the place, Monument Valley, at the Utah-Arizona line, northwest from

Puertocito. Here, from the sand, the deep-blazing rock plinths soar to hundreds, thousands of feet. A hogan, and in front of it a spacious brush sun shelter; near by, a sheep corral. Under the brush shelter, a young woman weaving; another young woman; and five little children of the two mothers are there. The fathers are somewhere in the Pacific theater of war. An adolescent boy is there, too; he will depart for the army next week. And the aged grandmother is there, and her aged sister; and two dogs, and a brood of kittens.

These are average Navajos, and as such, their per capita yearly income is about eighty-two dollars. No, in the barren splendor of Monument Valley the income will be lower than eighty-two dollars a year. But feeling of poverty there is none; squalor, graspingness, apology for obvious poverty, none. They smilingly accept some cookies, and offer coffee and bread to us. They bring forth letters from overseas—the two young mothers know English. They talk about the big meeting at Kayenta, twenty miles away, the day before; and will the closed government school at Kayenta be reopened soon? They joke about many things, but their jokes are in Navajo, the old and young joining in quiet laughter. But mainly their talk is concerned with a sick young man who is overstraining his family's resources by occasioning too many sings. Apparently the young man's disorder is decisively an organic one; the potent psychotherapy can dissipate its irradiations through body and mind but cannot cure the cause. But our Navajo hosts ask a subtle question: Has the young man become too much Americanized? Has he ceased, when his sings are not going on, to keep the Way? Is he doing his own part, outside the healing ceremonies? Is he running too hard after money, or girls, or drink? Or is he, perhaps, in the grip of some faithless diviner who maintains an illicit partnership with a medicine man? They do not judge, but only speculate. The troubled young man is a relative, living at the other end of the Navajo country; but these women, to whose hogan no road leads, appear to know all about the young man and his circumstances.

Here is true sophistication, and life richly lived within form; and the hogan seems enough for the abode of humans whose greater abode is Monument Valley and its shining immensities, and the whole rainbow-arched Navajo land. But now, to cite an authority on the subject of the hogan, lest my own testimony be considered overly romantic.

The authority is twofold: Clyde Kluckhohn, of Harvard University, and Dorothea Leighton, who, along with Alexander Leighton, of Cornell University, are the recognized authorities on Navajo facts. I quote from the Kluckhohn-Leighton book, *The Navaho*:

The hogan is an excellent simple adaptation to the climate. Its thick walls keep out cold in winter and, to some extent, heat in summer; the centrally placed fire keeps all parts of the dwelling warm, and there is room for more occupants to sit or sleep around the fire. We (the writers) have found hogans generally more comfortable than the thin-walled cabins of white homesteaders. . . .

To the white visitor, it is astonishing how many individuals can eat, sleep, and store many of their possessions within one room not more than twenty-five feet in diameter. As a matter of fact, livable order is attained only by adherence to a considerable degree of system with respect both to objects and persons. Women always sit on the south side of the hogan, men on the north. Small children stay close to their mothers. The male head of the family and the officiating medicine men (or other distinguished visitors) sit on the west side facing the doorway. The place of other persons, and the seating arrangements under special circumstances, are prescribed in considerable detail.

Goods have a fixed disposal which utilizes all available space. Herbs and small types of dried foods, ceremonial equipment, guns and bows and arrows, hats and articles of clothing in current use, are stowed away in corners of the rafters or suspended from beams by thongs or nails. Reserve clothing and bedding and prized jewelry and ceremonial articles, are stowed in trunks or suitcases, which are stacked against the walls where the roof is lowest. Pots and pans are stacked near the central fire or placed with the spoons and supplies of flour, lard, coffee, and sugar in crude cupboards made of boxes nailed to the wall by the door. . . .

To the Navahos (Dine, The People, in their own speech), their hogans are not just places to eat and sleep,

mere parts of the workaday world, as homes have tended
to become in the minds of white people, particularly in
cities. The hogan occupies a central place in the sacred
world also. The first hogans were built by the Holy People, of turquoise, white shell, jet, or abalone shell. Navaho
myths prescribe the position of persons and objects within;
they say why the door must always face the rising sun
and why the dreaded bodies of the dead must be removed
through a hole broken in the hogan wall to the north (always the direction of evil). A new hogan is often conse-
crated with a Blessing Way Rite or songs from it, and at
the very least, the head of the family will smear the sacred
corn pollen or meal along the hogan poles with some
such petition as *hozhoo telgoo ot'e*, "let this be assurance
that the place will be happy."

Kluckhohn's and Leighton's reference, above, to "the
north, always the direction of evil," and the "dreaded bodies
of the dead" occasions a remark of my own, to balance all
that has gone before in this chapter. The dominant note
which Navajo life strikes is joy, and buoyant confidence in
the powers within the breast and in the world. And active
happiness, positive health, are social duties among the
Navajos. But equally, the Navajos do not entertain, and
would scornfully reject, that view of life which is called
"pangloss," or willful, fact-denying, sentimental optimism.
Famine, war, drought, cold, and the dark storms that are
within the human soul, they have always known, and have
never tried to be oblivious toward them. Darkness and evil,
not only light and love and joy, are indwelling deep within
the nature of things, and their attempts to invade the soul
are never-ending. Once, for a long cosmic interval, gigantism
and darkness and evil predominated in the whole earth; then
through a mighty effort the forces of beauty, love and joy
subdued them, and scattered them afar, but never annihilated
or sought to annihilate them; and to man, then recreated or
newly born, the Blessing Way was given, and many other
symbols, precepts, rites and disciplines, and norms of conduct and feeling; and these, as lived by man, are the City of
God, but darkness and active evil assail the City and invade

it forevermore. Thus the cosmic and human drama is sustained by the Navajos, and the insecurity of things is wrought into a structure of beautiful security, a "dance over fire and water" whose rhythms are sometimes wildly impassioned but more often stately and gradual.

Navajo religion has its theological as well as its ethical and its aesthetic-emotional place among the fundamental religions of mankind. And Navajo religious art builds for eternity through building into the human and social tissue and soul, none the less for the fact that its material constructions are demolished on the very day that they are completed.

These material constructions of Navajo religious art are the dry paintings or sand paintings which are created as an element of the healing ceremonies and the ceremonies which renew the occult nature-man relationship. Sand painting is a misnomer, since often, as in the paintings which are an element in the Blessing Way ceremonial, the design and color materials are pollen, corn meal of various hues, and the crushed petals of dried flowers: in the curing ceremonials materials are charcoal and various pulverized stones. The background of the paintings usually is buckskin; sometimes it is sand.

Always the dry paintings are almost exclusively symbolic; often the design is a triumph of construction. A dry painting may be one or two feet across, or twenty feet or more, and each is the work of from two to fifteen or more ceremonial artists. A complete ceremonial requires four dry paintings, made on successive days; and always the painting is destroyed at the end of the day. The reason is not secrecy, for the Navajos have allowed more than five hundred dry paintings to be viewed and described, and a large number to be reproduced in paintings or colored photographs. Each of the five hundred recorded paintings is a precise complex of symbolism, of cosmic reference in the main; design and content have been passed down from generation to generation of healer-singers. A dry painting once perfected (and the hundreds of them were perfected in unknown times gone) may not be changed through whim or creative impulse, for it incorporates the Law from Old. In the chants of the ceremonials, innovation and experiment have quite a free play; but the dry paintings represent creative acts of a man or group of men long dead.

It is evident, now, what is the Navajos' treasure house and what is their most priceless treasure. Treasure house and treasure are one: the scores of "ritual ways," the many hundreds of dry paintings, the thousands of songs, and the thousands of *inities* who bear in their memories these secrets of earth and heaven. Let us note, then, a rather remarkable fact.

When we look at the Navajo tribe as a whole or at any part of it, we discover that there exists no formalized or institutionalized arrangement for building their vital treasure house or for guarding the treasure house or its contents. No machinery for forcing orthodoxy or for persuading it; none for insuring that a healer-singer, before he dies, shall vest his knowledge (which is just so much of the tribe's very life) in a worthy younger man. No machinery for insuring that a younger man shall choose to become a healer-singer and shall submit himself to the years of training which will be necessary before he becomes adept. From the beginning, as now, the Navajos have entrusted their most life-and-death public function to the completely unformalized and voluntary action of the aging healer-singer and of his self-elected disciples. Until now, at least, this public trust has been fully met by the young and the old; in current years, the unrecorded heritage seems to be dynamically alive and active in its entirety; the Navajos' ceremonial life is even reported by Kluckhohn and Leighton to have become intensified in the recent years.

The ready remark, certainly a superficial one, will be that healing-singing is a paid profession among the Navajos. The young man pays his healing-singing master for the years of requisite tutoring, and knows that upon graduation he will become a paid professional in his turn.

Actually, this answer does but restate the fundamentally impressive fact, that the Navajos' most important public service, the function which in the Navajo mind is life itself, is left to the free action of individuals, with no formalized or institutional provision to insure it. Of course, the healer-singer must live, therefore he must be paid. The Navajo man who is not a healer-singer devotes from one-fourth to one-third of his working time to religious activity, and the healer-singer, who also must meticulously train his successor, devotes a far greater share of his time. Among the Navajos, as among all Indians living within the ancient tribal zone, the mercenary motive is so casual, so devoid of prestige, or even nonexistent, that no major social reliance can be placed on it alone. No, our answer must be sought elsewhere than in the concept "paid professional."

And the answer, which I shall now try to give, leads far into an understanding of many things Navajo.

The Navajos, as previously stated, are the most numerous Indian tribe north of Mexico. They also are one of the tribes with the least of centralized or even centrally-tending organization.

They possess an unmistakable community of temperament, yet their physical type is heterogeneous; they are in fact a composite of many tribal bloods.

They have adopted all sorts of culture elements from other peoples, working them over into their own Navajo pattern of culture. From the Pueblos, weaving, agricultural methods, probably even their ritual dry painting. From the Spaniards and Mexicans, the horse and sheep, and the silverwork for which Navajos are famous. From the modern United States sundry technologies, trade practices, and notions and values which will enter into this account later on.

The Navajos commenced this appropriating activity at a time when they were mere single, isolated families or little groups of families, alongside the highly organized, richly cultured pueblo city-states. They continued the borrowing process through close contact with massive cultures whose quality was both definite and aggressive—Spain, and then the United States. All through these centuries they remained as they had begun, tribally inchoate; and then they became tribally subjected. Just after the American Civil War, they witnessed the destruction of all their crops, the cutting down of all their fruit trees (three thousand fruit trees in Canyon de Chelly alone), the slaughter of all their livestock, by the United States army, and were herded to exile far away, and knew that their last war had been fought and lost. And through all these events they remained tribally inchoate, nebulous, while in their individualities and in their local communities and their religious expression they also remained uniquely and buoyantly Navajo.

Thus, at their remote Athapascan beginning, somewhere up the Rocky Mountain plateau, perhaps within Canada or interior Alaska, whatever their genius became, it became a genius diffuse, not socially concentrated. Diffuse amid scattered small groups which often, for lifetimes perhaps, had no regular contact with one another. Diffuse, without institutional form, but through some extremely impressive ancient event or some innate determination, possessed in common by that sort of vision which their Book of Genesis, the Blessing Way, communicates even to us white people with a flashing power.

In the last eighty years, they have multiplied fourfold or sixfold. As a total tribe, a supposedly unified nation, they experienced the devastating shock of violent subjugation and forced exile. In all the years after, they have been pressed by necessities and emergencies national, tribal, over-all in their character. Still they have moved ahead without an institutional, tribal structure; they have not even moved in the direction of one, except very superficially at a white political level; they have relied on that diffuse instinct and genius which has been so uniquely theirs since a date far back in the Indian Stone Age.

That genius is the shaping of glad life through a multitude of highly structured rituals never integrated into a churchly religion, never removed from out of the play of unlimited free spiritual enterprise. There was no need for integration or regulation, because the spiritual winging along the old migration route of the Navajo soul was so strong and sure. Diffused vision, diffused purpose were enough; they required no centralized persuasion to insure the homing flight of the Navajo spirit, or the renewal of that flight from age to age.

Perhaps the Navajo shaman, diviner, diagnostician is a symbol of this diffuse genius of his race. The Navajo diviner is not trained in his art. He is called by the family of the sick person. Wide awake, the diviner waits. Then his arm and hand start trembling. He gropes a while, hesitating, in suspense; at length, the hand marks out on the scattered corn meal an ancient symbol. The malady is thus diagnosed, the particular healing ritual is indicated, the particular healer-singer is chosen.

We have looked at the undimmed rainbow of Navajo spiritual-aesthetic life. What sort of actualities, biological and economic, rest beneath its span?

When the Navajos were returned, in 1868, from their exile in eastern New Mexico, they numbered (including those never sent into exile) perhaps twelve thousand. They increase at two per cent a year—nearly twice as fast as the Indians of the country as a whole, more than twice as fast as the general population.

The government encouraged them—even, through indirection, compelled them—to multiply their livestock without any account taken of what amount of livestock load the range could support without being ruined. This livestock was sheep, goats, some cattle, and semi-wild horses to a maximum of two hundred thousand head at the peak of horse population.

The soil, trampled and eaten out to the roots of its vegetation, fought a rapidly losing battle. The wind blew it in dust clouds, flash floods swept it in rusty torrents toward the Colorado River, sheet erosion silently pilfered the topsoil. By the year 1933, a human population multiplied nearly fourfold since 1868 was subsisting on a land base whose potential had dwindled by more than one-half since 1868. The safe carrying capacity of the tribe's whole land area had fallen to some six hundred thousand sheep units. (A cow or horse represents four sheep units.) The sheep units on this land numbered one million three hundred thousand. That meant an erosion increasing at geometrical, not arithmetical speed; it meant near-impending doom.

At that time—May, 1933—a man who soon was to influence rural-life policy in many lands was obscurely stationed in the Department of Agriculture at Washington. His name was Hugh L. Bennett, chief of the Bureau of Soil Chemistry.

I had become Indian Commissioner, under Harold L. Ickes, who had become Secretary of the Interior. From Henry A. Wallace we borrowed Hugh L. Bennett's services. We made Bennett the chairman of a commission of forestry, range, and soils specialists; the commission went to the Navajo reservation. They found, in detail, the state of facts which is summarized above.

In July, 1933, at Fort Wingate, New Mexico, Bennett made his report directly to the Navajo tribe. We had not requested its prior clearance with the Washington office. Among other dread facts suddenly unrolled before the Navajo mind was the necessity that the livestock load on the total range should be cut in half, without delay.

The range must be saved or the Navajos must disperse into the white world. Dispersal would bring death to the Navajo spirit, the obliteration of the Navajo rainbow forever.

That meeting, July, 1933, launched a social, economic, and political struggle and effort well-nigh as intense and as dubious of outcome as any to be witnessed among men. It launched, also, the soil conservation movement of the United States; and that movement was to extend to every continent, in the years when there was dawning in the world's mind, through Hugh L. Bennett's leadership, the realization that mankind itself is faced by a silent crisis hardly less demanding than that which was facing the Navajo tribe. For the wastage of soil resource—of food potential—is going ahead on a world scale, and at an accelerating, catastrophic speed. But we will stay with the Navajos, and not enter upon the world story.

The unconcentrated, diffuse character of Navajo society has been told above. It was (and is) essentially a preliterate society, whose genius was oriented not toward organization nor toward technological achievement but toward imaginative and religious expression and the direct affirmation of buoyant life. All the years of governmental contact had not brought any tribe-wide organization into being, other than a small tribal council of very limited powers chosen by white electoral methods from large districts at infrequent elections.

The United States Government, on its side, to that date had scarcely sought to know, or to reach to, the obscure, informal, local embodiments of Navajo social order—the hundreds of extended families and local communities, where the deliberative processes of the Navajos went forward in ways of ancient Indian democracy and by the method of unanimous decisions slowly arrived at.

Tribe-wide synchronized action was demanded by the facts—action painful, and also complicated; for when the stage of critical erosion has been reached, as on much of the Navajo land, soil conservation requires more, much more, than merely the reduction of livestock overpopulation. How, when tribe-wide organization did not exist, could tribe-wide action, rapid, painful and complicated, be insured?

We in the Indian Service in 1933 knew that this enigma had three possible answers.

The first of the answers was: Direct compulsion by the government. The legal authority existed; and compulsion had been the traditional method of the Indian Service toward all Indians for eighty years.

The second of the answers was: To throw the whole staggering responsibility onto the Navajo Tribal Council—onto the almost phantom-frail political institution of the tribe. This choice would mean using federal governmental authority, if at all, solely to the end of carrying out the requests or ordinances of the Tribal Council.

The third answer was: Go with the facts to the hundreds of local communities of the Navajo people. Educate these communities through slow, patient conference and demonstration. Vest the responsibility for launching and guiding these huge, necessary adjustments, in the local headmen, in the healer-singers, the diviners, and ultimately, the heads of families.

We rejected the third of the choices because the ideal method was beyond our practical power, or because we believed it was beyond our practical power. In this rejection we may have erred profoundly; I shall touch upon that question later in this text.

We chose the second answer. We threw the burden squarely onto the Navajo Tribal Council. And the Council lifted the burden.

Then there commenced a political event rare if not unique in the history of popular government. The Council accepted and affirmed the conservation program, with its bitter requirement of a slashing stock reduction, because its intellect and conscience required it to. The Council's constituency did not accept the program, but resisted it with a bitterness sometimes sad, sometimes angry and wild. The Council stood firm, and the electorate threw it out of office. The successor Councilmen, confronting the implacable facts, reaffirmed and extended the conservation program, including the stock reductions. The electorate threw his successor Council out of office; and again the new Council affirmed the program and extended it. Thus, onward for ten years.

Not often do legislators, in the absence of corporation or big-money or other pressure-group influence, deliver themselves for electoral slaughter by going counter to the impassioned, even inflamed will of the vast majority of their constituents. That is what the Navajo legislators did. They did it under no sort of duress and bribery of the Indian Service; duress and bribery were not possible and were not attempted. They did it out of a political virtue of a high order, and under no compulsion except that of an overwhelming reality which they acknowledged after they entered on responsibility. They were helpless to communicate their understanding to the mass of the Navajos; but upward along the line of greatest unpopularity, greatest resistance, the Navajo Council moved.

The needful stock reductions have been practically completed now; the animal load is yielding a greater total value of meat and wool than the greater number of animals were yielding ten years ago. This, because of upbreeding, improved water supply, removal of surplus horses which were consuming the grass in the earlier years, and, in some parts of Navajo land, a healing and revegetation of the wounded range. The result has been paid for by anguish of spirit among most of the Navajos, extreme material hardship among thousands of them, and a truncating of the tribe's political development. The burden cast on the frail Tribal Council, and so bravely carried by it, was a burden too great. The disunion between the Council and the basic Navajo social order was altered, through the conservation struggle, from one of mere non-connection to one of resentment, fear, and active resistance.

Was, therefore, our choice made in 1933 a wrong choice? Should we in this one case have utilized sheer, direct authority, by-passing the Navajos' immature political institution and thus sparing it? Or should we, as the alternative, have depended solely on persuasion and education at the "grass roots"—in the many local communities?

In the whole restrospect, I answer that our choice was not wrong. As a basic policy, we had terminated the use of coercion upon Indian tribes. We could not, in the affairs of the largest tribe and in the most poignant of its issues, reinstitute coercion; for that would have been to betray the cause of all Indians. It was right to cast the burden on the Navajos' elected agents; these agents knew that it was right.

Our error was in another direction, and I dwell upon it briefly because it is the continuing error of the Navajo sector of Indian Service.[2]

We could not, or did not, move the conservation problem through and beyond the centralized political organ of the tribe, out to the local communities where the Navajos' real profundities and strengths have their abode. In the same way, we did not move the Navajos' health problems out there; and their schooling and adult education problems; and all of their other problems, and Indian administration itself.

There were many reasons, other than deficiency of effort, for this failure; they almost aggregated to impossibilities; there are many reasons why the failure continues still; and this text is not the place to discuss the intricacies of Indian Service budgeting, personnel, and institutionalism, the limitations placed in appropriation acts by Congressional prejudice and whim, the "pump priming" requirements of the

2. Now, in 1962, this error no longer is continuing. For the shining present, see the conclusion of this chapter.

depression years which compelled the spending of public monies at extreme speed. The idiosyncrasies of United States federal administration are not the subject of this work. But with the destiny of the Navajos, and their crisis, still unresolved, and their future, not yet spelled out, every reader will be concerned. I shall describe briefly this Navajo crisis of today, at the cost of some slight repetition. It exists in two aspects, inseparable from each other: the Navajo aspect, and the United States governmental aspect.

Immense effort, and much pain, across nearly sixteen years, have reversed the soil-wastage process on most of that part of the Navajos' land which had not been incurably wrecked before 1933. And, as stated above, the greatly diminished livestock load is returning larger money values than did the nearly one hundred per cent overload of fourteen years ago. Yet today, viewing the Navajo domain in its entirety, we find that one single sheep requires thirty acres for its browse. And we find that the entire livestock yield (meat and wool sold and consumed) supplies no more than 44 per cent of the average per capita yearly income of the Navajos; and the total per capita income is only $82. Farming accounts for 14 per cent of the total income; arts and crafts, 11 per cent; and wages for government and private labor, 30 per cent. Compare this Navajo per capita income with other (pre-World War II) per capitas: the United States as a whole, $597; Arizona, $473; New Mexico, $359; and the State of lowest income in the Union, Mississippi, $205.[3] Two items are added, as annotation. The Navajo pays all the federal taxes and most of the state taxes except the land tax, which for people of low incomes, in New Mexico and Arizona, is negligible anyway. He receives free schooling for about one-third of his children, and free medical service for a fraction of his population not larger than one-fourth. He gets few of the social-security benefits which the non-Indians in New Mexico and Arizona receive. If anyone has the idea that Navajos, and other Indians, "live off the government," or that Indian Service receives too much appropriated money, let him consider the items here set down.

3. 1949 figures. Ed.

Is this material poverty of the Navajos a fixed fact? No; for given the necessary capital, given administrative wisdom, and given time, the unused potentials of the country and also of the people can be brought alive. The irrigated farmland can be increased from 23,000 acres to more than 120,000. The per acre yield of farmland certainly can be doubled. With continued upbreeding of the livestock and continued revegetation of the damaged range, livestock income can be doubled in the generation ahead. The large timber wealth of the tribe can be manufactured into furniture, not merely cut into boards. The Navajo reservation contains many billion tons of accessible coal; and there is helium, and other minerals. The market demand for fine-quality Navajo blanket and silver and turquoise work is insatiable; here, the potential increase of Navajo income is indefinite. Payment of government wages to whites, and to Indians other than Navajos, in the Navajo Indian Service, totals some hundreds of thousands of dollars a year; and within a reoriented program and administrative system, most of this payment could go to Navajos.

Clearly, Navajo material poverty *is not* a fixed fact.

Wherein, then, rests the "crisis still unresolved," the "future not yet spelled out"?

First, and most obvious: Navajo population is not a fixed fact. Increase is at the rate of two per cent a year. Population is snowballing, as it has done since the Navajo's return from exile in 1868. Writes Clyde Kluckhohn: "There can be no doubt that the fecundity of the tribe is but one sympton of a generally radiant vitality. They want to live. They want children, many children." Let the Navajo death rate be brought down to that of the Indians of the country as a whole, and the population rise will approach three per cent, not two per cent, a year.

Second, and nearly as obvious: Many thousands of Navajos, women as well as men, through the war years were in the armed forces or in war industry. They became used to a material "standard of living" perhaps seven times higher than the average of their homeland. They became used to substituting this richer material standard for that very rich communal spiritual standard which no material poverty can dismay.

But unless the fullest of employment levels is maintained in the country, these Navajos will not be preferred in industry. With but few exceptions indeed, their rhythms are not those which industry requires; they will be viewed as a marginal labor supply. They will stay at home, entertaining material wants which the home world cannot supply now. Within a Navajo economic program wisely conceived and early launched, these returned veterans and war workers could be a decisive factor in terms of equipment, energy and ambition. Wanting that program (at this writing, 1949, it is still wanting), even the deep potency of the Navajo healing and reconciling ceremonials may not be enough to assuage them. They are one of their people's resources now; they can become its most troublesome disrupter and destroyer.

The really deep, controlling aspect of the Navajos' crisis has yet to be told. Population increase, and tensions brought home from the war and war industry, are among the precipitators of this deep and controlling aspect of the crisis, but they are not the essential part of it.

The deep, controlling crisis of Navajo life is found in the relationship between the United States Government and the Navajos. It is a crisis in Navajo Indian administration.

The main burden of this chapter has been to show where it is that the life treasure of the Navajos lies. It lies in the family and extended family, the local community, the headman who holds power only through democratic leadership, and the religious functioning—the healer-singer and his many helpers, the diviner, the wondrous ceremonials, the union of faith and prayer in joy, the many cooperative commonwealths of souls. Here, personality is formed, values and life attitudes are established, self-discipline, and that gallant buoyancy of spirit, that "radiancy" of the Navajo being, are communicated from man to man and from the elder to the younger generation.

Here the genius, the very existence of the Navajo is found. Here is no exclusiveness, but universal hospitality; no fear of new things or of change, since during hundreds of years the Navajos have changed and changed and changed again, have adopted new arts, new technologies, new industries, and have changed not at all at this life-generating core of their society.

And now, it must be added: Indian Service never has brought to bear the patience, perseverance, will and art needed to connect itself and its programs with the local complexes which really *are* the civilization and society of the Navajo. Hardly has it even tried factually to equate its programs with these basic Navajo facts.

Blind or hostile toward the Navajos' deep powers in their local embodiments, Indian Service has not been, at least not within recent years. But Indian Service has trafficked with Navajo individuals, and with Navajo electoral masses, in terms of this or that or the other program or service, without even trying, seriously, to communicate with the controlling sources of Navajo opinion, responsibility, power and genius. White personnel, Indian personnel from Oklahoma and the Great Plains and Lake States, few of them speaking the Navajo language, have received their Navajo Service assignments, brief or not quite so brief, and then have wended their way to other regions of Indian country, to be succeeded by newcomers who would prove to be as transitory as themselves. And always (as in the conservation effort recounted in this chapter), to those in charge of services and programs, it has seemed that there was not time enough to deal with the fundamental leadership among the Navajos, and with the local communities, and with the controlling intangibles of Navajo existence.

In earlier years, it did not matter very seriously that the government and its programs had not even a speaking acquaintance with the real centers of Navajo opinion and power. The programs were extremely circumscribed, and the great body of Navajo life remained untouched by them. But after 1933 the totality of Navajo existence became affected by the conservation program. And in the years now ahead, if the Navajos' economic crisis is to be met, the actions in the first instance must be governmental, and their consequences will reach through all of Navajo life. The continuing chasm between government Indian Service and the creative, responsible, potent parts of Navajo society therefore matters, now, very seriously indeed.

To make the above statement in another way. Are Navajos to do their own work, including the making of their own deliberative decisions? Are those of the Navajo people who have prestige, responsibility, wisdom, and leadership to be utilized in meeting a tribal crisis which plainly is a fateful one? Are the Navajos' social and spiritual energies and values to become harnessed for the great, difficult tasks ahead, or are these energies and values to be bypassed, dispensed with, kept in an outer darkness? The answer to these questions contains the very fate of the Navajos—certainly their spiritual, probably also their physical, fate.

How the question is answered will be of profound interest to workers throughout the colonial, preliterate, preindustrial world.

The right—the saving—answer will require of the Indian Service central headquarters a reoriented creativeness. It will lay that requirement intensely on the Navajo field service personnel. The saving answer will lead far and deep in ways of the good.

. . . And now (1962) the saving answer has been given. The Navajos have given it, helped by Allan Harper, Robert Young, and some others. But I wish that Americans could know the nonmaterial facts, of world significance. Here is a human group which a few years gone was nonliterate, nonindustrial, and virtually unexistent as a body corporate; incalculably rich in aesthetic and spiritual goods, but the goods were diffused into hundreds of informal and unintegrated organs. And here, now, after decades of painful travailing, is a human group which faces the modern challenges with a competence, a consistency of boldness, not equaled I believe, in any city or state of White America. Here is the worldwide human potential unfolding into great deeds from out of its unforsaken past. Here is an event for America and the world to be thankful for—and to know about.

Although most of the racial groups which have immigrated to America have in time been assimilated into the mainstream of our culture, there have been notable exceptions— isolated pockets of Southern mountaineers, Hassidic Jews residing in the Brownsville section of Brooklyn, New York, the inhabitants of the Chinatowns of New York and San Francisco, and the Old Order Amish of Pennsylvania, whose folkways are described in the following article. This summary is based primarily on Walter M. Kollmorgen's The Old Order Amish of Lancaster, Pennsylvania, issued in 1942 by the United States Department of Agriculture. A war and postwar economy and the increased mechanization of farming have exerted strong pressures on the Amish pattern of nonconformity. It would seem inevitable that like the Mormons of the past century— also a "peculiar people"—they will in time surrender to the process of acculturation which Gillin describes.

Born at Waterloo, Iowa in 1907, John Gillin graduated from the University of Wisconsin in 1927 and became a Ph.D. at Harvard in 1934. He has done anthropological field work in Algeria, British Guiana, Ecuador, Eastern Peru, and various sections of the United States. He joined the staff of the University of North Carolina in 1946, and became professor of anthropology at the University of Pittsburgh in 1959. He is the author of numerous monographs of The Ways of Men, from which the following selection is taken.

THE OLD ORDER AMISH OF PENNSYLVANIA

JOHN GILLIN

THE OLD ORDER AMISH of Pennsylvania constitute a nonconforming group which lives within the area of North American society and culture, but which up to the present has maintained a sharply distinguished subculture of its own. There are about 3,500 Old Order Amish in Lancaster County, Pennsylvania, and they occupy an area about 25 miles long by 15 miles wide on the "Limestone Plain" of this region. But they are closely surrounded and infiltrated by other Americans practicing general North American culture, and the Amish are of the same European physical stock (mainly

Swiss and German in origin) as the majority of their neighbors.

The sect known as the Swiss Brethren came into existence in the German-speaking part of Switzerland during the Zwinglian Reformation (of Lutheranism) shortly after 1520. Among the main tenets of their creed was insistence upon adult, rather than infant, baptism and a literal interpretation of the Bible by the communicants themselves without the interposition of an ecclesiastical hierarchy. The prevailing state churches, whether Roman Catholic or Lutheran, regarded the movement as heretical and hounded the Brethren from one religion to another, often using ruthless methods of exterminating them. The Brethren were a nonresistant people who refused to bear arms, and, since at this time Swiss mercenary soldiers were widely employed in Europe, the Swiss government also interested itself in persecuting the nonresisters, with the result that the major part of the Brethren group moved to the Rhineland region of Germany. At the same time that the movement was spreading in the upper Rhineland a similar religious group known as the Anabaptists arose in the Netherlands. There, about 1536, a leader by the name of Menno Simons appeared, whose followers became known as Mennonites. The Swiss Brethren of the upper Rhineland and the Mennonites of the lower Rhineland gradually fused, until by the latter part of the seventeenth century they were more or less united. However, among the Swiss Brethren a leader named Jacob Ammann arose who finally in 1693 led a schism, and his more conservative followers came to be called the Amish. These people were mainly from Alsace and the upper Rhineland area. The Amish, then, are an offshoot of the general Mennonite movement. In the early part of the eighteenth century, persecution of the group in Europe decided them to move to the New World and they came to Pennsylvania because of the advertised religious tolerance of William Penn. The bulk of the ancestors of the present-day Amish seem to have come to Lancaster County between 1710 and 1750.

In Europe the people belonged to the peasantry, and were thus both rural and lower class in background. They were determined to break completely with the social order of their place and time and to found a way of life based on the organization of the early Christians as set forth literally in the New Testament. The basic tenet of the Amish culture is that nothing is to be accepted or approved merely because it happens to be custom or law, but that all practices and activities must be based on the "Bible standard." The Bible is interpreted literally and the fitness of all customs must pass the Bible test. It appears, therefore, that the original movement represented a revolt by lower class, underprivileged people against the culture of their day in Europe, which had proved too punishing and too devoid of satisfactions to be followed longer. The Bible held forth the promise of reward after death and the anticipation of this type of reward was sufficient motivation to lead to the establishment of certain new customs.

The Amish[1] are an exclusively rural-dwelling group who live on their own farms in one of the better agricultural regions of southeastern Pennsylvania, the so-called Limestone Plain. They are highly successful farmers. The Amish are not conservative in the actual techniques of farming, except that they are prohibited from using tractors for field work; otherwise they have often been in advance of other farmers in the adoption of new methods of rotating crops, applying fertilizer, and developing commercial agricultural products.

Far from being ashamed of the opinion of outsiders, the Amish make a point of being a "peculiar people" who do not conform to the standards of the world.

All men wear their hair in a long bob with bangs over the forehead. Neither men nor women may part the hair anywhere except in the center. Unmarried men shave; married men wear a beard but may not grow a mustache. (A mustache is considered the mark of a military man.) No woman is permitted to cut or curl her hair and all comb their hair exactly alike except that unmarried girls are allowed to braid theirs and to wear it as a bun on the back of the head. Outer articles of clothing are exactly alike for all members of respective sex and age groups, and decidedly quaint in com-

1. We shall use the word in this chapter to refer to Old Order Amish although two other, more liberal, Amish groups have split off.

parison with current styles of outsiders, which by the Amish are considered marks of worldly ostentation.

Men and boys wear broadfall trousers with plain, home-made suspenders. Jackets worn for dress may have no lapels, no outside pockets, and no buttons—they are held together with hooks and eyes. (Work clothes may have buttons and even zippers, but these garments are considered strictly utilitarian.) Atop their bobbed hair, males wear broad, flat, black felt hats in winter and broad, flat, straw hats in summer. Women have no "styles," for all of the same age group must wear outer garments of identical pattern. None of these garments may be made of printed goods, and only solid colors are permitted. Full skirts and long-sleeved blouses are *de rigueur*. Married women wear aprons which match the color of their dresses, whereas unmarried girls wear white aprons. All females wear white devotional head coverings and identical homemade bonnets. "Store hats" are forbidden for women.

All of these peculiarities of dress are justified by biblical injunction, according to the interpretation of the Amish.

It is obvious that the customs and equipment concerned with dress serve at least two cultural functions: (1) they provide a constant and easily discriminated stimulus for both the group members and outsiders, which tends to evoke customs appropriate to this particular group, and (2) they tend to represent the symbolic patterns of "peculiarity" of this culture as based upon the Scriptures.

Except in emergencies, the Amish are not allowed to drive or ride in automobiles, particularly not for amusement or pleasure. The means of conveyance in use is the *open black buggy* with a single horse for unmarried men, and the rectangular topped, single-horse *gray buggy-wagon* which somewhat resembles an old-fashioned horse-drawn milk wagon, for married men. Dash boards and whip sockets are forbidden. Likewise the ownership or personal use of auto trucks for carrying loads is forbidden; only *wagons and teams* may be owned or operated. If an emergency requires one of the "worldly" type of conveyances, it may be hired with a driver. Telephones are not allowed in the houses, nor electricity or any of the farm or household conveniences operated on electric power. On the other hand, gasoline engines for pumping water are permitted and all types of modern farm machinery are in use, except tractors for field work. Tractors may be used only for belt power.

Houses follow the general patterns of the region, except that they are large, often with twelve to sixteen rooms, and are arranged with interior folding doors so that they may be opened up for the house religious meetings which frequently involve an attendance of over two hundred persons. Rugs may be only of the "rag" variety, and ostentatious furnishings, as well as most modern household appliances (except sewing machines), are eschewed.

Most clothing, except some underclothing and work clothes for men, must be made at home by the women.

Pictures and photographs are forbidden. "Thou shalt not make unto thee any graven image, or any likeness of any thing that is in heaven above, or that is in the earth beneath, or that is in the water under the earth." (Exodus, 20:4.)

The principal values of the Amish culture may be summarized as follows: (1) Nonconformity is held to be obligatory in everything in which "worldly" standards conflict with the Bible. This is known as the principle of the "unequal yoke," based on II Cor., 6:15: "Be ye not *unequally yoked* together with unbelievers: for what fellowship hath righteousness with unrighteousness? and what communion hath light with darkness?" (Italics ours.) In effect this means that social contacts with outsiders, which might lead to cultural diffusion from the outside world, are held to the minimum. The tabus upon cars, telephones, worldly amusements, marriage to outsiders, higher education, living in cities, in towns, and the joining of any associations other than the church are all consistent with this value. (2) The Bible, literally interpreted, is believed to be the source of all values. This in part explains the resistance of the Amish to education beyond the eighth grade. (3) The bearing of arms, going to war, and litigation in courts of law are all to be avoided on the authority of Jesus' command, "Resist not evil." It is, of course, possible to see this as a result of the persecutions which the group suffered in Europe: when the culture was in formation, it was early discovered that physical and legal resistance was nonrewarding, and a tabu upon such actions became established as part of the culture. (4) Farming constitutes the strongest positive interest and value of the people. The only suitable occupation for an Amish is farming, and it is the ambition of every man to own his own land. The Amish work longer hours than any of their neighbors, and since they spend no money on amusements and relatively little on clothing, mechanical conveniences, etc., young men are usually able to acquire land relatively early in life. (5) Money is valued only for the purpose of acquiring land and the necessities of life.

It is to be noted that the high values placed upon farming as an activity and land as property are not derived from Scripture, from which the other conscious values of the culture derive. Thus the total value system is not consistently unified in the strict sense of the word. Nevertheless, until recent times the two major systems of values have proved consistent with each other and mutually rewarding: the type of life required by the principle of nonconformity, etc., channeled the energies of the people into a single-minded devotion to agriculture which has produced success and rewards; on the other hand, devotion to rural life and unremitting labor on the farms has had the effect of isolating the people from the type of contacts and activities which might run counter to the religious values.

It would seem that Amish culture is dominated by two objectives. These two major objectives we might term (1) "the Christian way of life" (as defined in the cultural interpretation of the Bible) and (2) successful agriculture (in terms of abundant crops and agricultural products rather than in financial terms, which within the culture are more or less incidental). It should be recognized that the one objective is a "sacred" organization of cultural content, whereas the second is "secular." So far as our information goes neither the authority of the Bible nor the whole mental system of religious beliefs is functionally involved in the agricultural complexes, except in the prohibition of the use of field tractors. Planting, plowing, manuring, and all other techniques seem to be backed by a strictly secular (or "common sense") set of mental patterns.

The Amish eschew all forms of "worldly" amusement and

seek their relaxation in Sunday church meetings, in frequent visits between families, and in Sunday evening "sings" for young people. The effect of these customs is to maintain primary contact within the community. The Sunday evening sings are the mechanism of courtship: a young man sets out in the evening with his open buggy, picks up his young lady friend, and they drive (without chaperonage) to the house of some neighbor where the affair, consisting of hymn-singing around a table, takes place. Before marriage, the man is supposed to use a go-between to arrange the union with the girl's parents. Marriage with an outsider is forbidden. Weddings are elaborate affairs, and all social gatherings are characterized by the consumption of huge meals of home-cooked food. Marriage is said to be very stable, and divorces are unknown. The only permissible ground is adultery, of which no cases are reported. The younger son usually stays on the farm of his parents, and, when he takes over the management of the place, his father and mother retire from all except odd jobs. They live in an independent wing of the house, thus preserving close contact with the children, without imposing their presence upon the intimacy of the younger family. The family is patriarchal, and all decisions are supposed to be taken by the husband and father.

Smoking, drinking, card playing, and going to movies are prohibited. Amish are not allowed to read books for pleasure, but they are required to be literate, for every one must spend a certain amount of time "searching the Scriptures" for suitable texts. Thus the group approves elementary education in the three R's, but disapproves of consolidated schools and of all education above the eighth grade for its own members. The reasons for this are twofold: Once an individual has learned to read the Bible he is thought to need no further education, for the Bible is the source of all knowledge; likewise consolidated schools and higher education tend to bring the children into contact with "the world" and to take them away from their tasks about the farm, to which they should be inured at an early age. The result is that Amish children go to one-room "little red school houses" scattered about the countryside.

The literacy problem is complicated by the fact that the

Amish are bilingual. They speak English and also a German Rhenish dialect, now much mixed with English words. The Bible and the hymns, however, are read in German; thus, the children become literate in English in school, but their parents teach them to read German at home.

Another reason for being able to "search the Scriptures" is the fact that church officials are chosen by lot. It is believed that the Holy Spirit speaks through the mouth of any true believer, but since any man may be chosen as a minister, bishop, or deacon, he should be acquainted with the Bible so that he can preach according to the accepted patterns, which require heavy quotation from Holy Writ. Since speaking from notes is forbidden, men must have memories well stocked with Bible texts.

The Amish territory is divided into eighteen church districts; each contains one hundred adult persons and each is presided over by a bishop chosen by lot. Sunday meetings are held at the various houses in rotation. The bishop, ministers, and deacons form a sort of directing council of the district, but the whole membership decides matters of discipline, custom, and creed. The organization is on the congregational basis, with each district theoretically independent. In practice, decisions are expected to be unanimous.

Several mechanisms operate in a positive way to encourage compliance with the patterns of the culture. One is the custom of advice relationships. A man hardly ever takes a major step, such as buying a farm, getting a loan from a bank, and the like, without consulting some older man. Often the older men of his district congregation undertake to advise him as a group. Also a mutual aid system is in operation. The deacon of the district is responsible for collections for the poor fund and mutual aid fund, and a member who is the victim of misfortune is helped by the group without question, providing he is in good standing (has not broken the tabus). For this reason, no Amish were on relief or WPA during the depression. The advice relationship and mutual aid thus prove to be highly rewarding, particularly to the younger member of the society.

The question which arises in the mind of any outsider is, How can this culture so different from that about it be main-

tained in the group? We do not have a full account of the
patterns of socialization of the child, but even on the basis of
the data at hand, and our general knowledge of cultural dynamics, we may make some reasonable suggestions.

1. Competing customs have little chance to be presented
and tried out due to the operations of nonconformity and isolation. Members of the community are removed from contacts which would serve as stimuli or models for the learning
of outside customs and outside cultural drives. The joining of
associations, attendance at school beyond the eighth grade,
living in cities and towns, working in industry—all such possibilities of contact are expressly forbidden because they are
thought to be "contaminating."

2. Rewards for practicing the group culture and refraining
from outside "temptations" are very great. Through the advice relationship the individual is given group solidarity and
aid in his projects. In time of trouble or when starting out on
the purchase of a farm, etc., the community comes to the aid
of the individual with money, gifts of tools and stock, and in
other substantial ways. The desire for response is satisfied
from infancy exclusively by members of this society who
practice its culture, so that a strong motivation is acquired
for imitating the members of the group in order to secure
their approval and their attentions. In addition to such practical rewards, it must be remembered that a very strong acquired drive is inculcated in the members of the group,
namely, the desire for salvation after death. And the members are taught that the reward of this drive is only obtain-
able by practice of the group customs. Finally, the culture is
rewarding in the mundane business of farming, and a group
member has only to look about him to see that the Amish on
the whole are more successful agriculturists than nonbeliev-
ers. Thus a number of universal and acquired drives are op-
erative in the culture to motivate the practice of the customs
which, it is believed, bring satisfactions of the type desired.

3. The fear of punishment is also a powerful motivation.
The members are taught to believe that transgression of the
tabus violates the will of God and that its eventual aftermath
is certain punishment in the fires of Hell after death. A more
practical and immediate punishment is also provided by the

group. A member who violates any one of the tabus is brought to account by the church officials and the district church group. If he does not publicly confess and "mend his ways," he is henceforward "shunned." "Shunning" means that other members of the group withdraw from all social intercourse with the wrong-doer: they will not speak to him, cooperate with him, or enter into any intimate relationships with him. It amounts to social ostracism, and is said to be considered extremely painful. This type of punishment is particularly severe in a culture of this type, practically all of whose patterns imply primary contacts between individuals: there are no customs in the culture which fit the individual either to lead a solitary life or to "make his way" among strangers, so that the average individual cut off from contact with his kind by "shunning" is left almost without cultural resources.

If outside contamination were not punished by the group itself, attempts to mingle with outsiders would be punishing at least at the start, anyway. In fact, at the present time there is a certain tendency on the part of outsiders to treat the Amish with hostility and ridicule on account of their "peculiarities." Thus the Amish individual who endeavors to enter into social relations with outsiders is apt to find the experience disagreeable in contrast to the warm atmosphere of self-righteous mutual understanding which he finds in his own group.

4. The cultural situation is so arranged that so long as isolation is maintained, the learning of all acquired drives labeled as "worldly" is inhibited. The process is not essentially different from that whereby the "regular" American culture inhibits the development of an acquired drive, say, for morphine. The average Amishman, once he has settled down, apparently no more desires to go to movies than the average North American in general desires to take morphine. If the "worldly" acquired drives can thus be prevented from developing, "worldly" customs for their satisfaction have no motivation on which to be built.

Although Amish culture apparently arose in Europe out of a conflict situation, its success depends upon cultural isolation. As a closed system of custom, it seems to work well and to perpetuate itself and its society.

On the whole, the culture seems to be remarkably compatible with the various components of its situation, with the exception of the social and outside cultural components. The technical procedures are adapted to the land and climate of the region; the customs are well adapted to the artifacts in use, and this compatibility has been the more maintained because new artifacts have not been hastily introduced. The culture seems to be fitted to the capabilities of the group, for long life and health are characteristic of the Amish. The psychological component is well managed within the isolated culture so that the customs are well learned, and conflicts, either within the individual or within the group, seem to be remarkably few. Within the group itself the culture is adapted to its social potentialities, except for the fact that at present no successful solution for increased population has been found. The traditional solution is more land for more farms, but the Amish are finding increased difficulty in acquiring the needed land. Since business or industry is ruled out of consideration for members, a cultural crisis is arising. Some cultural change or innovation will have to be introduced to solve the maladjustment between the patterns of the culture, the increasing population, and the limited supply of available land.

The outstanding incompatibilities of the Amish culture are, of course, with the foreign cultural component. This is not entirely accidental, for the Amish culture explicitly states as one of its major objectives the maintenance of "peculiar" customs. Now, two cultures may exist side by side without necessarily being in conflict with one another. It is possible for the system of Culture A to contain patterns which render it perfectly compatible with Culture B. It would appear that on the whole this has been true of the Amish culture until recently. Patterns of withdrawal and nonresistance enabled it to exist compatibly within the area of general North American rural culture. Recently the "outside cultural component" has developed some innovations which have changed the situation. We may mention only two which Kollmorgen analyzes in some detail. One is the developing movement for consolidated schools, supported by state laws and state and federal funds. This has been evaded by the Amish through establishing parochial one-room neighborhood schools, but this evasion of course doubles the cost of Amish education. Furthermore, it is entirely likely that before long the state law will require longer years of schooling for children, so that the Amish will be required to go to high schools or at least to remain in school beyond the fourteenth year. This would be inconsistent with the pattern of putting children to full-time work at age fifteen. Another change in the outside cultural component of the situation is the new program of agricultural cooperative and relief measures initiated by state and federal agencies during the 1930's. The Amish refuse to cooperate because they are forbidden to join associations of any kind outside their church, but such refusal places them at a competitive disadvantage in relation to non-Amish farmers, and is inconsistent with one of the major objectives of the culture, namely, successful agriculture.

Other incompatibilities with the changing outside cultural situation may be mentioned. The outsiders have hard-surfaced the country roads, so that buggy horses are "pounded to pieces" in the course of a year or eighteen months' use. Also not a few buggies and horses have been smashed up in serious accidents by speeding motorists on the highways. In short, the horse and buggy patterns are no more adapted to the new roads than they are to the new distances involved in the social factor. Likewise, the ban upon the use of motor trucks and field tractors places the Amish farmers under a heavy competitive burden as compared with others, for, without these inventions, more time and man power is required to do the same work.

So long as the Amish society and culture maintained isolation, it would seem from information available to us that the elements of the culture were remarkably consistent with one another. None of the major patterns of the culture seems to have run counter to one another and all goals and objectives appear to have been mutually consistent.

It might be noted that the two major objectives of the culture, "the true Christian life" and successful agriculture, are consistent with each other and support each other, but that the one does not penetrate the other. Religious patterns of action or representation do not appear in the agricultural customs and complexes (except for the prohibition of field tractors). The whole agricultural sector of the culture is secular and its mental systems are of the common-sense types. For example, the Amish scorn "book farming," for they believe that one learns the proper agricultural techniques only by practice, but they employ manure and commercial fertilizer, rotation of crops, planting of legumes to restore nitrogen to the soil, and so on. There are no religious rites or beliefs associated with this work.

This case illustrates that a consistent and well-knit cultural system is possible without the complete pervasion of religious beliefs into all aspects of the system. It is true, that, among the Amish, the religious beliefs have some influence on the fact that the people are almost exclusively agricultural, but the religious element is a negative one. The principle of the "unequal yoke" interdicts mingling with outsiders, and farming one's own land or that of other believers is the only practical road open for the avoidance of the unequal yoke. Yet this is a negative influence of the religious beliefs. The religion does not demand the practice of agriculture on biblical or other supernatural authority. It simply prohibits types of work which would require Amishmen to work with non-believers. Agriculture happens to fit this requirement under the circumstances, and was also established in the historical circumstances of the original founders of the culture.

If it is true that the integrity and continued existence of a cultural system are, as we have assumed, dependent upon the compatibility between a culture and its situation, one of three possibilities for the future lie before the Amish culture. (1) Recent changes in the cultural situation may be eliminated and the situation may be restored to its former condition to which the present culture is well adapted by isolating patterns. This possibility does not seem at all likely. The outside world "moves on": agricultural cooperatives, consolidated schools and higher education, paved roads and automobiles, are here to stay, and further innovations are probably on the way. (2) The Amish culture may fail to change in any significant adaptive particular. If this happens, it seems inevitable that the incompatibilities and resulting inconsistencies of the culture will bring about its disintegration, if the group continues to live in its present situation. At least two times in history the group has avoided incompatibilities with its situaton by migrating to a new situation. This solution, however, is much more difficult and impractical at the present time. (3) Certain changes in patterns and organization of the culture are inevitable if the culture is to remain in its present situation. Customs of family limitation would solve some of the problems attendant upon spatial and numerical expansion of the society, but would probably run counter to biblical injunctions. What seems more likely is the development of certain impersonalized patterns of custom which would enable Amishmen to mingle with and interact with outsiders, while not identifying with them.

If this proves impossible, we may expect to see a gradual infiltration of Amish culture by outside patterns. This process is generally known as "acculturation." The end result, if it runs its course, will be the substitution of Amish cultural elements and organization by those of general North American culture, and the eventual disappearance of Amish culture as a discrete system and of Amish society as a social unit.